Tenured Radicals

Roger Kimball is co-editor and publisher of *The New Criterion* and president and publisher of Encounter Books. He contributes widely to periodicals in Britain and America and is a regular columnist for Pajamas Media. Among his other books are *The Rape of the Masters: How Political Correctness Sabotages Art*; *Art's Prospect: The Challenge of Tradition in an Age of Celebrity*; *Lives of the Mind: The Use and Abuse of Intelligence from Hegel to Wodehouse*; *Experiments Against Reality: The Fate of Culture in the Postmodern Era*; and *The Long March: How the Cultural Revolution of the 1960s Changed America*.

TENURED RADICALS

How Politics Has Corrupted
Our Higher Education

ROGER KIMBALL

Third Edition, with a New Introduction by the Author

Ivan R. Dee, Chicago

TENURED RADICALS. Copyright © 1990, 1991, 1998, 2008 by Roger Kimball.
All rights reserved, including the right to reproduce this book or portions
thereof in any form. For information, address: Ivan R. Dee, Publisher, 1332
North Halsted Street, Chicago 60642, a member of the Rowman & Littlefield
Publishing Group. Manufactured in the United States of America and printed
on acid-free paper.

www.ivanrdee.com

Library of Congress Cataloging-in-Publication Data:
Kimball, Roger, 1953–
    Tenured radicals : how politics has corrupted our higher education
    / Roger Kimball. — 3rd ed.
        p. cm.
    Includes index.
    ISBN-13: 978-1-56663-796-1 (pbk. : alk. paper)
    ISBN-10: 1-56663-796-1 (pbk. : alk. paper)
  1. Education, Humanistic—United States. 2. Education, Higher—United
    States. 3. Education—Political aspects—United States. 4. Radicalism—
    United States. I. Title.
    LC1023.K56 2008
    370.11'2—dc22

                                                          2008024909

To Hilton Kramer

Contents

Reflections on *Tenured Radicals*, 2008

*After the Vietnam War, a lot of us didn't just crawl back into
our literary cubicles; we stepped into academic positions. With
the war over, our visibility was lost, and it seemed for a
while—to the unobservant—that we had disappeared. Now we
have tenure, and the work of reshaping the universities has
begun in earnest.*
—Jay Parini, *The Chronicle of Higher Education*

I Death of the counterculture?

WHEN *Tenured Radicals* was first published in 1990,
I noted that, "with a few notable exceptions,"

> our most prestigious liberal arts colleges and universities
> have installed the entire radical menu at the center of their
> humanities curriculum at both the undergraduate and the
> graduate levels. Every special interest—women's studies,
> black studies, gay studies, and the like—and every modish
> interpretive gambit—deconstruction, post-structuralism,
> new historicism, and other postmodernist varieties of

what the literary critic Frederick Crews aptly dubbed "Left Eclecticism"—has found a welcome roost in the academy, while the traditional curriculum and modes of intellectual inquiry are excoriated as sexist, racist, or just plain reactionary.

The intervening years have done nothing to gainsay that observation, but with the passage of time I realize that, critical though I was in 1990 (and again in 1998 when I published an updated edition of the book), I had in some respects underestimated the severity or at least the extent of the problem.

What has happened to the universities, I realized, could not be understood apart from its cultural context. It was part—a large part, perhaps—of that "long march through the institutions" that the Italian Marxist Antonio Gramsci recommended and whose American lineaments I chronicled in *The Long March: How the Cultural Revolution of the 1960s Changed America*. "The Age of Aquarius," I wrote in the Introduction to that book, "did not end when the last electric guitar was unplugged at Woodstock. It lives on in our values and habits, in our tastes, pleasures, and aspirations. It lives on especially in our educational and cultural institutions, and in the degraded pop culture that permeates our lives like a corrosive fog."*

Whether American culture has begun to recover from that assault has become a matter of debate. But the fact that the situation has become debatable may be an en-

---

* Roger Kimball, *The Long March: How the Cultural Revolution of the 1960s Changed America* (San Francisco: Encounter Books, 2000), page 5.

couraging sign. Seven or eight years ago, few serious observers were registering signs of cultural health in American society. The terrorist attacks of September 11
changed that. The fires at the World Trade Center were
not yet extinguished when some commentators proclaimed that the cultural revolution of the 1960s was, at
long last, finally over. In his book *South Park Conservatives: The Revolt Against Liberal Media Bias*, Brian C.
Anderson of *City Journal* reinforced the optimism, citing
the rise of conservative talk radio, the popularity of Fox
News, the new visibility of conservative publishers, and
the spread of interest in the internet with its many right-
of-center populist weblogs.* Taken together, these and
kindred phenomena have helped inspire the thought that,
at last, there is beginning to be a widespread counter to
the counterculture.

These are heartening signs. Nevertheless, as it was with
Mark Twain's announced demise, I suspect that reports of
the death of the counterculture have been greatly exaggerated. *Something* changed on 9/11—of that I have no
doubt—but it seems to me to have affected the assumptions of elite culture sporadically at best. Moreover, the
institution that has proved the most resistant to change is
the one most publicly committed to "innovation": the
university.

It is a peculiar moment in academia. In many ways,
things have never been worse. All those radical trends
that got going in the 1960s and gained steam in the 1970s
and 1980s are now so thoroughly entrenched that they

* Brian C. Anderson, *South Park Conservatives: The Revolt Against
Liberal Media Bias* (Washington, D.C.: Regnery Publishing, 2005),
pages 164–165.

are simply taken for granted. Consider, for example, the case of "transgender" students at Smith College. As the *Financial Times* reported, the whole issue of "transgender" is a growth industry at Smith—as indeed it is at many colleges and universities around the country. "Transgender"? The term, as the *FT* notes, "is a catch-all that includes a wide spectrum of people who don't identify with their birth sex; from transsexuals, who use surgery to change their sex, to those who change their appearance cosmetically—cross-dressers, as they used to be known, though such a term is considered old-school today."* There aren't—not yet, anyway—many university health services that will cover the cost of hormone therapy and surgery for those who wish to make the "transition" to the other (I suppose one is now supposed to say *an* other) sex, but the *FT* reported that the University of California is considering covering the procedures. (Arnold Schwarzenegger take note: a breast reduction alone can cost $10,000.) The subject is particularly complicated—or, depending on how you look it it, particularly risible—at Smith, the elite, all-female college whose founder, Sophia Smith, wanted the college to be a place where women "could develop as fully as may be the powers of womanhood."

"All-female"? There's the rub. What does a progressive institution like Smith do when Barbara decides to become Bert? It's a problem. I thought it was a joke when someone told me that Stanford had added "other" to the check boxes "male" and "female" on their application form.

* Craig Offman, "A Class Apart," *The Financial Times* April 16, 2005. Article available at http://www.ft.com/cms/s/0/99065352-ae13-11d9-9c30-00000e2511c8.html

According to the FT, many schools now eschew the old "binary way" of looking at sex and make do with the catchall "gender," a much more plastic term: "M," "F," "Neither," "Both," "Trans" (the preferred shorthand). Wesleyan College in Middletown, Connecticut, has experimented with a "gender blind" dormitory in which "transgender" students could live in a single room or with roommates who didn't care if it was Robert or Roberta in the bunk above. Some Smithies complain that if people "want to be boys, they should go to a co-ed school." But the Smith administration, being progressive, nervously embraces its two dozen or so "transgender" students. The college, the FT observes, "has long been tolerant of sexual difference. Notably tolerant."

No doubt. Still, the phenomenon of "transgender" raises all sorts of questions. Consider, for example, the pedestrian issue of how one should label the restrooms? And for parents, there is the deeply pragmatic question of why they should spend upwards of $50,000 per year to finance such "experiments in living" (to borrow John Stuart Mill's forward-looking expression).

It might seem that in wandering into the issue of "transgender" we have arrived at some bizarre byway of contemporary university life. This is only partly true. As Irving Kristol observed in his essay "Countercultures,"

"Sexual liberation" is always near the top of a counter-cultural agenda—though just what form the liberation takes can and does vary, sometimes quite wildly. Women's liberation, likewise, is another consistent feature of all countercultural movements—liberation from husbands, liberation from children, liberation from family. Indeed, the real object of these various sexual heterodoxies is to disestablish the family as the central institution of human society, the citadel of orthodoxy.*

Yesterday the slogan "free sex"; now, ironically, it is something closer to "free from sex." The *FT* quotes Paisley Currah, an associate professor of political science at Brooklyn College of the City University of New York and a board member of the Transgender Law and Policy Institute: "Just as Herbert Marcuse's theories were important on campus in his day, gender theory is important now." Ms.—or is it Mr.?—Currah is quite right to conjure up Herbert Marcuse. The German-born radical, who died in 1979, was indeed an important Sixties guru. But he was more than that. In his "protests against the repressive order of procreative sexuality" and insistence that genuine liberation requires a return to a state of "primary narcissism," Marcuse sounds a very contemporary note. Such a "change in the value and scope of libidinal relations," he wrote in *Eros and Civilization*, "would lead to a disintegration of the institutions in which the private interpersonal relations have been organized, particularly the monogamic and patriarchal family."† Marcuse would be as at home at Smith College in 2008 as he was at Brandeis in the 1960s.

The chief issue is this: should our institutions of higher education be devoted primarily to the education of citizens—or should they be laboratories for social and

* Irving Kristol, "Countercultures," in *Neoconservatism: The Autobiography of an Idea* (New York: The Free Press, 1995), pages 141–142.

† Herbert Marcuse, *Eros and Civilization: A Philosophical Inquiry into Freud* (Boston: Beacon Press, 1966), pages 168, 201.

political experimentation? Traditionally, a liberal arts education involved both character formation and learning. The goal was to produce men and women who (as Allan Bloom put it) had reflected thoughtfully on the question "'What is man?' in relation to his highest aspirations as opposed to his low and common needs."* Since the 1960s, however, colleges and universities have more and more been home to what Lionel Trilling called the "adversary culture" of the intellectuals.† The goal was rejection, not reflection.

The English novelist Kingsley Amis once observed that much of what was wrong with the twentieth century could be summed up in the word "workshop." Nowadays, "workshop" has been largely replaced by the word "studies." Gender Studies, Ethnic Studies, Afro-American Studies, Women's Studies, Gay, Lesbian, and Transgender Studies: these are names of political grievances, not disciplines. They exist not to further liberal education but to nurture the feckless antinomianism that Jacques Barzun dubbed "directionless quibble."‡

---

* Allan Bloom, *The Closing of the American Mind: How Higher Education Has Failed Democracy and Impoverished the Souls of Today's Students* (New York: Simon and Schuster, 1987), page 21.

† Lionel Trilling, Preface to *Beyond Culture* reprinted in *The Moral Obligation to Be Intelligent: Selected Essays*, edited by Leon Wieseltier (New York: Farrar, Straus & Giroux, 2000), page 554.

‡ Jacques Barzun, *The House of Intellect: How Intellect, the Prime Force in Western Civilization, Is Being Destroyed by Our Culture in the Name of Art, Science and Philanthropy* (New York: Harper and Brothers, 1959), page 119.

II The significance of Ward Churchill

Think back to the case of Ward Churchill, the professor of "ethnic studies" at the University of Colorado whose comparison of the victims of the 9/11 terrorist attacks to the Nazi bureaucrat Adolf Eichmann sparked outrage across the nation. Professor Churchill made the comparison in an essay he wrote in 2001,* shortly after the murderous attacks on New York and Washington, D.C. But his remarks did not attract much attention until he was invited to speak at Hamilton College in upstate New York and some public-spirited individuals unearthed and publicized his rebarbative anti-American effusion. The closer one looked into the case of Ward Churchill, the worse it got. This tenured radical had been battening on the public purse for decades—and for what? A congeries of radical political diatribes masquerading as scholarship in a bogus discipline. Much of what Churchill published was simply fabricated. Much else turned out to have been plagiarized.

Churchill had been invited to Hamilton College by "the Kirkland Project for the Study of Gender, Society and Culture," a left-wing, activist redoubt that for the decade of its existence has devoted its considerable resources to transforming a liberal arts education into an exercise in radical repudiation of American society, its manners, morals, and political filiations. It was the Kirkland Project, for example, that invited Susan Rosenberg, the felon and former member of the Weather Underground, to be an "artist- and activist-in-residence" and

* The essay in question, "Some People Push Back," is available at http://www.kersplebedeb.com/mystuff/s11/churchill.html.

teach a seminar on "Resistance Memoirs: Writing, Identity and Change."* It was a satellite of the Kirkland Project that had ago invited Annie Sprinkle, the former prostitute and porn star, to preside over a workshop (but of course) designed to educate "students and faculty on how better to pleasure themselves."†

Now the point about the Kirkland Project is not how extreme it is but how ordinary.‡ (I use the term "ordinary" in its statistical, not its normative, sense.) There are hundreds, maybe thousands of similar organizations at American colleges and universities. Their undeclared goal is to radicalize American society by betraying the intellectual and moral standards whose general observance they depend upon for their very existence. When challenged, proponents of such organizations will instantly retreat to the mantras of "free speech" and "academic freedom." But it has long been obvious that the academic notion of "free speech" is like the academic notion of "diversity": it means strict intellectual and moral con-

---

* Roger Kimball, "Meet the Newest Member of the Faculty," *The Wall Street Journal* December 3, 2004, page W15.

† Roger Kimball, "Academic Freedom for Me But Not for Thee," *The New Criterion*, November 2002, page 1.

‡ In the wake of the nationwide scandal over Ward Churchill, the Kirkland Project finally reaped some of the obloquy it deserved. In response, the college, together with the protagonists of the Kirkland Project, engaged in some serious soul-searching. The result was a long-winded report and, in place of a change of heart, a change of name to—it is almost too good to be true, but it *is* true—the Diversity and Social Justice Project. So: slightly repackaged sclerotic anti-American leftism—that is to say, business as usual in academia these days.

formity on any contentious issue: Free speech for *me* but not for *thee*. As the historian Robert Paquette—perhaps the only self-identified conservative at Hamilton College—observed, in all of its history the Kirkland Project has never invited anyone to Hamilton who was "libertarian, conservative or even centrist."* In other words, the notion of "academic freedom" has mutated from being a protection into being a weapon.†

John Silber, the former president of Boston University, summed up the fate of academic freedom in his essay "Poisoning the Wells of Academe." Originally, Silber observed, academic freedom

> entailed an immunity for what is said and done by dedicated, thoughtful, conscientious scholars in pursuit of truth or the truest account. Now it came to entail, rather, an immunity for whatever is said and done, responsibly or carelessly, within or without the walls of academia, by persons unconcerned for the truth; who, reckless, incompetent, frivolous or even malevolent, promulgate ideas for which they can claim no expertise, or even commit deeds for which they can claim no sanction of law.‡

This is what Silber referred to as "the absolute concept of

* Robert L. Paquette, "Of Liberty and License," *The Washington Times*, February 7, 2005, page A19.

† For a *tour d'horizon* of the assault on academic freedom, see Alan Charles Kors and Harvey A. Silveglate's book *The Shadow University: The Betrayal of Liberty on America's Campuses* (New York: The Free Press, 1998).

‡ John Silber, "Poisoning the Wells of Academe," *Encounter*, August, 1974, page 34.

academic freedom," according to which "the academic can say whatever he pleases about whatever he pleases, whenever and wherever he pleases, and be fully immune from unpleasant consequences."

In themselves, the Hamilton follies are scarcely noteworthy. The story that American colleges embrace left-wing radicals with no discernible scholarly accomplishment is a dog-bites-man piece of news—which is to say that it is not news at all but merely business as usual. Nevertheless, the controversy over the Rosenberg and Churchill episodes may have marked the beginning of a new chapter in the public's understanding of what goes on in American universities. In this sense, they may represent not only a scandal but also an opportunity. For the first time since the onslaught of the 1960s, a critical mass may be forming against the ready acquiescence to the politically correct imperatives of academic radicalism.

This resistance is crystallizing around two issues. One involves the distinction between free speech (the right to peaceful political dissent) and academic freedom (the more limited right to pursue, teach, and publish about the truth). This is a distinction that was often lost in the controversy over Ward Churchill. As the sociologist Edward Shils noted, academic freedom is "the freedom to seek and transmit the truth." It does not, he noted, "extend to the conduct of political propaganda in teaching."

Academic freedom is the freedom of university teachers to perform their academic obligations of teaching and research. These are obligations to seek and communicate the truth according to "their best lights." Academic freedom is not the freedom of academic individuals to do just anything, to follow any impulse or desire, or to say anything that occurs to them. It is the freedom to do academic things: to teach the truth as they see it on the basis of prolonged and intensive study, to discuss their ideas freely with their colleagues, to publish the truth as they have arrived at it by systematic methodical research and assiduous research.*

"That," Shils concludes, "is academic freedom proper." A number of corollaries follow. One is that one assesses academic things according to academic or intellectual criteria, "regardless of the person's political or religious beliefs, his or her sex, ethnic origin, personal qualities, kinship connections, friendship or enmity toward the individual or the work assessed." It also follows (and here what Shils has to say is particularly relevant to the case of Ward Churchill) that academic freedom is limited in certain ways. For example, "An academic is not free to falsify the record of his observations; he is not free to forge or misrepresent the contents of documents and inscriptions." Shils also goes on to argue that although "Academic freedom includes political freedom," it is nonetheless "desirable that teachers should not expound their own political or moral preferences and values in their classes," and, if they do, that "they should take care to distinguish evaluative judgments from their statements of fact."

The distinction between free speech and the more limited privilege of academic freedom is not novel. But it

---

* Edward Shils, "Academic Freedom," in *The Order of Learning: Essays on the Contemporary University* (New Brunswick: Transaction Publishers, 1997), pages 220–221.

is one that Joan Stewart, the president of Hamilton, had difficulty wrapping her mind around. In an open letter to the Hamilton community, Stewart invoked Hamilton's belief that "open-ended and free inquiry is essential to educational growth."* Well, fine. But surely a college president should understand that "open-ended and free inquiry" is one thing, political agitation and proselytizing is another. Our society provides many outlets for the expression of political opinions. Thank God for that. It has also taken care to provide for educational institutions whose purpose is learning, scholarship, and pedagogy. *Pace* President Stewart, academic freedom is not the same thing as free speech. It is a more limited freedom, designed to nurture intellectual integrity and to protect those engaged in intellectual inquiry from the intrusion of partisan passions. The very limitation of academic freedom is part of its strength. By excluding the political, it makes room for the pursuit of truth.

This is a point that was articulated well by the British philosopher Kenneth Minogue in *The Concept of a University*.

Universities were based, like all social institutions, on something valued—on a "value judgment," to use the current jargon. They were based (if I may use an old formula) on "the disinterested pursuit of truth." It was this pursuit, as it were, that constituted the moral basis of their authority. They had no direct concern with justice, and no one was ever sent to a university to make him courageous.

* "President Stewart Sends Message to Hamilton Community" is available at http://www.hamilton.edu/news/more_news/display.cfm?ID=9011.

Their excellence was to be found in their limits. Academia dealt in the virtues of truth and exactitude.*

What happened? In the 1960s, universities collapsed "in the face of a little juvenile swagger." They never recovered, most of them, and now Hamilton College (among many others) is reaping the fruit. Which leads us to the second, and more general, issue raised by the Hamilton follies, an issue I often advert to in these pages: the politicization of higher education.

What has become increasingly obvious in the aftermath of the Hamilton College follies is that the politicization advocated by the Kirkland Project and its successor at Hamilton College is also advocated by similar organizations at many, indeed most, other institutions of higher education in this country. Higher education has long been an important front in the culture war that began in the 1960s, a war whose aim is to remake American society according to a left-wing, antinomian blueprint.

The use and abuse of academic freedom to indemnify not the expression of unpopular opinions but political incitement of various kinds is one symptom of the degradation of American academic life. The newfound impatience with some extreme examples of that abuse is a heartening sign. Nevertheless, the whole issue of academic freedom is only part of a much larger phenomenon. Academics have an unspoken compact with society. As scholars, their charge is to pursue the truth in their chosen discipline; as teachers, their charge is to help preserve and transmit the truth by encouraging thought-

---

* Kenneth Minogue, *The Concept of a University* (New Brunswick: Transaction Publishers, 2005), page xv.

ful study and candid discussion. The largely unspoken nature of this compact was part of its glory—it underscored the element of freedom that has always been a central ingredient in liberal education. To a large extent, that freedom has been violated. How has this happened?

III Larry Summers and the girls

Consider the case of Lawrence Summers, the former president of Harvard University. A few years ago, Summers caused a ruckus when he suggested that Cornel West, who was then the Alphonse Fletcher, Jr., University Professor of Afro-American Studies at Harvard, buckle down to some serious scholarship (West's most recent production had been a rap CD called "Sketches of My Culture") and that he lead the way in fighting the scandal of grade inflation at Harvard where one of every two grades is an A or A-.

Summers was quite right. Cornel West (who figures prominently below in Chapter Two) is one of the most ridiculous figures in contemporary academia. He calls himself a philosopher but really is just a political sermonizer. He acts like an old-time revivalist minister. But his revival meetings feature not hellfire and brimstone but the racist failings of American society. What Summers did not understand was that college presidents are not allowed to criticize black professors. No sooner had Summers opened his mouth than West went into a snit, followed by the entire politically correct community at Harvard and beyond. Charles J. Ogletree, another professor of Afro-American Studies at Harvard, thundered that "It's absolutely critical that the president make an unequivocal public statement in support of affirmative action."* And *The New York Times*, natch, lumbered into support West and criticize Summers.

You might ask, why is it "critical" that the president of Harvard support "affirmative action"? After all, that is just a fancy phrase for discrimination on the basis of race, sex, or some other PC category. Isn't Harvard an institution of higher education where what matters is accomplishment, not skin color, sex, or ethnic background?

Summers evidently thought so, but he was quickly disabused of the notion. When West and his buddies in the Afro-American Studies department whined and threatened to leave Harvard, Summers collapsed. The whole thing, he said, was "a terrible misunderstanding." He told everybody how "proud" he was of "the Afro-American Studies program at Harvard, collectively and individually. We would very much like to see them stay at Harvard and will compete vigorously to make this an attractive environment." In other words, "Name your price, boys. I give up." Writing about the West v. Summers affair in *National Review*, I suggested that readers send Larry Summers a copy of Ralph Buchsbaum's zoological classic, *Animals Without Backbones*. I am happy to report that several did.

It didn't do any good, though. No sooner had the case of Cornel West died down than Mr. Summers found himself embroiled in another, and far more toxic, politically correct controversy. Speaking at a conference on "Diversifying the Science & Engineering Workforce" at MIT in

---

* Jacques Steinberg, "At Odds with Harvard President, Black-Studies Stars Eye Princeton," *The New York Times*, December 29, 2001. Article available at http://query.nytimes.com/gst/fullpage.html?res= 9F06E4D71F31F93AA15751C1A9679C8B63

2005, Summers speculated on why there are not more women scientists at elite universities. He touched on several possibilities: maybe "patterns of discrimination" had something to do with it. Maybe most women preferred to put their families before their careers. And maybe, just possibly, it had something to do with "different availability of aptitude at the high end."*

My, what a storm that last comment sparked! "I felt I was going to be sick," sniffed Nancy Hopkins, a professor of biology at the Massachusetts Institute of Technology, who then walked out on Summers. Oh, the poor dear. "My heart was pounding and my breath was shallow," Hopkins said. "I was extremely upset."† So take some Midol, Nancy, and lie down.

Of course, Summers was right. There are innate differences between men and women. Everyone knows this, even the feminists who most loudly deny it. But the wailing and gnashing of teeth that greeted Summers's comments pushed him into full retreat. He instantly published an open letter to the Harvard Community in order to abase himself: "I deeply regret the impact of my comments," he said, "and apologize for not having weighed them more carefully."‡ Mea culpa, mea culpa, mea maxima culpa. Naturally, he also claimed that he had been

* His remarks are available at http://www.president.harvard.edu/speeches/2005/nber.html.
† Quoted in Christina Hoff Sommers, "Summers Storm: A Feminist Show Trial at Harvard," in *National Review* February 14, 2005, pages 26–28.
‡ "Letter from President Summers on Women and Science," January 19, 2005. Available at http://www.president.harvard.edu/speeches/2005/womensci.html.

misunderstood: "Despite reports to the contrary, I did not say, and I do not believe, that girls are intellectually less able than boys, or that women lack the ability to succeed at the highest levels of science."

Now, I know some pretty smart women. I'm sure you do as well. Maybe, Dear Reader, you yourself are a very intelligent woman. That's not the issue. The issue is whether we are even allowed to ask if the innate differences between the sexes might express themselves in differences in intellectual aptitude and interest as well as in other ways.

As Larry Summers discovered to his sorrow, that interesting question is essentially unaskable in today's politically correct academic environment. Why is it unaskable? Well, let's see. That there *are* fewer women scientists is indubitable, even if it is impolite to mention the fact. But how can that be? For the last three decades, and especially in the last two decades, every college and university whose administrators can pronounce the phrase "affirmative action" has been scouring the world for girls who aren't actually brain dead and have showered them with any job their hearts desire. Jobs traditionally the preserve of males—engineering, say—were especially open to "talent," i.e., people of the right, i.e., the female, sex. So where are the female Einsteins and Freges and Hertzes and Bohrs? Where are the female Darwins and Mendels and Faradays? Where are the female . . . "Marie Curie, don't forget about Marie Curie, and . . . and . . . and . . . , well don't forget about Marie Curie!" OK, I won't. But Larry Summers embarrassed his oh-so-sensitive faculty with his well-meant but bumbling raising of the issue, and so he must suffer ritual humiliation and expulsion from the tribe. By May 2005, his faculty had returned a vote of no confidence by a margin of 218 to 185, with 18 abstentions. By February 2006, he had been forced to announce his resignation.* Harvard's motto is *Veritas*, "Truth." But truth-in-advertising should require them to add an asterisk: "*Veritas*—so long as the truth in question fully accords with the politically correct dictates of the day. Otherwise, *falsum* is the order of the day."

IV Duke, lacrosse, and the new racism

The virus of political correctness poisons the atmosphere of higher education in other ways as well. On April 11, 2007, Roy Cooper, the North Carolina attorney general, announced that he was dropping all charges against the three Duke lacrosse players who had been indicted for kidnapping and raping a black stripper in March 2006. As Mr. Cooper stressed, he was dropping the case not because there was insufficient evidence—often a euphemism for "probably guilty, but we can't prove it"—but because the three players were completely innocent of the charges that had recklessly been brought against them. Mr. Cooper went further: not only had there been "a tragic rush to accuse and a failure to verify serious allegations," but the case also showed "the enormous consequences of overreaching by a prosecutor."†

* Lawrence Summers, "Letter to the Harvard Community," February 21, 2006. Available at http://www.president.harvard.edu/speeches /2006/0221_summers.html.

† "Comments by Attorney General Roy Cooper: State vs. Finnerty, Evans, Seligmann," April 11, 2007. Document available at http://

In fact, the Duke lacrosse case showed a number of things. Yes, there was the issue of the disgraced district attorney Michael Nifong running amok, suppressing evidence and cynically bartering the lives of three white lacrosse players in his populist bid to win reelection in racially divided Durham. Nifong was certainly part of that "tragic rush to accuse." As was Syracuse University, which decided not to accept as transfers any students from the Duke lacrosse team—not just the three accused chaps, mind you, but *anyone* contaminated by having played lacrosse for Duke. "I think it would be inappropriate," sniffed Syracuse athletic director Daryl Gross.* But there are at least two other aspects of the case that deserve comment. One is the role of the media, which pounced on the story with unseemly delight. Oh, how *The New York Times*, *The Boston Globe*, and countless other bastions of liberal self-satisfaction loved it! Race. Class. Sex. Victimhood. It was the perfect morality tale. Those white jocks at "the Harvard of the South" just *had* to be guilty. And what a good time we were all going to have lacerating the malefactors while at the same time preening ourselves on our own superior virtue!

The editorials, the op-eds, the comments, the analyses poured forth non-stop, demonstrating that one of the deepest human passions is the urge to self-righteous pontification. The novelist Allan Gurganus epitomized the

---

www.ncdoj.com/DocumentStreamerClient?directory=PressReleases/&file=Dismissal%20Statement%20Press.pdf.

* "Syracuse refuses Duke lacrosse transfers," NBCSports.com, April 20, 2007. Report available at: http://nbcsports.msnbc.com/id/12407016/from/RS.2/.

tone in an op-ed for the *Times* in April 2006: "The children of privilege," he thundered, "feel vividly alive only while victimizing, even torturing."* You don't say? Even sports writers got into the act. Selena Roberts located Duke University "at the intersection of entitlement and enablement, . . . virtuous on the outside, debauched on the inside."† By August 2006, as Nifong's case was betraying worrisome fissures, the *Times* published a 6,000-word article arguing—"praying" might be a more apposite term—that, whatever weaknesses there might be in the prosecution's case, "there is also a body of evidence to support [taking] the matter to a jury."‡ As the *Times* columnist David Brooks ruefully noted after the tide had begun to turn, the campaign against the athletes had the lineaments of a "witch hunt."§

Not, of course, that the *Times* was alone. Even after the lacrosse players had been declared innocent, *The Boston Globe* began an editorial stating that "three members of the Duke lacrosse team may have been louts, but all the

---

* Allan Gurganus, "Blue Devils Made Them Do It," *The New York Times*, April 9, 2006. Article available at http://www.nytimes.com/2006/04/09/opinion/09gurganus.html.

† Selena Roberts, "When Peer Pressure, Not a Conscience, Is Your Guide," *The New York Times*, March 31, 2006. Article available at http://select.nytimes.com/2006/03/31/sports/31roberts.html

‡ Duff Wilson and Jonathan D. Glater, "Files from Duke Rape Case Give Details But No Answers," *The New York Times* August 25, 2008. Article available at http://www.nytimes.com/2006/08/25/us/25duke.html

§ David Brooks, "The Duke Witch Hunt," *The New York Times*, May 28, 2006. Article available at http://select.nytimes.com/2006/05/28/opinion/28brooks.html.

evidence suggests they were not rapists."* "Suggests," you see. Not "shows" or "demonstrates," even though the attorney general declared the athletes innocent of all charges. And what evidence is there to suggest that they are "louts"? They *have to be* louts, countless character references and testimonials to the contrary, otherwise the story wouldn't go according to script.

The other aspect of the Duke lacrosse fiasco that deserves special scrutiny is the behavior of university officials, especially the faculty. So let's see: there is a wild allegation of gang rape. What does Richard Brodhead, Duke's president, do? He remembers that in America there is the fundamental principle that one is innocent until proven guilty, so he urges patience and discretion, and displays statesmanlike leadership in helping Duke negotiate the troubled waters stirred up by the incident.

Just kidding. What President Brodhead really did was to suspend the accused students, fire the lacrosse coach, cancel the rest of the team's season, and pander to every possible interest, but especially to those baying for the heads of the accused. (One commentator estimated that only 3 percent of Brodhead's statements could be construed as supporting the accused students.)

And then there is the Duke faculty. As Vincent Carroll, writing in the *Rocky Mountain News*, noted, "the most astonishing fact, hands down, was and remains the squalid behavior of the community of scholars at Duke itself. For months nearly the entire faculty fell into one of two camps: those who demanded the verdict first and the

* "Short fuse," *The Boston Globe*, April 13, 2007. Article available at http://www.boston.com/news/globe/editorial_opinion/editorials/articles/2007/04/13/short_fuse/.

trial later, and those whose silence enabled their vigilante colleagues to set the tone."*

Particularly egregious was the behavior of the "Group of 88," a congeries of faculty activists and fellow-travelers who signed "What Does a Social Disaster Sound Like?," a full-page manifesto published in April 2006 in the Duke student newspaper.† The statement, which purported to be "listening" to students on campus, mingled anonymous student comments with racialist agitprop. "Regardless of the results of the police investigation," ran part of the introductory comment, "what is apparent everyday now is the anger and fear of many students who know themselves to be objects of racism and sexism." There followed a mosaic of histrionic proclamations: "We want the absence of terror," one student is supposed to have said. "But we don't really know what that means." "This is not a different experience for us here at Duke University. We go to class with racist classmates, we go to gym with people who are racists . . ."

The Group of 88 had clearly mastered the art of feigning shock in order to rivet attention and generate anxiety. But as Richard Bertrand Spencer noted in *The American Conservative*,

> Far from coming as a shock, the accusations that white students gang-raped a black stripper reached the Group as a kind of fulfillment of a dream. The case was, for them,

---

* Vincent Carroll, "Duke's Sorry Faculty," *Rocky Mountain News*, April 12, 2007.

† The document is available at http://www.dukenews.duke.edu/mmedia/pdf/socialdisasterad.pdf

an affirmation of what they always knew about Duke, Durham, and American society in general.*

According to the Group of 88, the alleged rape of a black woman by three white men was just business as usual in racist America. In fact, as the journalist Robert VerBruggen reported, "white-on-black rape is so rare there really isn't any way to measure its ups and downs."† For five of the last ten years, the National Crime Victimization Survey put the number at zero for its respondents.

But reality counts for little in the febrile world of the Group of 88. How little? Wahneema Lubiano, a tenured associate professor of literature and African-American studies, summed it up with all possible clarity when she wrote that "regardless of the 'truth,' whatever happens with the court case, what people are asking is that something changes."

Note the deflationary scare quotes around the word "truth." For Professor Lubiano, truth is expendable (if, indeed, it even exists). What matters is political action. So: it doesn't matter what those lacrosse players actually *did*. What matters is who they happen to be: i.e., where they fit into the politically correct racial-sexual-ethnic constellation of merit. As Professor Lubiano gleefully noted on her webblog, members of the lacrosse team "are almost perfect offenders" because they're "the exemplars

* Richard Bertrand Spencer, "Rotten in Durham," *The American Conservative*, February 26, 2007. Article available at http://www.amconmag.com/2007/2007_02_26/article5.html.

† Robert VerBruggen, "The Duke Case and Interracial Rape," posted January 15, 2007 at http://robertsrationale.blogspot.com/2007/01/duke-case-and-interracial-rape.html

of the upper end of the class hierarchy . . . and the dominant social group on campus."*

Some of the Group of 88 are common or garden-variety academic liberals—timid souls whose long tenure in the protected purlieus of the university surrounded by adolescents has nurtured their risible sense of self-importance and political enlightenment. But a good percentage are radicals more devoted to political activism than to scholarship. Indeed, one scandal that still has not received sufficient publicity is the preposterous pseudo-scholarship purveyed by many trendy academics. A look at the CVs of many members of the Group of 88 provides a case in point, partly shocking, partly embarrassing.† It's 99 percent race-class-gender gibberish embroidered with a toxic dollop of ill-digested lit-crit-speak and infatuation with the dregs of pop culture. "Shuckin' Off the African-American Native Other: What's PoMo Got to Do with It?," *Soul Babies: Black Popular Culture and the Post-Soul Aesthetic*, etc. This is scholarship at one of America's best universities?

One of the central players in the scandal was Houston A. Baker, Jr. You'll be hearing more about him below, especially in Chapters One and Seven. A former president of the Modern Language Association, Baker has built his career through a carefully orchestrated fabrication of race scandals and juvenile cultural relativism. (Choosing between Shakespeare and Jacqueline Susann, he once wrote, is "no

* Quoted in Kurt Andersen, "Rape, Justice, and the 'Times,'" *New York*, October 9, 2006. Article available at http://nymag.com/news/imperialcity/22337/.

† See, for example, the CVs of faculty in the Department of African & African-American Studies: http://fds.duke.edu/db/aas/AAAS/faculty.

different from choosing between a hoagy and a pizza," adding that "I am one whose career is dedicated to the day when we have a disappearance of those standards."* Soon after the lacrosse scandal broke, Professor Baker called for "immediate dismissals of those principally responsible for the horrors of this spring moment at Duke. Coaches of the lacrosse team, the team itself and its players, and any other agents who silenced or lied about the real nature of events." He joined the other members of the Group of 88 in signing a "thank you" letter to campus radicals who had distributed a "wanted" poster of the lacrosse players and publicly branded them "rapists." After the more serious charges against the three students were dropped in December, the mother of another member of the team emailed to ask if he would reconsider his comments. Professor Baker's response is illuminating:

> LIES You are just a provacateur [sic] on a happy New Years [sic] Eve trying to get credit for a scummy bunch of white males! . . .
>
> I really hope whoever sent this stupid farce of an email rots in . . . umhappy [sic] new year to you . . . and forgive me if your [sic] really are, quite sadly, mother of a "farm animal."†

Houston Baker was the George D. and Susan Fox Beischer Professor of English at Duke. How proud the Beischers must be. In the aftermath of the Duke scandals he decamped to a distinguished professorship at Vander-

---

* See below, page 5.

† See KC Johnson, "Baker: In His Own Words" at http://durham-wonderland.blogspot.com/2007/01/baker-in-his-own-words.html.

bilt University. What does that tell us about the state of American academia?

The story of this tawdry melodrama at Duke deserved an entire book, and it got a very good one in *Until Proven Innocent: Political Correctness and the Shameful Injustices of the Duke Lacrosse Rape Case* by KC Johnson, a professor of history at Brooklyn College, and the journalist Stuart Taylor. They show in horrifying detail how "many professors and, to a lesser extent, administrators at one of the nation's finest universities chose to grind their radical political axes at the expense of both their own students' well-being and the academy's traditional fidelity to due process."* Many people suffered because of the Duke farce. But what of the Professor Bakers and Wahneema Lubianos in the case? What of the Group of 88? They wrap themselves in the mantle of "academic freedom" and proceed as if nothing had happened. What a travesty.

V Academia and infantilization

Academic life, like the rest of social life, unfolds within a frame of rules and permissions. At one end, there are things that one must (or must not) do; at the other end, there is rule of whim. The middle range, in which behavior is neither explicitly governed by rules but is not entirely free, is that realm governed by what the British

---

* Stuart Taylor, Jr., and KC Johnson, *Until Proven Innocent: Political Correctness and the Shameful Injustices of the Duke Lacrosse Rape Case* (New York: Thomas Dunne Books/St. Martin's, 2007), page 387.

jurist John Fletcher Moulton, writing in the early 1920s, called "Obedience to the Unenforceable."

This middle realm is a place governed not by law or mere caprice, but by virtues such as duty, fairness, judgment, and taste. In a word, it is the "domain of Manners," which "covers all cases of right doing where there is no one to make you do it but yourself." A good index of the health of any social institution is its allegiance to the strictures that define this middle realm. "In the changes that are taking place in the world around us," Moulton wrote, "one of those which is fraught with grave peril is the discredit into which this idea of the middle land is falling." One example was the abuse of free speech in political debate: "We have unrestricted freedom of debate," say the radicals: "We will use it so as to destroy debate."*

The repudiation of obedience to the unenforceable is at the center of what makes academic life (and not only academic life) today so noxious. The contraction of the "domain of Manners" creates a vacuum that is filled on one side by increasing regulation—speech codes, rules for all aspects of social life, efforts to determine by legislation (from the right as well as from the left) what should follow freely from responsible behavior—and on the other side by increased license. More and more, it seems, academia (like other aspects of elite cultural life) has reneged on its compact with society.

One of the great ironies that attends the triumph of political correctness is that in department after department of academic life, what began as a demand for

---

* John Fletcher Moulton, "Law and Manners," *The Atlantic Monthly*, July 1924, pages 2–3.

emancipation recoiled, turned rancid, and developed into new forms of tyranny and control. As Alan Charles Kors noted in a recent essay,

> under the heirs of the academic Sixties, we moved on campus after campus from their Free Speech Movement to their politically correct speech codes; from their abolition of mandatory chapel to their imposition of Orwellian mandatory sensitivity and multicultural training; from their freedom to smoke pot unmolested to their war today against the kegs and spirits—literal and metaphorical—of today's students; from their acquisition of young adult status to their infantilization of "kids" who lack their insight; from their self-proclaimed dreams of racial and sexual integration to their ever more balkanized campuses organized on principles of group characteristics and group responsibility; from their right to define themselves as individuals—a foundational right—to their official, imposed, and politically orthodox notions of identity. American college students became the victims of a generational swindle of truly epic proportions.*

What, as Lenin memorably asked, is to be done?

As with any disease, the malady besetting academia requires two stages of therapy: first accurate diagnosis, then effective treatment. In some ways, the diagnostic stage is the most difficult, because it is the hardest to sustain. One corollary of society's natural obedience to the unenforceable is the tendency to assume that those institutions in which we have invested great trust are in-

---

* Alan Charles Kors, "On the Sadness of Higher Education," *The New Criterion*, May 2008, page 11.

herently trustworthy. "Academic institutions are expensive, socially respected bodies whose imprimatur is a powerful door-opener and tool of accreditation, ergo they *must* be doing a good job." Some such sentiment is the prevailing one, so when someone like Ward Churchill comes along to remove the scab, the shock is great—and unwelcome. One of the chief tasks for critics of what has happened to academic life in this country is to show the extent to which Ward Churchill, the Kirkland Project, the transgender follies at Smith College and elsewhere, and similar deformations are not exceptions but the predictable result of institutions that have gradually abandoned their commitment to education for the sake of radical posturing. The prime difficulty of facing the aspirant diagnostician is not the elusiveness of symptoms—they are florid and ubiquitous—but the patience required to set forth chapter and verse repeatedly and in language that effectively conveys the depredations on view.

The bright side of the Ward Churchill affair was the fact that public scrutiny brought dramatic, if local, changes. The melancholy side of the affair lay in the fact that the scrutiny had to be enormous and unremitting and that, as the media's attention wandered so did the public's interest. If real change is going to come to academic culture, criticism must be ceaseless, pointed, and deep. It is not enough to expose Ward Churchill. The academic culture that breeds and rewards such figures—and their name is legion—must be exposed for what it is: a thoroughly politicized rejection of the principles that inform liberal learning.

In one sense, the diagnosis of the calamity that has befallen academic culture is inseparable from the task of treatment. Which is to say that the job of criticism is never finished. Basic questions, the answers to which one could once have assumed were taken for granted, must be asked anew. To whom is the faculty accountable? To the extent that it holds itself accountable to its pedagogic duties, it is accountable to itself. To the extent that it repudiates those duties, it is accountable to the society in which it functions and from which it enjoys its freedoms, privileges, and perquisites. Faculties often take it amiss when critics appeal over their heads to alumni, trustees, or parents. But ultimately teachers still stand *in loco parentis*, if not on everyday moral issues then at least with respect to the content of the education they provide. Many parents are alarmed, rightly so, at the spectacle of their children going off to college one year and coming back the next having jettisoned every moral, religious, social, and political scruple that they had been brought up to believe. Why should parents fund the moral decivilization of their children at the hands of tenured antinomians? Why should alumni generously support an alma mater whose political and educational principles nourish a worldview that is not simply different from but diametrically opposed to the one they endorse? Why should trustees preside over an institution whose faculty systematically repudiates the pedagogical mission they, as trustees, have committed themselves to uphold? These are questions that should be asked early and asked often.

VI Tenure and other conundrums

It is time to revisit several large issues—the issue of tenure, for example. An arrangement that was intended to protect academic freedom and intellectual diversity has mutated into a means of enforcing conformity and excluding the heterodox. And for those representing establishment opinion in the academy, the institution of tenure has the added advantage that, like a virus, it tends to be self-perpetuating. In July 2008, under the headline "The '60s Begin to Fade as Liberal Professors Retire," *The New York Times* reported that "there are signs that the intense passions and polemics that roiled campuses during the past couple of decades have begun to fade."* But the truth is, *pace The New York Times*, what has happened is that those passions and polemics have been institutionalized, not abandoned. Faculties attract, promote, and grant tenure to candidates less on the basis of intellectual vigor or scholarly accomplishment than because they exhibit ideological like-mindedness. Indeed, one recent study suggests that faculties are if anything *more* left-leaning today than was previously thought. At one elite university, fully 87 percent of the faculty identifies itself as liberal.† For those few conservatives who have managed to obtain tenure, it doubtless functions to protect them. But for the faculty in general it seems to have become a prescription for political correctness and intellectual lassitude: get tenure, stop working.

Of course, the American academy is not entirely bereft of positive examples. Indeed, the task of reforming higher

* Patricia Cohen, "The '60s Begin to Fade as Liberal Professors Retire," *The New York Times*, July 3, 2008. Article available at http://www.nytimes.com/2008/07/03/arts/03camp.html.

† Howard Kurtz, "College Faculties a Most Liberal Lot, Study Finds," *The Washington Post*, March 29, 2005. Article available at http://www.washingtonpost.com/wp-dyn/articles/A8427-2005Mar 28.html

education has become a vibrant cottage industry, with think tanks, conferences, and special programs, institutes, and initiatives cropping up like mushrooms after a rain. I think, for example, of the Manhattan Institute's Center for the American University, The American Council of Trustees and Alumni, Robert George's Madison Center at Princeton University, The Tocqueville Forum on the Roots of American Democracy at Georgetown University, the Center for the Study of Western Civilization and American Institutions at the University of Texas, and the Alexander Hamilton Institute for the Study of Western Civilization in Clinton, New York.

Naturally, many of these initiatives—those whose home is at a college or university, anyway—run into stiff resistance. For example, when a couple of dissident professors at Hamilton College wanted to start a center named for Alexander Hamilton and dedicated to "excellence in scholarship through the study of freedom, democracy, and capitalism," the roof caved in on them. Hamilton was only too happy to invite the "post-porn feminist" Annie Sprinkle to campus to demonstrate sex toys for the young scholars; it wanted Susan Rosenberg—the former Weather Underground member whose 58-year sentence was commuted by Bill Clinton on his last day in office—to be an "artist- and activist-in-residence"; and it endeavored mightily to bring Ward Churchill to enlighten Hamilton students about 9/11 and American culture. But just let someone try celebrating the *achievements* of America and, bang, the predominantly left-wing faculty at Hamilton, terrified that there might be an initiative they didn't control, began whining about "governance" and "accountability." Fifteen minutes later, the administration capitulated and killed the center.

This particular story has a happy ending, however, because the Alexander Hamilton Institute for the Study of Western Civilization went ahead anyway—but not at Hamilton College. It's just down the street in Clinton, New York, in the old Alexander Hamilton Inn, a separate educational entity with no official ties to the college.*

I applaud all of these initiatives—indeed, I am involved in one way or another with some of them. But I wonder what lasting effect they will have on the intellectual and moral life of the university. They are important in any event because, even if they remain relegated to the sidelines of academic life, they demonstrate that real alternatives to reflexive academic left-wingery are possible.

I suspect, however, that they will remain minority enterprises, a handful of gadflies buzzing about the left-lunging behemoth that is contemporary academia. Why? There are several reasons.

One reason is that the left-wing monoculture is simply too deeply entrenched for these initiatives, laudable and necessary though they are, to make much difference. For the last few years, I have heard several commentators from sundry ideological points of view predict that the reign of political correctness and programmatic leftism on campus had peaked and was about to recede. I wish I could share that optimism. I see no evidence to support it. Sure, students are quiescent. But indifference is not instauration, and besides, faculties nearly everywhere form a self-perpetuating closed shop.

---

* The story of the travails of of this sorry episode is told by Robert Paquette, one of the Institute's founders in "The World We Have Lost: A Parable on the Academy," *The New Criterion* May 2008, pages 15–20.

It is the same with the fashion of "theory"—all that anemic sex-in-the-head politicized gibberish dressed up in reader-proof "philosophical" prose. It is true that names like Derrida or Foucault no longer produce the frisson of excitement they once did. Yet that is not because their "ideas" are widely disputed but rather because they are by now completely absorbed into the tissues of academic life. (Something similar happened with Freud a couple decades ago: it's not that his silly ideas were no longer influential; on the contrary, they had merely become commonplace assumptions: still toxic but by now taken for granted.)

In September 2002, *American Enterprise* magazine created a small stir when it published "The Shame of America's One-Party Campuses," providing some statistical evidence to bolster what everyone already knew: that American colleges and universities were overwhelmingly left-wing. You know the story: out of 30 English professors at college X, 29 are left-leaning Democrats and 1 is an Independent, while in the economics department of college Y, 33 profs are left-leaning Democrats and 1 is, or at least occasionally talks to, Republicans.* Etc., etc.

Well, that's all old hat now. As the 2008 presidential campaign was gearing up in the fall of 2007, *The Yale Daily News* ran a story revealing that faculty and staff at Yale contributed 45 times more to Democratic candidates than to Republications. "Most people in my department," said the one doctor known to have contributed to the

---

* Karl Zinsmeister, "The Shame of America's One-Party Campus," *American Enterprise*, September 2002. The article is available online at http://www.taemag.com/issues/articleid.17443/article_detail .asp

campaign of Rudolph Giuliani, "are slightly to the left of Joseph Stalin.""*

The key issue, I hasten to add, is not partisan politics but rather the subordinating of intellectual life to non-intellectual, i.e., political imperatives. "The greatest danger," the philosopher Leszek Kolakowski wrote in "What Are Universities For?," "is the invasion of an intellectual fashion which wants to abolish cognitive criteria of knowledge and truth itself. . . . The humanities and social sciences have always succumbed to various fashions, and this seems inevitable. But this is probably the first time that we are dealing with a fashion, or rather fashions, according to which there are no generally valid intellectual criteria."† Indeed, it is this failure—a failure to check the colonization of intellectual life by politics—that stands behind and fuels the degradation of liberal education. The issue is not so much—or not only—the presence of bad politics as the absence of non-politics in the intellectual life of the university.

At the end of *Until Proven Innocent*, their masterly account of the Duke lacrosse scandal, KC Johnson and Stuart Taylor describe the "assault on excellence" currently taking place in the academy. They quote from *Excellence Without a Soul: How a Great University Forgot Education*, a study of Harvard by Harry R. Lewis, a former dean at Harvard College:

---

* Andrew Mangino, "Profs donate heavily to Dems," *Yale Daily News*, September 10, 2007. The article is available at http: //www.yaledailynews.com/articles/view/21235.

† Leszek Kolakowski, "What Are Universities For?," in *My Correct Views on Everything* (South Bend: Saint Augustine's Press, 2005), page 241.

xliv

There is absolutely nothing that Harvard can expect students will know after they take three science or three humanities courses freely chosen from across the entire course catalog. The proposed general-education requirement gives up entirely on the idea of shared knowledge, shared values, even shared aspirations. In the absence of any pronouncement that anything is more important than anything else for Harvard students to know, Harvard is declaring that one can be an educated person in the 21st Century without knowing anything about genomes, chromosomes, or Shakespeare.

Johnson and Taylor comment that "Absent outside intervention—from alumni, trustees, parents, the media—academic culture is likely to grow more, not less, extreme."* I suspect that they are right about the ideological drift and "dumbing down" of the academy, the "assault on excellence." Consider, to take two interrelated examples, the decreasing popularity of merit scholarships and the increasing popularity of "diversity" initiatives and "open" curricula in which students approach education as if it were a smorgasbord. But I am not so sanguine about the remedy they propose. I used to think that appealing over the heads of the faculty to trustees, parents, alumni, and other concerned groups could make a difference. I have become increasingly less confident about that strategy. For one thing, it is extremely difficult to generate a sense of emergency sufficiently alarming that those groups will actually take action, let alone maintain that sense of emergency long enough to allow action to develop into meaningful, large-scale reform.

* *Until Proven Innocent*, page 401.

What's more, those groups are increasingly impotent. Time was when a prospective hiccup in the annual fund would send shivers down the spine of an anxious college president. These days, as James Piereson pointed out in an essay on the Left University in *The Weekly Standard*, many colleges and universities are so rich that they can afford to cock a snook at parents and alumni. Forget about Harvard and its $30 billion, or Princeton or Yale, or Stanford, or the other super-rich schools. Even many small colleges are sitting on huge fortunes.

Consider tiny Hamilton College once more. When I reported on the Susan Rosenberg case in *The Wall Street Journal*, the story appeared on the day that Hamilton kicked off a capital campaign at the New York Historical Society. My article was highly critical and generated a lot of comment. Donations to Hamilton, I am told, simply dried up. But so what? The college enjoys an endowment of some $780 million. That is more three-quarters of a billion dollars.† So what if the annual fund is down a few millions this year? Big deal. They can afford to hunker down and wait out the outcry.

Deep and lasting change in the university depends on deep and lasting change in the culture at large. Undertaking that task is a tall order. Criticism, satire, and ridicule all have an important role to play, but the point is that such criticism, to be successful, depends upon possessing an alternative vision of the good.

---

* James Piereson, "The Left University, *The Weekly Standard*, October 3, 2005. The article is available on-line at http://www.weeklystandard.com/Content/Public/Articles/000/000/006/120xbklj.asp.

† http://www.hamilton.edu/hamilton_at_a_glance/financial_information.html

Do we possess that alternative vision? I believe we do. We all know, well enough, what a good liberal education looks like, just as we all know, well enough, what makes for a healthy society. It really isn't that complicated. It doesn't take a lot of money or sophistication. What it does require is candidness and courage, moral virtues that are in short supply wherever political correctness reigns triumphant. The bottom line is that those who want to retake the university must devote themselves cultivating those virtues and perhaps even more to cultivating the virtue of patience, capitalizing wherever possible on whatever local opportunities present themselves.

Tenured Radicals
Preface to the Second Edition, 1998

A *cultivated intellect, a delicate taste, a candid, equitable, dispassionate mind, a noble and courteous bearing in the conduct of life; these . . . are the objects of a University.*
—John Henry Newman, *The Idea of a University* (1852)

The idea that the curriculum should be converted to any partisan purposes is a perversion of the ideal of the university. The objective of converting the curriculum into an instrument of social transformation (leftist, rightist, centrist, or whatever) is the very opposite of higher education.
—John Searle, *The New York Review of Books* (1991)

IT WAS not all that long ago that these preeminently liberal propositions drawn from Cardinal Newman and the philosopher John Searle could have been embraced as mottos by the American academic establishment. This is not to say that our institutions of higher education necessarily lived up to the ideal that Newman enunciated, or that they always avoided the perversion against which Professor Searle warned. But the ability to recognize an ideal as an ideal, or a perversion as a perversion, had not yet atrophied. Indeed, until at least the early 1960s there was robust agreement about the intellectual and moral goals of a liberal arts education even if those goals seemed impossible to achieve. Above all, there was a shared commitment to the ideal of disinterested scholarship devoted to the preservation and transmission of knowledge pursued in a community free from ideological intimidation. If we inevitably fell short of the ideal, the ideal nevertheless continued to command respect and allegiance.

There is perhaps no more dramatic index of the disaster that has befallen liberal arts education in this country than the contempt in which the new academic orthodoxy holds this constellation of ideas about the nature and goals of higher education. It would be difficult to overstate the resulting intellectual carnage. Because the degradation of education implies the degradation of the future, "disaster" may be too weak a word. Everything about Newman's description—from its lucid diction and lofty tone to its praise of the dispassionate cultivation of the intellect—is an object of derision in the academy today. Likewise, Professor Searle's insistence that the curriculum not be reduced to a tool for partisan propaganda, "leftist, rightist, centrist, or whatever," is now widely derided as hopelessly naïve or insidiously reactionary.

Are there exceptions? Yes, of course. But by the time I published the first edition of *Tenured Radicals* in 1990, they had already become just that, exceptions. And although a small but steady stream of books and articles has appeared to take issue with one or another dimension of the academic assault on truth, the situation is far graver today than it was a decade ago when exotic phenomena such as Afrocentrism, Queer Theory, Critical

1

Legal Studies, and the attack on science by so-called humanists were just beginning to gather steam. Now more than ever those dominating the discussion in academia are committed to discrediting the ideals of objectivity and disinterested scholarship by injecting politics into the heart of the educational enterprise.

The much-publicized controversy over attempts to enforce "politically correct" thinking on American campuses in the name of "diversity" and higher virtue, for example, has underscored the extent to which higher education has been transformed into a species of ideological indoctrination—a continuation of politics by other means.* The politics in question are the politics of victimhood. Increasingly, academic study is organized not around intellectual criteria but simply to cater to the demands of various politically approved "marginalized" groups. Anyone still harboring doubts about the extent of the damage is invited to try the experiment of proposing the gist of either of my epigraphs to the humanities faculty at any major college or university in the country. There may be a handful of professors who will agree privately—some will whisper their support afterwards if no one is looking—but most will sit in abject silence as you are informed by their politically correct colleagues that these ideas are reactionary, white, male, elitist, Western, and exclusionary, not to say outmoded. If the institution is up-to-date, you may even be directed to a sensitivity

* See Alan Charles Kors and Harvey A. Silverglate *The Shadow University: The Betrayal of Liberty on America's Campuses* (New York: The Free Press, 1998) and Roger Kimball "Political Correctness Or, The Perils of Benevolence" *The National Interest*, No. 74, Winter 2003–2004, pages 158–165.

training class in order that you might avoid such transgressions in the future.

Like most modern tyrannies, the dictatorship of the politically correct has freely used and abused the rhetoric of virtue in its effort to enforce conformity and silence dissent. This is part of what makes it so seductive. How gratifying to know that one is automatically on the side of Virtue simply because one espouses the party line! But the union of moralism and radicalism, while hardly a novel marriage—it was pioneered by Jean-Jacques Rousseau and perfected by his disciple Maximilien Robespierre—is particularly destructive when applied to institutions dedicated to intellectual inquiry. Not only does it foster an atmosphere of intimidation and encourage slavish conformity, but it also attacks the very basis for the free exchange of ideas. As the philosopher Allan Bloom observed, "now the universities have become the battleground of a struggle between liberal democracy and radical, or, one might say, totalitarian, egalitarianism."*

It goes without saying that the new academic elite—the tenured or soon-to-be-tenured radicals now controlling nearly all of the most prestigious humanities departments in this country—constantly object that the academy's critics have overstated the case. Really, they say, there is nothing amiss, nothing has happened that need concern parents, trustees, alumni, government or private funding sources. On the issue of enforcing politically correct behavior on campus, for example, they will assure you that the whole thing has been overblown by "conservative"

---

* Allan Bloom, "The Democratization of the University," in *Giants and Dwarfs: Essays 1960–1990* (New York: Simon and Schuster, 1990), page 367.

journalists who do not sufficiently admire Michel
Foucault and cannot appreciate that the free exchange of
ideas must sometimes be curtailed for the higher virtue of
protecting the feelings of designated victim groups. And
the curriculum, they will say, has not been politicized, it
has merely been democratized: opened up to reflect the
differing needs and standards of groups and ideas hitherto insufficiently represented in the academy.

The aim of such tendentious arguments is not to enlighten or persuade but to intimidate and pre-empt criticism. This of course is something that our new academic
mandarins cannot bring themselves to acknowledge. But
the truth is that what we are facing today is nothing less
than the destruction of the fundamental premises that
underlie our conception both of liberal education and of a
liberal democratic polity. Respect for rationality and the
rights of the individual; a commitment to the ideals of
disinterested criticism and color-blind justice; advancement according to merit, not according to sex, race, or
ethnic origin: these quintessentially Western ideas are
bedrocks of our political as well as our educational system. And they are precisely the ideas that are now under
attack by politically correct academics intoxicated by the
coercive possibilities of inherent in the ideology of virtue.

How bad is it? You be the judge. Item: Richard Delgado, a law professor and proponent of the influential
Critical Legal Studies movement, neatly epitomized one

* One politically correct academic even went so far as claim that
political correctness was a "myth," i.e., that it didn't exist. See John
K. Wilson *The Myth of Political Correctness: The Conservative
Attack on Higher Education* (Durham: Duke University Press,
1995).

aspect of the current orthodoxy when he insisted that "racism and enlightenment are the same thing" and went on to argue that the concept of merit is "a prominent example" of "the kind of racism evident in facially [sic] neutral laws." Another law professor, the radical feminist Catharine MacKinnon, summed up a different aspect of the situation when she declared that feminism's "critique of the objective standpoint as male is a critique of science as a specifically male approach to knowledge. With it we reject male criteria for verification."*

"Male criteria for verification"? Oh dear. Of course, the assault is not undertaken solely by law professors. Michael Harris, a professor of religious studies at the University of Tennessee, put it this way: "when you see the word 'qualifications' used, remember that this is the new code word for whites."† Sandra Harding, the author of *The Science Question in Feminism*, among other works, blithely described Isaac Newton's *Principia* as a "rape manual." The Afrocentrist Hunter Adams assured his readers that "early African writings indicate a possible understanding of quantum physics and gravitational theory."‡ Jonathan Culler, a professor of literature at Cornell

---

* Quoted in Daniel A. Farber and Suzanna Sherry, *Beyond All Reason: The Radical Assault on Truth in American Law* (New York: Oxford University Press, 1997), *seriatim*, pages 29, 32, 26.

† Quoted in Dinesh D'Souza, *Illiberal Education: The Politics of Race and Sex on Campus* (New York: Free Press, 1991), page 4.

‡ Quoted in Paul Gross and Norman Levitt, *Higher Superstition: The Academic Left and Its Quarrels with Science* (Baltimore: Johns Hopkins University Press, 1994), *seriatim*, pages 131, 208. Since *Tenured Radicals* was first published, attacks on the cogency of scientific rationality have emerged as one of the most toxic growth

and a follower of the French deconstructionist Jacques Derrida, solemnly wrote that "since no reading can escape correction, all readings are misreadings."* In a similar spirit, the historian Simon Schama told his readers that "the claims for historical knowledge must always be fatally circumscribed by the character and prejudices of its narrator."† And if these examples seem too abbreviated, consider as a final instance this more extended quotation from a book called *Feminism and Geography: The Limits of Geographical Knowledge*, "a sustained examination of the masculinism of contemporary geographical discourses":

> Women's exclusion is not only a question of the themes of research, nor even of the new concepts with which feminists work to organize those themes, but rather a question related to the very nature of hegemonic geographical knowledge itself. . . . I argue that to think geography—to think within the parameters of the discipline— is to occupy a masculine subject position. Geography is masculinist. . . . After examining many of the founding texts of philosophy, science, political theory and history,

---

industries in the academy. *Higher Superstition*, written with great wit and clarity by a biologist and a mathematician, is a classic anatomy. Its work is carried further by Alan Sokal and Jean Bricmont's *Fashionable Nonsense: Postmodern Intellectuals' Abuse of Science* (New York: Picador, 1998).

* Jonathan Culler, *On Deconstruction: Theory and Criticism after Structuralism* (Ithaca: Cornell University Press, 1982), page 178.
† Simon Schama, *Dead Certainties (Unwarranted Speculations)* (New York: Vintage, 1992), page 322.

feminists have argued that the notion of reason as it developed from the seventeenth century onwards is not gender neutral. On the contrary, it works in tandem with white bourgeois heterosexual masculinities.*

The important point to understand about these examples—and they could easily be multiplied tenfold—is not how extravagant but, on the contrary, how common they are. Such vertiginous nonsense—ranging over disciplines as various as literature, law, history, and the social sciences—now constitutes a large proportion of what is taught and pursued as "scholarship" in the academy. Typically combining hermetic jargon and a profound animus against the achievements of the Western moral and intellectual tradition, such politicized rhetoric governs the teaching of the humanities from the ground up. And it is in this sense, as the philosopher Roger Scruton has pointed out, that "the radical curriculum is not so much a *reformed* curriculum as an anti-curriculum," one designed to short-circuit the humanities by redefining them as a species of political grievance-mongering.†

From the Marxist literary critic Fredric Jameson to the post-structuralist philosopher Michel Foucault, from Jacques Derrida to the legions of lesser-known feminist "theorizers," devotees of "cultural studies," and all-purpose academic radicals, you'll find slightly different arrangements of the same old song: All cultural and intellec-

---

* Quoted in William A. Henry, III *In Defense of Elitism* (New York: Doubleday, 1994), page 117.

† Roger Scruton, "On Humane Education," a lecture presented at Boston University in December 1992 (Boston: Boston University, 1993), page 23.

tual life is "really," at bottom a coefficient of power relations. There is, according to this dour philosophy, no truth untainted by political ambitions, no realm of intellectual or artistic endeavor not subordinated to ulterior passions. This is part of what many academics mean when they say—and they never stop saying it—that all art and literature, indeed, that all "discourse," including science, including even sexuality, is "socially constructed."

As I show below in Chapter Six, in essentials the argument is as old as Thrasymachus's insistence, in Plato's *Republic*, that "might makes right," though it got a major overhaul when Marx came along with his theory of ideology. John Ellis, an emeritus professor of German literature, put it neatly when he observed that "as Marxism is to the economic sphere, so cultural political correctness is to the cultural sphere."* Just as the one promised abundance and everywhere brought penury and wretchedness, so the other promises greater freedom and diversity and winds up demanding a lock-step conformism in intellectual as well as moral matters. The great irony, of course, is that whereas Marxism as a political force has been shown the world over to be both barbarous and morally bankrupt, its prestige in Western universities remains undiminished.

Indeed, for the gender-race-class cadres that now dominate the discussion in the university, all social, artistic, and intellectual life must be subjected to a battery of political tests. This marks what we might call the Sovietization of intellectual life, where the value or truth of a work is determined not by its intrinsic qualities

---

* John Ellis, *Literature Lost: Social Agendas and the Corruption of the Humanities* (New Haven: Yale University Press, 1997), page 31.

(many deny that "intrinsic qualities" even exist) but by the degree to which it supports a given political line. In some ways, this approach to cultural life is highly moral—or, rather, highly moralistic. Although it is thoroughly anti-bourgeois and thoroughly anti-traditional in its morality, it nevertheless seeks to judge every product of the human spirit by the degree of "virtue" it exhibits—where "virtue" is defined beforehand by whatever sexual, feminist, Marxist, racial, or ethnic agenda to which the particular critic has declared his allegiance.

This extraordinary, if perverted, moralism is of course one of the great appeals of contemporary academic radicalism. Few things are more titillating to modern intellectuals—who grow up being told that their pursuits are of limited social utility—than the prospect of infusing their work with high moral purpose. How edifying to think that one is not simply teaching a novel by Jane Austen but is somehow also striking a blow for female emancipation! How exciting to believe that one is not just reading Shakespeare but is somehow challenging the evils of imperialism at the same time!

There is, however, a problem with this moralistic approach: like all totalitarian impulses, it winds up being terribly simple-minded and philistine, unfitting the mind for serious thought. Moralistic tests of cultural achievement always wind up being reductive, and the more ruthlessly applied, the more reductive are their tenets. This is where the jargon of deconstruction, post-structuralism, and kindred Continental imports has been a godsend for "cutting edge" academics. It has allowed them to indulge their moralism to the hilt while at the same time appearing to be intellectually sophisticated (or incomprehensible, which is often just as effective).

Unfortunately, the moralism is as unconvincing—it is preachily moralistic rather than genuinely concerned with moral issues— as the sophistication is bogus. The anti-Western and (in particular) anti-American animus of so much academic radicalism has its origins in a utopian Romanticism that goes back at least to Rousseau. It was disastrous then and it is disastrous now. As the distinguished historian Jacques Barzun observed, "the current obscurantism, which attacks the Western tradition with the zeal of censorship, comes not from those supposedly unrepresented in the curriculum, but from academics and other intellectuals who *are* represented and hate their own heritage."* It should be said, too, that in extolling the virtues of societies and civilizations other than our own—and at the expense of our own—today's tenured radicals are merely following in the footsteps of intellectually disgruntled figures as diverse as the eighteenth-century German Romantic Johann Herder, the anthropological fantasist Margaret Mead, and beyond.

The most ironic aspect of this whole phenomenon is that what appears to its adherents as bravely anti-Western is in fact part of the West's long tradition of self-scrutiny. Indeed, criticism of the West has been a prominent ingredient in the West's self-understanding at least since Socrates invited his fellow Athenians to debate with him about the nature of the good life. No civilization in history has been as consistently self-critical as the West. The very concept of "ethnocentrism," which is used like a sledge-hammer to disparage the West, is a Western inven-

---

* Jacques Barzun, *Begin Here: The Forgotten Conditions of Teaching and Learning*, edited by Morris Philipson (Chicago: University of Chicago Press, 1991), page 129.

lix

tion. Susan Sontag once charged that the white race was "the cancer of human history."* But the civilization represented by that much-maligned race has been considerably less ethnocentric—and considerably more enlightened politically—than any other civilization in world history. Of course the West is not perfect; but perfection is not given to humanity. And the insistence that perfection can be achieved is a prescription for engendering misery. Professor Ellis is very persuasive on this point.

> Our Western cultural inheritance is not perfect, but it has succeeded in raising us from the barbarism of a state of nature. It has managed to abolish many forms of human cruelty, has given us forms of democratic government that actually work, and has a record of human thought in literature and philosophy that offers extraordinary range, depth, and complexity. Far from debasing human beings, it has enhanced their dignity in a thousand different ways. We can build on it, extend it, modify it; but if we allow the politically correct to pull it down with their characteristic utopian promises about what they can replace it with, we have only ourselves to blame. We can be sure that if we allow their destructive resentment to destroy yet again so that they can create perfection, we shall witness the destruction but never see the benefits promised.†

If the claims of the politically correct to greater moral sensitivity and insight cannot stand, neither can their as-

---

* Susan Sontag, "What's Happening in America (1966)," in *Styles of Radical Will* (New York: Farrar, Straus and Giroux, 1969), page 203.

† *Literature Lost*, page 32.

sumption of superior intellectual sophistication. One of the first things one notices about today's academic writing is how drab and unvarying it is. Works of literature are read not for what they are in themselves but for predetermined political lessons about some form of racial injustice, sexual oppression, or class warfare. The result is formulaic criticism that never really engages its subject. In other words, what is left out of a politicized view of literature is literature. As Roger Scruton observed,

> behind the many pseudo-sciences that have recently dominated literary criticism . . . you will find the same suspicion of literature, a desire to sever our relation to it by denuding it of meaning. The "methods" proposed are laughable caricatures of science; and the results delivered are useful to no one. But that was not the point. The methods of the new literary theorist are really weapons of subversion: an attempt to destroy humane education from within, to rupture the chain of sympathy that binds us to our culture. That is why the new schools of criticism have acquired a following: they promise to release us from the burden of study by showing that there is nothing after all to learn.[*]

Trivializing the nature of aesthetic experience—which in its highest sense binds us to a larger community by educating that most social of faculties, taste—politicized criticism reduces everything to politics. And—yet another irony—even the operative idea of politics is simplistic, for, to quote Professor Ellis once more,

[*] "On Humane Education," page 18.

a meaningful politics must recognize other important values in human life. Indeed, politics makes no sense when it stands by itself. If the question who wields political power is not broadened to take account of what that power is to be used for—that is, what human values it will serve—then it reduces to a matter of who manages to subdue whom.*

In other words, the result is a brutish, one-dimensional view of human relations that is not so much political as a barbaric parody of politics.

Writing about the literary scene of the late nineteenth-century, the novelist William Dean Howells once re-marked that the chief problem for a critic was not making enemies but keeping them. By that measure, anyway, *Tenured Radicals* must be judged a success, since it quickly became, with Allan Bloom's *Closing of the American Mind* and Dinesh D'Souza's *Illiberal Education*, one of the books that contemporary academics most loved to hate. If there was an undeniable satisfaction in that ac-complishment, it was a melancholy satisfaction; for what is at stake in the controversy over the politicization of the humanities is a profound diminishment of our culture and, ultimately, of ourselves.

RK *Easter 1998*

* *Literature Lost*, page 63.

Introduction

I

I T IS no secret that the academic study of the humanities in this country is in a state of crisis. Proponents of deconstruction, feminist studies, and other politically motivated challenges to the traditional tenets of humanistic study have by now become the dominant voice in the humanities departments of many of our best colleges and universities. And while there are important differences and even struggles among these various groups, when seen from the perspective of the tradition they are seeking to subvert—the tradition of high culture embodied in the classics of Western art and thought—they exhibit a remarkable unity of purpose. Their object is nothing less than the destruction of the values, methods, and goals of traditional humanistic study. This book is a chronicle of the progress of that destruction.

Whether one turns to Princeton University's Elaine Showalter, who has called for a "complete revolution" in the teaching of literature in order to enfranchise "gender as a fundamental category of literary analysis," or to Houston Baker, the Albert M. Greenfield Professor of Human Relations at the University of Pennsylvania and president of the Modern Language Association in 1992, who touts the black power movement of the 1960s as a desirable alternative to the "white Western" culture he sees enshrined in the established literary canon, or to Duke University's Fredric Jameson who propounds a Marxist vision of criticism that takes the "extreme position" that "the political perspective" is the "absolute horizon of all reading and all interpretation," one finds a thoroughgoing animus to the traditional values of Western thought and culture. ("Everything," Jameson writes in a phrase that has become a rallying cry of the new academic radicalism, "is 'in the last analysis' political.")*

The same is true—albeit in a more rarefied way—of the legions of deconstructionists, post-structuralists, and other forbiddingly named academics who congregate in departments of English, French, comparative literature, history, and other disciplines. With their criticism of the "logocentric" and "phallocentric" Western tradition, their insistence that language always refers only to itself, and their suspicion of logic and rationality, they exhibit a species of skepticism that is essentially nihilistic and deeply at odds with the ideals of a liberal arts education—ideals, it must be

---

* Fredric Jameson, *The Political Unconscious: Narrative as a Socially Symbolic Act* (Ithaca: Cornell University Press, 1981), *seriatim*, pages 17, 20. Since this was written, Houston Baker (who also figures in chapter one below) went on to fancy professorships at Duke and, most recently, Vanderbilt University, where he is "a distinguished university professor."

added, that also underlie the democratic institutions and social life of the West. The conviction uniting these disparate groups received dramatic expression at Stanford University in the late 1980s when Jesse Jackson and some five hundred students marched chanting, "Hey hey, ho ho, Western culture's got to go." The influential philosopher Richard Rorty, a professor at the University of Virginia and himself a champion of everything chic and postmodern in the humanities, accurately summed up the situation when he noted that "a new American cultural Left has come into being made of deconstructionists, new historicists, people in gender studies, ethnic studies, media studies, a few left-over Marxists, and so on. This Left would like to use the English, French, and Comparative Literature Departments of the universities as staging areas for political action."* Identifying himself as a proponent of "liberal irony," Rorty applauds this development, seeing in it a means of distracting philosophy from its traditional concern with old-fashioned ideas like truth and justice. Indeed, he looks forward to a time when philosophy as a distinct discipline will have disappeared altogether, and he aims to hurry its demise by "blurring the literature-philosophy distinction and promoting the idea of a seamless, undifferentiated 'general text,'" in which, say, Aristotle's *Metaphysics*, a television program, and a French novel might coalesce into an exciting object of hermeneutical scrutiny.†

* Quoted in Sidney Hook, "Civilization and Its Malcontents," *National Review*, 13 Oct. 1989, pages 30–33. Rorty moved on from Virginia to Stanford in 1998 and died in June of 2007.
† Richard Rorty, *Contingency, Irony, and Solidarity* (Cambridge: Cambridge University Press, 1989), pages xiii–xvi.

II

In this war against Western culture, one prime object of attack within the academy is the traditional literary canon and the pedagogical values it embodies. The notion that some works are better and more important than others; that some works exert a special claim on our attention; that "being educated" requires a thoughtful acquaintance with these works and an ability to discriminate between greater and lesser—all this is anathema to the forces arrayed against the traditional understanding of the humanities. The very idea that the works of Shakespeare (for example) might be indisputably greater than the collected cartoons of Bugs Bunny is often rejected as "antidemocratic" and "elitist," an imposition on the freedom and political interests of various groups.*

At many colleges and universities, students are now treated to courses in which the products of popular culture—Hollywood movies, rock and roll, comic strips, and the like—are granted parity with (or even precedence over) the most important cultural achievements of our civilization. Typical is the philosopher Stanley Cavell's seminar at Harvard University on the movies of Katharine Hepburn and Spencer Tracy or a graduate course at Columbia University on Victorian and modern British literature that repeatedly took time to ponder the relevance of the pop singer Bruce Springsteen and the

---

* For a wide-ranging critical assessment of this attack on intellectual standards, see *In Defense of Elitism* by William A. Henry, III (New York: Doubleday, 1994) and my review essay of Henry's book, "What's Wrong with Equality?" in *The New Criterion*, Oct. 1994, pages 4–10.

television series "Star Trek" to the issues at hand. Instead of aspiring to gain a thoughtful acquaintance with (as the Victorian poet and critic Matthew Arnold famously put it) "the best that has been thought and said," these new forces in the academy deliberately elide the distinction between high culture and popular culture. They pretend, to quote Houston Baker again, that choosing between Pearl Buck and Virginia Woolf, for example, or between Shakespeare and Jacqueline Susann is "no different from choosing between a hoagy and a pizza." Professor Baker added, "I am one whose career is dedicated to the day when we have a disappearance of those standards."*

Even the most cursory glance at what passes for humanities offerings at colleges and universities across the country will serve to corroborate these impressions. With a few notable exceptions, our most prestigious liberal arts colleges and universities have installed the entire radical menu at the center of their humanities curriculum at both the undergraduate and the graduate levels. Every special interest—women's studies, black studies, gay studies, and the like—and every modish interpretive gambit—deconstruction, post-structuralism, new historicism, and other postmodernist varieties of what the literary critic Frederick Crews aptly dubbed "Left Eclecticism"—has found a welcome roost in the academy, while the traditional curriculum and modes of intellectual inquiry are excoriated as sexist, racist, or just plain reactionary.†

---

* Joseph Berger, "U.S. Literature: Canon Under Siege," *The New York Times*, 6 Jan. 1988.

† Although I have occasion to cite Professor Crews and his notion of "Left Eclecticism" more than once in *Tenured Radicals*, it is worth noting that in his subsequent writings Crews has been careful to

Thus what began as an intoxicating intellectual spree at a few elite institutions—places such as Yale, Johns Hopkins, Brown, and certain campuses of the University of California—has quickly spread to many other institutions. This metastasis is indeed one of the most troubling developments in the story of the crisis of the humanities. Increasingly, second- and third-tier schools are rushing to embrace all manner of fashionable intellectual ideolo-

distance himself from conservative critics of the trends he himself criticizes. Thus in a collection of essays on American fiction, he dismisses "such cultural nostalgics as William Bennett, Allan Bloom, Lynne Cheney, and Roger Kimball" as "people who conceive of the ideal university as a pantheon for the preservation of great works and great ideas" and who "implicitly subscribe to a 'transfusion' model of education, whereby the stored-up wisdom of the classics is considered a kind of plasma that will drip beneficially into our veins if we only stay sufficiently passive in its presence." Professor Crews goes on to assure his readers that he wants "keen debate, not reverence for great books." Never mind that none of the critics he cites, including myself, has ever endorsed anything like the simplistic "transfusion" model conjured up here; nor do any of the critics he cites wish to replace "keen debate" with unquestioning "reverence." The main point is that, like many academics, Professor Crews is willing to countenance "keen debate" only when it comes from certified segments of the academic brotherhood. Interlopers—especially conservative interlopers—are to be excluded from participating, keenly or otherwise, in the discussion. See Frederick Crews, *The Critics Bear It Away: American Fiction and the Academy* (New York: Random House, 1992), page xiv, and *Postmodern Pooh* (Evanston: Northwestern University Press, 2001).

gies as so many formulas for garnering prestige, publicity, and "name" professors (and hoping thereby to attract more students and other sources of income) without having to distinguish themselves through the less-glamorous and more time-consuming methods of good teaching and lasting scholarship. One case in point was Duke University, which in the late 1980s and early 1990s conducted a tireless—and successful—campaign to arm its humanities departments with assorted academic radicals from the Marxist Fredric Jameson to Barbara Herrnstein Smith, Stanley Fish, and Eve Kosofsky Sedgwick, author of "Jane Austen and the Masturbating Girl," a founding document in the annals of "Queer Theory."

It has often been observed that yesterday's student radical is today's tenured professor or academic dean. The point of this observation is not to suggest that our campuses are littered with political agitators. In comparison to the situation that prevailed in 1968, when colleges and universities across the country were scenes of violent demonstrations, the academy today seems positively sedate. Yet if the undergraduate population has moved quietly to the Right in recent years, the men and women who are paid to introduce students to the great works and ideas of our civilization have by and large remained true to the emancipationist ideology of the Sixties.

III

Indeed, it is important to appreciate the extent to which the radical vision of the Sixties has not so much been abandoned as internalized by many who came of age then and who now teach at and administer our institutions of higher education. True, there is no longer the imminent prospect of universities being shut down or physically destroyed by angry radicals. But when one considers that the university is now supplying many of those erstwhile radicals with handsome paychecks, a pleasant working environment, and lifetime job security, then their quiescence is perhaps not so very extraordinary.

Besides, why shouldn't they act contentedly? To an extent unimaginable a decade or two ago, their dreams of radical transformation have been realized. Even if we leave aside the enormous changes that have occurred in social life at our institutions of higher learning, it is patent that the transformation of the substance and even goals of the typical liberal arts program has been staggering. Who could have guessed that the women's movement would have succeeded in getting gender accepted as "a fundamental category of literary analysis" by departments of literature in nearly every major university? Who could have guessed that administrators would one day be falling over themselves in their rush to replace the "white Western" curriculum of traditional humanistic studies with a smorgasbord of courses designed to appeal to various ethnic and racial sensitivities? Who could have predicted that the ideals of objectivity and the disinterested pursuit of knowledge would not only be abandoned but pilloried as products of a repressive bourgeois society? No, the radical ethos of the Sixties has been all too successful, achieving indirectly in the classroom, faculty meeting, and by administrative decree what they were unable to accomplish on the barricades.

The political dimension of this assault on the humanities shows itself nowhere more clearly than in the attempt to restructure the curriculum on the principle of "equal time." More and more, one sees the traditional literary canon ignored as various interest groups demand that there be more "women's literature" for feminists, "black literature" for blacks, "gay literature" for homosexuals, and so on. The idea of literary quality that transcends the contingencies of race, gender, and the like, or that transcends the ephemeral attractions of popular entertainment, is excoriated as naïve, deliberately deceptive, or worse.

One recent example is "Vision 2000," a document prepared by the women's studies programs at the University of Massachusetts at Amherst and the five other land-grant universities of New England. Under the guise of promoting "diversity" and "gender equity," "Vision 2000" advocates the transformation of these six universities into radical feminist fiefdoms in which "gender equity"—i.e., "equal numbers of men and women" in every program and subject area, from business administration and biology to physics and zoology—would be enforced by college administrators. "Faculty whose students identify their courses, teaching styles, and mentoring as failing to be inclusive," the document warns, "do not receive teaching prizes, satisfactory teaching evaluations, or merit raises." As the commentator John Leo noted in his report on "Vision 2000," three of the five university presidents—in Vermont, Maine, and New Hampshire—have already signed on to its recommendations "in spirit."*

The insinuation of political imperatives into higher

---

* John Leo, "No Takeovers, Please," *U.S. News & World Report*, 19 Jan. 1998, page 13. "Vision 2000" is available from the Women's Studies Program at the University of Massachusetts at Amherst.

education shows itself in other, more subtle, ways as well. At many colleges and universities today, traditional precepts about the methods and goals of humanistic study are rejected as hopelessly *retardataire*. Basic questions such as "What does it mean to be an educated person?" are no longer entertained as worthy of serious attention. *Reading* is no longer seen as an activity that aims at construing the meaning of books and ideas, but as an elaborate interpretative game that seeks to expose the impossibility of meaning. And—as anyone with even a passing acquaintance with the products of the new academic scholarship knows—*writing* no longer means attempting to express oneself as clearly and precisely as possible. On the contrary, writing is pursued as a deliberately "subversive" activity meant to challenge the "bourgeois" and "logocentric" faith in clarity, intelligibility, and communication. Mas'd Zavarzadeh, a follower of the French deconstructionist Jacques Derrida, put it bluntly when he declared in a review of a rival critic that "his unproblematic prose and the clarity of his presentation" were "the conceptual tools of conservatism."* Even more disturbing is the widely commented-on phenomenon of "political correctness," in which demands for ideological conformity have encroached on basic intellectual and social freedoms. At many campuses across the country, university administrations have enacted "anti-harassment" rules that provide severe penalties for speech or action deemed offensive to any of a wide range of officially designated "victims." Ostensibly designed to prevent sexual, ethnic,

---

* Quoted in John Ellis, *Against Deconstruction* (Princeton: Princeton University Press, 1989), page 10.

and racial harassment, these rules actually represent an effort to enforce politically correct attitudes by curtailing free speech. By now, examples of political correctness on campuses and elsewhere in American society are legion. Dinesh D'Souza's book *Illiberal Education: The Politics of Race and Sex on Campus* is only the best-known compendium of examples.* At one campus, the entire press run of a conservative student newspaper was stolen and destroyed because it contained an editorial that offended the sensibilities of some black students. At Smith College, a brochure is distributed to incoming students rehearsing a long list of politically incorrect attitudes and prejudices that will not be tolerated, including the sin of "lookism," i.e., the prejudice of believing that some people are more attractive than others. At the University of Pennsylvania, when a student on a panel for "diversity education" wrote a memorandum to her colleagues in which she expressed her "deep regard for the individual and . . . desire to protect the freedoms of all members of society," a university administrator responded by circling the passage just quoted, underlining the word "individual," and commenting "This is a 'RED FLAG' phrase today, which is considered by many to be RACIST. Arguments that cham-

---

* Dinesh D'Souza, *Illiberal Education: The Politics of Race and Sex on Campus* (New York: The Free Press, 1991). See also Richard Bernstein, *Dictatorship of Virtue: Multiculturalism and the Battle for America's Future* (New York: Knopf, 1994) for many additional examples of the baneful effects of political correctness on campus. The definitive study of the assault on free speech on campus is the previously cited book by Alan Charles Kors and Harvey A. Silverglate, *The Shadow University: The Betrayal of Liberty on America's Campuses.*

pion the individual over the group ultimately privileges [*sic*] the 'individuals' belonging to the largest or dominant group."* Such examples could be multiplied indefinitely. What they portend is nothing less than the effort to institute a new form of thought control based on a variety of New-Left slogans and attitudes.

Nor is the effort to enforce politically correct attitudes and behavior on our campuses confined to new forms of university legislation. At the beginning of 1990, a front-page article in *The New York Times* reported that the Supreme Court ruled that the confidentiality of independent evaluations and other material collected to assess an individual's qualifications for academic tenure is no longer inviolate. The article noted that henceforth "universities accused of discriminating in tenure decisions must make the relevant personnel files available to Federal investigators." As it happens, the Court's decision was based on a complaint filed against the University of Pennsylvania in 1985 by a Chinese-American woman who was denied tenure at the university's Wharton School of Business. The *Times* gleefully described the decision as "a decisive victory for the Equal Employment Opportunity Commission and for many civil rights groups" that have complained that the confidentiality of the tenure process has functioned as "a shield for discrimination that has kept women and minority candidates out of the tenured ranks."†

The Court's decision is thus being hailed as a triumph

---

* Alan Charles Kors, "It's Speech, Not Sex, the Dean Bans Now," *The Wall Street Journal*, 12 Oct. 1989.

† Linda Greenhouse, "Universities Lose Shield of Secrecy in Tenure Disputes," *The New York Times*, 10 Jan. 1990.

for what Associate Justice Harry A. Blackmun, who wrote the majority opinion, called the "compelling government interest" in "ferreting out" racial and sexual discrimination. But as with the virtuous-sounding anti-harassment legislation, one wonders. The *Times* reported that some university officials have expressed concern that the new policy will make it "harder to get the candid scholarly assessments needed to make the best decisions." And indeed, one cannot but suspect that the net result of this attack on confidentiality will be to politicize the appointment and promotion process even further. Now that any academic who is denied tenure—and who happens to be female or a member of an approved racial or ethnic minority—has a legal basis upon which to contest the denial, can we really expect that scholarly accomplishment or effective teaching will be the main criteria for promotion? On the contrary, not only can we look forward to a greater reluctance on the part of scholars to provide honest assessments of their colleagues' work; we can also confidently predict a further erosion of intellectual standards—what once upon a time could be referred to without irony as academic standards—as tenure decisions come increasingly to be exercises in affirmative action and virtue-mongering.

IV

The institutionalization of the radical ethos in the academy has brought with it not only an increasing politicization of the humanities, but also an increasing ignorance of the humanistic legacy. Instead of reading the great works of the past, students watch movies, pronounce on the depredations of patriarchal society, or peruse second- or third-rate works dear to their ideological cohort; instead of reading widely among primary texts, they absorb abstruse commentaries on commentaries, resorting to primary texts only to furnish illustrations for their pet critical "theory." Since many older professors have themselves been the beneficiaries of the kind of traditional education they have rejected and are denying their students, it is the students who are the real losers in this fiasco. Presumably, they enrolled in a liberal arts curriculum in the first place because they wished to be educated; alas, after four years they will find that they are ignorant of the tradition and that their college education was largely a form of ideological indoctrination. It may well be the case that the much-publicized decline in humanities enrollments over the last couple of decades is due at least in part to students' refusal to devote their college education to a program of study that has nothing to offer them but ideological posturing, pop culture, and hermetic word games.

The issues raised by the politicization of the humanities have application far beyond the ivy-covered walls of the academy. The denunciations of the "hegemony" of Western culture and liberal institutions that are sounded so insistently within our colleges and universities these days are not idle chatter, but represent a concerted effort to attack the very foundations of the society that guarantees the independence of cultural and artistic life—including the independence of our institutions of higher education. Behind the transformations contemplated by the proponents of feminism, deconstruction, and the rest is a blueprint for a radical social transformation that would revolutionize every aspect of social and political life, from the independent place we grant high culture within society to the way we relate to one another as men and women. It is precisely for this reason that the traditional notion of the humanities and the established literary canon have been so violently attacked by *bien-pensants* academics: as the cultural guardians of the ideals and values that Western democratic society has struggled to establish and perpetuate, the humanities also form a staunch impediment to the radical vision of their new academic enemies.

It is my aim in *Tenured Radicals* to expose these developments in the academic study of humanities for what they are: ideologically motivated assaults on the intellectual and moral substance of our culture. To that end, I have attempted to present a "report from the front" on some of the most important and representative radical campaigns currently being waged in the academy. In order to give as concrete and specific a picture as possible, I have not scrupled to spare the reader many examples of academic absurdity. Because simply describing what goes on in the academy today often produces blank incredulity in those not acquainted with its workings, I have drawn on conferences and symposia as well as books, journal articles, and various academic movements in an effort to convey a vivid and immediate sense of both the arguments and the often rebarbative rhetoric that fill the lecture halls and publications of our most prestigious colleges and universities.

To those of my readers who may have heard of the developments I discuss but have not had occasion to become acquainted with them first-hand, I regret to report that the situation is far worse than they are ever likely to have imagined.

CHAPTER ONE

The Assault on the Canon

I Cultural literacy

O F THE many issues that have commanded the public's attention regarding the state of the humanities in this country, perhaps none has been more hotly contended than the issue of the academic canon. Since the late 1980s, the battle over the fate of the canon has been waged in myriad academic books, journal articles, and conferences; it has been bruited about in the popular and high-brow cultural press; and it has been settled and resettled concretely in curricular changes that have taken place on campuses from Yale to Stanford.

The term "canon" originally referred to an official rule or decree of the Church, a particular section of the Mass, or the list of canonized saints. Today, as applied to colleges and universities, "canon" refers to the unofficial, shifting, yet generally recognized body of great works that have stood the test of time and are acknowledged to be central to a complete liberal arts education. That this ideal of education can never be fully realized has also been generally acknowledged, as this passage from the Yale College Bulletin for the academic year 1958–1959 suggests:

> The purpose of the program of distribution is to provide the student with a broad view of the world he lives in and to equip him with the means of understanding it. This entails a knowledge of inanimate and animate nature through the appropriate sciences, a large view of man in the perspective of time, an acquaintance with the great ideas which have influenced the actions of men in the past, and continue to do so in the present, and a knowledge of the significant institutions of modern society. It also entails a comprehension of the art, the ideas, and the aspirations of men. To obtain so large a view in all its fullness is properly the occupation of a lifetime.*

Just fifty years ago, but how many things presupposed by this sober bit of academic prose have been called into question! Especially with respect to the humanities, the idea that college students should acquaint themselves with the "great ideas which have influenced the actions of men in the past, and continue to do so in the present" would instantly elicit a whole range of objections, from the feminist complaint about the use of "man" and "men" to the more general complaint that there is no agreed-upon set of "great ideas" that speaks equally to every ethnic and racial constituency.

In fact, the current debate over the canon—its origins, its composition, the desirability of preserving the values

* *Yale University Bulletin, 1958–1959*, page 2.

and traditions it represents—really poses two interrelated questions: What should our colleges and universities be teaching? And *how* should they be teaching the material they present? For the assault on the canon is not simply a matter of diluting the curriculum—of replacing, say, Plato with Navaho folk tales or Shakespeare with Jacqueline Susann. It also shows itself in the aggressively opaque jargons favored by many contemporary academics as well as in the widespread insinuation of patently political criteria into teaching. Together, these developments have helped to transform liberal studies into an ideological battleground that is also, all too often, an intellectual wasteland.

The enormous public controversy that was generated in the 1980s by Stanford University's decision to drop its required year-long course in Western culture in favor of a new requirement called "Culture, Ideas, and Values" shows that both questions have the capacity to arouse considerable passion in and out of the academy. And this is as it should be. For what is at stake in these difficult questions is more than an academic squabble over book lists and pedagogy. What is at stake is nothing less than the traditional liberal understanding of democratic society and the place of education and high culture within it. The ruling by the Stanford Faculty Senate that every course in the university's new program must include "works by women, minorities and persons of color," and that at least one work each quarter must address issues of race, gender, or class may be seen by the supporters of the "Culture, Ideas, and Values" program as a triumph for intellectual diversity, social relevance, and ethnic sensitivity. For some of us, however, this self-righteous emphasis on "diversity," "relevance," and "sensitivity" provides a graphic example of the way in which the teaching of the humanities has been appropriated by special interests and corrupted by politics.

The situation at Stanford, which I examine in more detail below, is hardly unique. All across the country, colleges and universities have been busy revamping their educational programs according to criteria that a couple of decades ago would have been considered blatantly political and therefore inappropriate for determining the educational program of a respectable institution of higher learning.

As the German scholar John Ellis noted in *Literature Lost,* "twenty years ago no one would have believed it possible that professors, of all people, would one day argue that the universities should have an overtly political function."* And the reason for this, of course, is that the traditional ideal of disinterested intellectual inquiry makes sense only to the extent that one believes that truth does not play political favorites. Similarly, the whole realm of literary-aesthetic experience exercises an important claim on us only to the extent that it transcends the vagaries of contemporary political squabbles.

For the race-class-gender lobby, however, all social, artistic, and intellectual life must be subjected to a battery of political tests. It's the Sovietization of intellectual life, where the value of a work is determined not by its intrinsic qualities but by the degree to which it supports a given political line. It is a measure of how drastically things have changed that although the ubiquitous triumvirate of gender, race, and class is still considered to be patently

* John Ellis, *Literature Lost: Social Agendas and the Corruption of the Humanities* (New Haven: Yale University Press, 1997), page 7.

political, it is now for that very reason increasingly held to furnish the *only* appropriate criterion for determining the content of the curriculum and the focus of pedagogical interest.

As it happens, the most widely noticed contributions to the debate over the canon have also been among the most reviled in the academy. It all started in the late 1980s with E. D. Hirsch's *Cultural Literacy: What Every American Needs to Know** and Allan Bloom's *The Closing of the American Mind: How Higher Education Has Failed Democracy and Impoverished the Souls of Today's Students.*† Indeed, Professor Bloom's book, after an extraordinarily positive reception in the the non-academic press, was subjected to an unremitting barrage of criticism and abuse from the academic Left, including the charge that it is "Hitleresque."‡ Nonetheless, though they boast many common enemies, these are very different sorts of books. Professor Hirsch's study is a cross between a research report and a primer, while Professor Bloom's book is more in the way of a philosophical meditation on the fate of liberal education in contemporary American society.

---

* E. D. Hirsch, Jr., *Cultural Literacy: What Every American Needs to Know* (Boston: Houghton-Mifflin, 1987).

† Allan Bloom, *The Closing of the American Mind: How Higher Education Has Failed Democracy and Impoverished the Souls of Today's Students* (New York: Simon and Schuster, 1987).

‡ The term was used at a seminar on "Innovations in Education" at Columbia University by Frank Moretti, then assistant headmaster of the Dalton School, one of the most prestigious primary and secondary schools in New York City. See my account of the session in "Guns and Other 'Hermeneutical Acts' at Columbia," in *The New Criterion*, May 1988, pages 77–79.

But both books are highly critical of the current situation in the academy. And both garnered extraordinary public attention. *The Closing of the American Mind* was number one on *The New York Times* best-seller list for the better part of a year, while *Cultural Literacy* followed close behind at number two. Whether all or even most of those who bought the books also took the trouble to read them—especially Professor Bloom's book, which is not exactly what is usually meant by light reading—is of course another question. Yet there can be no question that both books touched a nerve and continue even now, ten and more years later, to be much discussed and cited. Their commercial success is one of many suggestions in contemporary cultural life of how widespread is the concern about the state of American higher education.

Much of this concern originally crystallized around former Secretary of Education William J. Bennett's monograph *To Reclaim a Legacy: A Report on the Humanities in Higher Education*. This report was published by the National Endowment for the Humanities in November, 1984, when Secretary Bennett was chairman of the Endowment. Retailing the recent tribulations of the humanities in the academy—ignorance and apathy on the one hand, overt politicization on the other—the report insisted that "the nation's colleges and universities must reshape their curricula based on a clear vision of what constitutes an educated person." The goal was "a common culture rooted in civilization's lasting vision, its highest shared ideals and aspirations, and its heritage." Secretary Bennett did not hesitate to name Western civilization as the repository of these "ideals and aspirations" or to provide a list of books that help define the "lasting vision" of that common culture.

The response to Secretary Bennett's report from the academy was a combination of disbelief and rage: disbelief that anyone could still seriously speak of such things as "civilization's lasting vision" and "its highest shared ideals and aspirations," rage that a Reagan appointee (albeit one with a Ph.D. in philosophy) should dare to criticize . . . well, *them*: the self-appointed intellectual and moral elect. Judging from the abuse showered upon William Bennett, one would have thought that he represented a monstrous threat to the survival of academic freedom, scholarly creativity, and true culture. His vision of a common culture, the notion that the West's cultural, intellectual, and political achievements have a special claim on our attention and allegiance, the criticism of importing politics into the humanities, the effrontery of suggesting that some books are fundamental to any sound education in the humanities: all this drew—and continues to draw, as a quick glance at the Internet shows—sharp denunciations from *bien-pensant* academics across the country. Let us begin, then, by examining some representative responses.

II Goodbye to all that

In the fall of 1986, *Salmagundi*, an influential quarterly of the humanities published by Skidmore College, featured a lengthy exchange entitled "On Cultural Literacy: Canon, Class, Curriculum."* Professor Robert Scholes of Brown

* *Salmagundi*, No. 72, Fall 1986, pages 101–165. Quotations from this exchange in the following paragraphs are from this issue of *Salmagundi*.

University set the tone and agenda of the exchange with an essay coyly entitled "Aiming a Canon at the Curriculum." Several academics, including Professor Hirsch, Marjorie Perloff of Stanford University, Elizabeth Fox-Genovese of Emory University, and John P. Sisk of Gonzaga University in Spokane, Washington, responded.

Professor Scholes began with some portentous etymological speculations on the relation between the terms "canon" and "cannon," concluding ominously that "Where the Empire went, the cannon and the Canon went too." But the real focus of his essay was Secretary Bennett's report, especially its advocacy of a literary canon, and Professor Hirsch's miscellaneous writings on "cultural literacy" (the book had not yet appeared). About *To Reclaim a Legacy*, Professor Scholes wrote that "I am opposed to the establishment of a canon humanistic studies because I believe such a move to be fundamentally undemocratic: a usurpation of curricular power by the federal government." He then proceeded to invoke Adolf Hitler, writing that

> the leader who will reclaim a legacy is a potent image, ranging in Western cultural history from the Once and Future King drawing Excalibur from its stone scabbard to Adolf Hitler reviving the spirit of a fallen people by finding suitable scapegoats upon whom to blame their fall. William Bennett's cry for strong leadership from those on top, combined with the charge that the loss of our legacy is the fault of a "failure of nerve and faith" strongly suggests that the first move of an educational leader should be a purge of those lacking in nerve and faith.

What does it mean, one might ask, that an eminent

scholar and a U.S. Secretary of Education should be blithely compared to one of the greatest monsters of all history simply because they dared advance some criticisms of the academy? Is this an example of the "tolerance" for "diversity" that one hears so much about? Even more troubling—because more likely to be taken seriously—is the suggestion that "the establishment of a canon in humanistic studies" is "fundamentally undemocratic." This idea is as pernicious as it is common, implying as it does that political democracy is essentially inimical to authority, tradition, and rigor in its cultural institutions. At bottom, it is another way of suggesting that "being democratic" means abandoning any claim to permanent intellectual or cultural achievement.

It should also be noted that the substance of *To Reclaim a Legacy* is not the result of Secretary Bennett's private whims but a reflection of the deliberations of a distinguished panel of twenty professors and university administrators whose numbers included figures as diverse as the late William Arrowsmith, the well-known translator and professor of classics who was then teaching at Boston University; William M. Banks, professor of Afro-American Studies at the University of California, Berkeley; Hannah H. Gray, at that time the president of the University of Chicago; and Paul Oskar Kristeller, the eminent philosopher and longtime professor of philosophy at Columbia University. Are these figures also to be understood as upholding a Hitlerite position on humanistic education?

Then, too, Professor Scholes implied that Secretary Bennett had wanted the list of books included in the report to be dogmatically imposed on the nation's colleges and universities. The truth is precisely the opposite.

"In providing a list of these works and authors," we read in *To Reclaim a Legacy*, "it is not my intention (nor is it my right) to dictate anyone's curriculum. My purpose is not to prescribe a course of studies but to answer, as candidly as I can, an oft-asked question." I do not see how Secretary Bennett could have put it more clearly. The responses to Professor Scholes's essay covered a fair range of opinion but may be described as generally supportive. No one, at any rate, did much to defend *To Reclaim a Legacy*. Marjorie Perloff, for one, praised Professor Scholes's "eloquent, humane" critique of the report's defense of the canon, agreeing that "educational philosophy always masks political ideology." To her credit, however, she did point out that there is an unacknowledged, yet nonetheless rigidly adhered to, alternative canon already in place in the academy. This is the canon whose founders are Freud, Marx, and Nietzsche, and whose contemporary representatives champion a motley variety of "avant-garde" criticism based on a combination of radical political pieties and the half-digested tenets of the latest intellectual fads. As if in illustration of Professor Perloff's claim, Elizabeth Fox-Genovese began her response, entitled "Gender, Class, Race, Canon," with an admiring reference to the black revolutionary Frantz Fanon. Professor Fox-Genovese has lately emerged as an articulate scourge of radical feminism; but on this occasion she seemed taken by Fanon's ideal of "purging violence," observing that the notions of "imperialism and colonialization . . . nicely capture the relations between many students and the official culture that is taken to constitute a liberal education." "The canon," she concluded, "can best be taught if it is recognized at least in part as a kind of political spoil." In other words, for her, today's college students stand in the same relation to their culture as do the victims of colonial exploitation.

Professor Hirsch's response took the form of an *apologia* explaining why Professor Scholes's attacks on his work had been misplaced. Of course, the chief reason that Professor Scholes troubled to criticize Professor Hirsch in the first place is that Professor Hirsch's work on cultural literacy has been widely described as "conservative"—a tag earned in part because it was early on endorsed by Secretary Bennett (Professor Hirsch was even cited admiringly in *To Reclaim a Legacy*), in part because it scrupled to point out what a shambles our country's educational system is in. Professor Hirsch's efforts helped to make the litany of horrors familiar. At the time of his writing, one-half of our high school seniors did not recognize the names of Winston Churchill or Joseph Stalin, nor could they locate the correct half century in which the First World War occurred, and so on.*

Professor Hirsch is to be commended for bringing the shocking state of our educational system to public notice so effectively. He helped start an important debate that continues to this day. At the same time, it must be said that his defense against Professor Scholes's attack was really a capitulation. The truth is that although Professor Hirsch's writing on cultural literacy has been generally associated with the spirit of *To Reclaim a Legacy*, his responses, in the pages of *Salmagundi* and elsewhere, have been little more than a series of attempts to distance himself from Secretary Bennett, the report, and everything they stand for. In retrospect, we can now see that Profes-

---

* *Cultural Literacy*, page 218.

sor Hirsch's capitulation in the pages of *Salmagundi* was only the beginning of a long career of repudiating his earlier positions. But already in the *Salmagundi* exchange, we find him replying to one of Professor Scholes's main charges by insisting that, in his view, "*The common background knowledge required for literacy does not depend upon specific texts. . . . To be culturally literate, one does not need to know any specific texts.*" It follows naturally, he continued, that "it's acceptable to take one's entire knowledge of *Romeo and Juliet* from *Cliff Notes*" [*sic*], that is, from a crib.

Now think about that for a moment: "it's acceptable to take one's entire knowledge of *Romeo and Juliet* from *Cliff's Notes.*" Acceptable to whom? Acceptable to Professor Hirsch, perhaps, but is it acceptable to the students who wish to be educated, not merely appear to be educated? Is it acceptable to the students' parents, who are paying for their children to be educated, and not merely to acquire a superficial patina of knowledge?

Professor Hirsch's disregard for the substance of humanistic knowledge points to the crippling weakness of *Cultural Literacy*: its thoroughgoing philistinism and superficiality. In some ways, the most questionable part of Professor Hirsch's book is also the most controversial—I mean The List: the sixty-odd page, alphabetically ordered confection appended to the main text. Entitled "What Literate Americans Know," it is a startling hodgepodge of dates (1066, 1492, 1776, etc.), names, phrases, acronyms, titles, and technical terms. Liberal critics complained that Professor Hirsch was acting in an authoritarian fashion here, attempting to lay down the law, to dictate what should count as knowledge indispensable for "cultural literacy" in our society. But really they should have been heartened by his efforts. Far from laying down the law about cultural literacy, what his notorious list confirms is that he has abandoned the effort to establish anything of the kind. Consider the sorts of things that make it on to the list. Towards the end of the Bs, for example, we encounter

Bryan, William Jennings
bubble (economic)
Bucharest
buck stops here, The
Budapest
Buddha
Buddhism
Buenos Aires
Buffalo, New York
Buffalo Bill
buffer (chemistry)
build castles in the air

And on and on, from "abbreviation (written English)," "abolitionism," and "abominable snowman" to "Zola, Emile," "zoning," and "Zurich." What does this random inventory of cultural trivia have to do with genuine education or cultural literacy? Well, about as much as *Cliff's Notes* has to do with Shakespeare. It is—to use a phrase that Professor Hirsch favors—simply a promiscuous blend of general "background knowledge." It is humanistic Muzak, mastery of which might help one excel in crossword puzzles, quiz games, or faculty cocktail parties, but which is totally alien to the spirit of serious humanistic education. Consider only the entry "Am I my brother's keeper?" How many eager but ill-informed students will absorb the phrase but neglect the context—and thereby utterly misconstrue the meaning, taking it for an expression of bold if sour self-absorption rather than a fratricide's evasion?

It should be noted that Professor Hirsch has been quite frank about the rudimentary nature of his enterprise. In the preface to his book, he tells us that "to be culturally literate is to possess the basic information needed to thrive in the modern world"—which is to say that in his terms being culturally literate is more or less like having a plumber's license. He has endeavored to be even more specific about the nature of that "basic information" in his sequel to *Cultural Literacy*, *The Dictionary of Cultural Literacy: What Every American Needs to Know,** which is essentially a hypertrophied version of the list that appears at the end of his earlier book. It is unfortunate indeed that many people have continued to assume that books featuring the term "Cultural Literacy" in their title must have something to do with high culture and genuine learning.

III The cult of theory

While many academics continue to keep their distance from Professor Hirsch, the attitudes expressed by Professor Scholes and most of his respondents about the canon are so deeply ingrained in elite opinion in the academy these days that they are simply taken for granted. Still,

* E. D. Hirsch, Jr., Joseph F. Kett, and James Trefil, *The Dictionary of Cultural Literacy: What Every American Needs to Know* (Boston: Houghton-Mifflin, 1989).

when one steps back to consider the countless publications, symposia, and administrative declarations informing us that the traditional literary canon is an instrument of repression and so on, there are some few that stand out as exemplary summaries of contemporary academic opinion. One illustrative event took place in New Haven one Saturday early in May, 1987, when Yale's Whitney Humanities Center sponsored a day-long public symposium to examine the subject of "Literary Theory and the Curriculum."

That the topic was of more than casual interest was clear from the enthusiastic audience of about three hundred students, teachers (from Yale and elsewhere), and curious outsiders that crowded the Center's modest lecture hall to overflowing. In a notice announcing the symposium, Sheila Murnaghan, then assistant director of the Center and associate professor of classics at Yale, explained that "After two decades of intense debate sparked by structuralism, post-structuralism, feminism, Afro-American and Third World Studies, and a resurgence of Marxism, teachers of literature find themselves in a bewildering situation."* The symposium, Professor Murnaghan promised, "will bring together some of the most thoughtful members of the profession to compare notes on the current state of literary study and to assess the possibility of finding a common ground from which to respond to these challenges."

It is difficult to quarrel with the accuracy of Professor Murnaghan's list of "challenges" or her diagnosis of bewilderment. Yet whether what we have witnessed in

---

* Unless otherwise noted, quotations in this section are taken from the presentations and responses delivered at this symposium.

literary studies in the past two or three decades is properly termed an "intense debate" is itself highly debatable. A more plausible term might be "usurpation," motivated partly by intellectual fashion (structuralism, post-structuralism, deconstruction), partly by politics (feminism and the rest). And looking back on the event, one would also have to quibble with Professor Murnaghan's description of what the majority of those "most thoughtful" members of the profession had to contribute to the discussion: "compare"? "assess"? "respond"? "Proselytize" was much closer to the truth.

Peter Brooks, who, among other titles at Yale, is the Chester D. Tripp Professor of the Humanities, opened the festivities with a few words about the ways in which recent literary theory has called into question traditional approaches to literature and "what we do as teachers of literature." Do we, he asked, still have any fixed point of reference or any common ground in the teaching of English? Has anything like a new consensus emerged from "challenges" of the sort that Professor Murnaghan rehearsed? Or have literary studies become caught up in the logic of the "post-, post-, post-; post-structuralist, post-modernist, post-disciplinary"? Without attempting to answer these questions, Professor Brooks did suggest something of a common project when he observed at the end of his remarks that the task he and his colleagues now faced was that of "rewriting" tradition "in a more suspicious manner." As it happened, though, what one witnessed as the event proceeded were sundry attempts to "rewrite" the tradition in a manner that, far from being simply "suspicious," was blatantly tendentious and ideological.

Though lamenting the loss of consensus in the

humanities, the participants that day nonetheless shared a number of important assumptions about what was and wasn't wrong with the academy, the ends of education, and the tasks currently facing literary criticism. A superficial diversity masked a considerable unity of purpose. Taken together, the contributions more or less summarized the range and style of mainstream opinion in the academy on these issues, and so it is worth reviewing the proceedings in some detail.

The symposium was divided into three sessions. The morning session was devoted to "The State of the Curriculum in the Wake of Two Decades of Literary Theory." J. Hillis Miller, for many years professor of English at Yale but by then ensconced at the University of California at Irvine, and Michael Riffaterre, Professor of Comparative Literature at Columbia University, each presented papers that purported to deal with the announced subject. They were followed by Professors Paul Fry of Yale and Barbara Johnson, lately of Yale but now installed at Harvard, who responded to the papers. As it happened, the participants dealt with the subject of the curriculum only obliquely; but, as is often the case these days, their critical methods and assumptions told us a good deal about how the assault on the canon may proceed as much by trivializing or obscuring great works of literature as by ignoring or replacing them with inferior works.

Professor Miller's contribution was entitled "From the Theory of Reading to the Example Read." He began by describing the "spectacular proliferation of powerful and incompatible theories" that have swept contemporary literary criticism and have fundamentally changed the way the subject is taught. In his view, perhaps the most important change wrought by these "spectacular" theories is in the relationship between theory and example. Where in traditional literary criticism the "example"—that is, particular works of literature—clearly took precedence over "theory," today the relationship is reversed; now, as Professor Miller cheerfully explained, the example is "arbitrarily chosen." That is to say, it is chosen not for its historical importance, not for its literary value, not for any truth or moral clarity it might be supposed to communicate, but solely for its aptness in illustrating the current pet theory of the critic.

Professor Miller went on to point out that this reversal in the relationship between example and theory has had profound implications for the way in which we read. The reader of this book might respond that Professor Miller's "we" is fortunately still far from universal. But the reversal of theory and example that he heralds certainly has had profound implications for the way in which books— or, to use the preferred term, "texts"—are read in the academy. There, as Professor Miller notes, it is widely held that a "resistance to theory is in fact a resistance to reading." This slogan, which Professor Miller took care to repeat two or three times in the course of his presentation, may be said to summarize the burden of his paper. The idea comes from the late Paul de Man, who, along with the celebrated French philosopher Jacques Derrida, was among those chiefly responsible for institutionalizing the tenets of deconstruction in literary studies. By the time he died in 1983, de Man's reputation as a literary theorist was stratospheric. His death catapulted it into orbit, though the discovery that this connoisseur of deconstruction had written scores of articles for newspapers that openly supported the Nazi cause in World

War II has had a noticeably diminishing effect on his stature. Nevertheless, even today, in many academic circles, to invoke the authority of Paul de Man is to confer an unimpeachable aura of critical sophistication upon one's words, so naturally he is alluded to continuously in the books and articles—and symposia—of his acolytes.

"The resistance to theory is in fact a resistance to reading"—a prize de Manian specimen, that. And whatever "theory" might mean in this context—it is bad form to indulge in anything so pedestrian as a definition in these intellectual precincts—the rest of Professor Miller's presentation clearly showed that his own resistance to theory is approximately nil. He proceeded to exemplify the triumph of theory over literature with a prolix and convoluted meditation on Nathaniel Hawthorne's short story, "The Minister's Black Veil." Among much else, his presentation featured a turgid discussion of the notion of personification, a good deal of solemn talk about "the act of reading," and the enlightening revelation that "the story is the unveiling of the possibility of the impossibility of the unveiling." So much for Hawthorne.

While Professor Miller's meditations really had little to do with the question of "The State of the Curriculum in the Wake of Two Decades of Literary Theory," his *approach*, which grants explicit priority to "theory" over literature, represents one of the chief ways by which the assault on the canon is carried out in the academy today. Unlike many of the participants in the symposium, however, Professor Miller did at least make some gesture toward addressing the announced topic. In outlining what he described as the "practical implications" of his paper, he warned that the rejection of theory is "reactionary or stupid or both" and suggested that universities ought to arrange their curricula in such a way as "to make possible the teaching of reading in its uneasy relation to theory."

Professor Miller didn't specify exactly what he meant by this "uneasy" relation; but he was clearly concerned that his colleagues were backsliding on their commitment to the priority of theory. Indulging in a gloomy pun, he wondered if we weren't witnessing the "wake of literary theory" in a sense quite different from that intended by the title of the session. His concern seemed misplaced, it must be said, for, as he also noted, deconstruction and its offshoots had by then firmly established themselves not only in literary studies but also throughout the humanities, history, and certain social sciences. Such "theoretical" approaches have gained a notable foothold in legal studies, for example, with the Critical Legal Studies and Critical Race Studies movements, which— ensconced as they are at Duke, Harvard and elsewhere— are busy applying the teachings of deconstruction to legal texts and theories. The vertiginous tenets of deconstruction have even made headway in some schools of business management and accounting. In the intellectual slums— among sociologists, educationists, and the like—the damage done by deconstruction has been terrific. Consider *Postmodernism, Sociology and Health* (1993) by one Nicholas Fox, a sociologist who lectures in English medical schools. Mr. Fox assures readers that such terms as "patient" and "illness" are "sociological fictions" that can be cleared up by "elements of feminist theory and Derridean concepts of *différance* and intertextuality."*

---

* Quoted in Keith Windschuttle, *The Killing of History: How Literary Critics and Social Theorists Are Murdering Our Past* (New York: Free Press, 1997), page 13.

The truth is that by the late 1980s, postmodernist "theory" was well advanced on all fronts. Nevertheless, Professor Miller lamented that Yale no longer deserved its reputation as a bastion of theoretical criticism. Anyone who is at all familiar with the faculties of the departments of English, French, and Comparative Literature there would find the notion that Yale suffers from a dearth of scholars smitten by the virus of deconstruction simply laughable. But who knows: perhaps Professor Miller felt that his own departure deprived the university of its place on the frontiers of advanced thought? In any case it was his view that if Yale wanted to recapture its former glory it must not only appoint more senior professors who are sympathetic to the cause of theory—he mentioned several possible candidates—but it must also give tenure to more of their younger disciples—again, he favored us with several names. As things stand, Professor Miller concluded darkly, it might already be too late to stop what he described as the "Harvardization" of Yale.

The next two installments of this session continued in the same vein. Michael Riffaterre performed a kind of set piece entitled "Relevance of Theory/Theory of Relevance." "What we must be after is the *je ne sais quoi* that makes literature literary," he told us. But literature got quite lost as he proceeded, employing an extraordinary congeries of categories and distinctions to deduce the six "necessary properties" of "literariness" and apply them to a reading of *Madame Bovary*. For his part, Paul Fry concentrated on elaborating the theme of the "undecidability of language" that he found expressed in different ways in both Professors Miller and Riffaterre's papers. His delivery was very rapid and often hard to follow; but one caught various fragments, such as his call for an "onto-poetic" theory that would "revise Miller and impose a little specificity on Heidegger" by viewing personification as a "relay station" between being and language. His response was full of such pretentious nonsense, which reminds one, as John Ellis observed in *Literature Lost*, that "what is wrong here is not theory but *bad* theory."* My favorite moments were when Professor Fry dropped phrases like "from Aristotle to [Jonathan] Culler" and "from Schleiermacher to de Man" as if it were only natural that such illustrious names should be so linked. If nothing else, Professor Fry's response ought to have reassured Professor Miller about the state of theory in the Yale English department.

IV The feminist assault

And indeed, Barbara Johnson, the next respondent, also made one wonder what Professor Miller had to fear from the "Harvardization" of Yale. For if her views are at all typical of her colleagues,' he needn't have worried that books are being read primarily as literary documents or that theory is getting short shrift in Cambridge, Massachusetts. In fact, Professor Johnson provided us with our first example of what may be the single biggest challenge to the canon as traditionally conceived: radical feminism. As with the cult of theory, with which it is often in collusion, radical feminism does not undermine the canon only or even primarily by proposing an alternative canon—one, for example, in which female authors are read in place of male ones. Instead, it seeks to subordinate literature to ideology by instituting a fundamental change in the way

---

* *Literature Lost*, page 181.

literary works are read and taught. As Brigitte Berger pointed out in a perceptive article in the quarterly *Academic Questions*, feminism in the academy has had the effect of "a revolutionary intellectual movement. Encouraged by initial successes and unfettered by any serious intellectual resistance, professional feminists are driven by their presuppositions toward ever more radical conceptualizations. At the end of their road stands the formulation of a distinctive *feminist standpoint*, which in essence is nothing less than an imperialism of feminist sentiments."*

Professor Johnson offered a preliminary illustration of Professor Berger's thesis. Taking as her epigraph "Theory is quicker," she began with a few theoretical curlicues and then turned to examine Professor Riffaterre's discussion of *Madame Bovary*. That Flaubert's book deals with adultery was a great boon to her presentation, of course, because that opened up an unlimited field for pronouncements about the baleful condition of women. Nor was Professor Johnson lax in capitalizing on this wonderful opportunity. Blending a deconstructionist's obsession with language and a feminist's obsession with male dominance, she summed up Professor Riffaterre's paper as a "masterful demonstration" of "the fact" that "gynophobia" (i.e., the fear of women) "is structured like a language" and, conversely, that "language is structured like gynophobia."

Women themselves conspire in this dread process, she told us, for "the collective linguistic psyche exists in symbiotic relation to the fallen woman." We also learned, by a similarly elusive logic, that the "literary canon is a defense against its own femininity," a defense "against the

---

* Brigitte Berger, "Academic Feminism and the 'Left'," *Academic Questions*, Spring 1988, pages 6–15; this quotation, page 13.

woman within." What any of this could possibly mean was never revealed, but no one seemed to mind: it all sounded so exquisitely chic. The assertion that "gynophobia is structured like a language," for example, echoes the French psychoanalyst Jacques Lacan's equally absurd statement that the unconscious is structured like a language; and in this company such a pedigree was warrant enough to present even patent drivel as fact.

The agenda of the radical feminist assault on the canon showed itself even more clearly at the second session of the Yale conference on Literary Theory and the Curriculum, which was devoted to "The Literary Canon and Anti-Canonical Criticism." Elaine Showalter, then chairman (or rather, "chairwoman") of the English department at Princeton University, and Houston Baker of the University of Pennsylvania each presented papers— Professor Baker's presentation was largely *ex tempore*— and Professors Geoffrey Hartman and J. Michael Holquist of Yale responded.

Professor Showalter, who has achieved a position of great power and influence in the academy, read a paper entitled "The Other Bostonians: Gender and Literary Study." It was, quite simply, a call for "a transformation of the curriculum" that would accept "gender as a fundamental category of literary analysis." Professor Showalter is obviously nothing if not ambitious, for by pursuing the notion of "gender as a fundamental category of literary analysis" she hopes for nothing less than the triumph of feminist ideology over literature. She hopes, that is to say, that "literary knowledge itself will be redefined" by the feminist crusade. What she wants is not merely "mainstreaming," not merely the inclusion of many more women authors in the standard college curriculum—though that, certainly, is a prerequisite for the kinds of change she has in mind. She also wants to enshrine the recognition of "sexual difference" as a "crucial element in the way we all read and write." Only thus could she realize the dream of a "female vernacular" out of which "women can name their own experience." And despite multifarious setbacks, which Professor Showalter was careful to enumerate, progress was being made.

Among the indications of progress she alluded to we must include the institution of women's studies programs at colleges and universities across the country. Many of these programs offer majors in "women's studies," and all take Professor Showalter's insistence that gender is "a fundamental category of literary analysis" as their basis. Consider, for example, how the official bulletin of Yale University for 1988–1989 put it in its description of the Women's Studies program:

> Recent scholarship makes it clear that a full understanding of human behavior, culture, and society cannot be attained without investigating women's experiences. The critical perspective of women's studies establishes gender as a fundamental category of social and cultural analysis, linking gender with class, race, ethnicity, and sexual identity to analyze the diversity of women's experience.*

The tone and diction ("Recent scholarship makes it clear . . .") of this passage may be typical of traditional academic officialese—even if it relies on notions ("establishing" "fundamental categories," etc.) that many versions

* *Bulletin of Yale University*, Series 84, Number 7, August 1, 1988, "Yale College Programs of Study," page 423.

of feminism will attack as "patriarchal." But despite its relatively sedate tone, the message of this description—that sexual, racial, and ethnic politics should henceforth determine or at least strongly influence the curriculum—is deeply at odds with the presuppositions of traditional humanistic study.*

That of course is the point, as one can see from other areas of "progress" that Professor Showalter cited. Already there is daring "new research" underway, she told us, that promises to result in "new curricular experiments" and "genuine knowledge" of a field. Like what? Well, like the proliferation of current feminist studies of eating disorders that, among other wonderful things, "creates new interest in the binge/purge syndrome" as it relates to the American poet Sylvia Plath's development. Lest you think that Professor Showalter was exaggerating, note that among the many sessions dealing with feminist subjects at the Modern Language Association meeting in 1988 was a panel devoted to "Food and the

---

* A decade later, in 1998, the official brochure describing Yale's Women's Studies program suggests the extent to which the tenets of radical feminism have become thoroughly institutionalized. The program, we read, "is based not only on reclamation of women's presences and voices but fundamentally on the premise that gender *matters*, that the social construction of maleness and femaleness, masculinity and femininity, forms an appropriate, indeed a necessary, subject for social, cultural, political, and historical investigation." Among the classes offered to further these enterprises are "History and Sexual Identity," parts I and II ("Examination of . . . the types of gender and sexual behaviors associated with the modern gay and lesbian identities"), "Introduction to Lesbian and Gay Studies," "Power, Resistance, and Marginalization," etc.

Construction of Femininity in Drama by Women." Here, for example, one could listen to R. L. Widmann of the University of Colorado, Boulder, deliver a paper called "Sugar Shock in the Plays of Hroswitha and Beth Henley's *Crimes of the Heart*," in which such evils as "dichotomized sex" and "compulsory heterosexuality" were roundly denounced. Professor Showalter herself did not participate in that session, doubtless because she was busy preparing her talk about George Eliot as a "female androgyne" and the "delegitimization" of "patriarchal poetics" that she delivered later in the day.*

Such a "delegitimization" was high on Professor Showalter's agenda that day in New Haven, too. Feminism cannot rest content with championing female (one could hardly call it feminine) experience, she told us. Male experience must also be scrutinized. Professor Showalter

---

* The annual meetings of the MLA, the largest academic organization in the country, provide a good barometer—or perhaps one should say "fever chart"—of what's happening in academic literary studies. In 1994, for example, one was treated to papers on such subjects as "The Epistemology of the Queer Classroom: A Roundtable"; a panel on Henry James that included "'A Queer Confusion of Yearning and Alarm': Disavowing the Family Fiction in James's 'The Pupil'"; "Feminism and the Unspeakable" (parts one and two); a panel on "The Politics, Ethics, and Erotics of Collaborative Scholarship," which featured "Marital Methodologies or Heterosexual Habits" and "The Queerness of Collaboration." See my essay "The Periphery vs. the Center: The MLA in Chicago" in *Debating P.C.: The Controversy over Political Correctness on College Campuses*, edited by Paul Berman (New York: Dell, 1992), pages 61–84, and (co-authored with Hilton Kramer) "Farewell to the MLA" in *The New Criterion*, Feb. 1995, pages 5–16.

named "the defamiliarization of masculinity" "one of the most important tasks facing feminist criticism in the next decade." If "male experience" has hitherto been understood to be "natural" and "unproblematic," a mode of experience that represents "humanity in general," it must now be exposed as a biased, ideologically-laden construction. Men, too—perhaps especially men—must be enlisted in this attempt to "open up the discourse of masculinity." And good news: for those men who have abandoned "the myth of objectivity and transcendence," who have "the courage to become vulnerable" and "realize that they are embodied," this new recognition of masculinity "will be a transformation of volcanic force." "Simply to think about masculinity is to become less masculine oneself," we were assured—and, after all, what could be better than that?

As Professor Showalter enthusiastically proclaimed, her envisioned program implies a "complete revolution" in the teaching of our literary heritage, a revolution that would also establish "gay criticism," "black criticism," "post-colonial criticism," and so on as equal partners in the academy. In fact, Professor Showalter's proposals provide a sterling illustration of the way in which feminism has provided a kind of blueprint for special interests that wish to appropriate the curriculum in order to achieve political goals. As the philosopher Thomas Short pointed out in an excellent anatomy of radical trends in the academy, one result of the academic feminist agenda is a situation in which "every course will be Oppression Studies."* For if gender is a "crucial element in the way

* Thomas Short, "'Diversity' and 'Breaking the Disciplines': Two New Assaults on the Curriculum," *Academic Questions*, Summer 1988, pages 6–29; this quotation, page 24.

we all read and write," then why not sexual orientation, race, and class? Why not any political interest? Presumably, the only criticism that would not be nurtured as a minority interest in this feminist utopia is *literary* criticism, tainted as it is by an allegiance to the "myth" of disinterested inquiry and a notion of scholarship that deliberately strives to transcend political differences.

V An introduction to oppression studies

In order to understand how the principles at work in Professor Showalter's presentation can be applied by ideologies other than feminism, let us turn to Houston Baker's presentation, entitled "The Promised Body," in which the privileged category was race, not gender. Professor Baker, whom we shall have occasion to meet again at the end of this book, began with a bit of ideological throat-clearing, invoking Marx to the effect that the canon is determined to some extent by class interests and reminding us that the past is always an "ideologically conditioned version of events gone by." In the American academy today, he told us, the entire fabric of literary study, including the determination of the literary canon, is the function of a biased reading of the recent and the distant past, especially our own past. In his view, the "most penetrating and reverberant" sound in canon formation in the last three decades in the United States is the sound of civil rights marchers chanting—and here Professor Baker himself began to chant—"we shall not be moved, we shall not be moved."

This brought Professor Baker to his main point: that the black-power and black-art movements of the Sixties and early Seventies challenged dominant "white Western" cultural values in a uniquely productive and promising way. It was then, he told us, that the black experience "found its way onto the stage of the American academy and the black initiative became a reality for every man, woman, or student, every administrator, professor, resident advisor, security guard, or secretary." Professor Baker's oratory included quotations from Washington and Jefferson meant to portray them as racists, charges that the Constitution of the United States is a racist document (a "Gothic romance," as he memorably put it), readings from the writings of former slaves to show what terrific literature we've missed, and many references to what Professor Baker referred to as "the African diaspora."

Though delivered with unusual pathos, all this was in fact the most predictable fare imaginable. But Professor Baker concluded with a twist that was new to me, comparing the black experience in this country to the Roman Catholic Mass. Central to both, he told us, is the notion of a sacrifice and also the "materialization and engorgement of the body as a manifested covenant of a new order." He also described black Americans as "the African Body," noting, among much else, that "the African Body emerges as a canonical announcement of a promised or covenanted body." It need hardly be said that the audience was spellbound by Professor Baker's performance, especially by his concluding litany of recent outbreaks of violence and racial prejudice against "the African Body" on several campuses around the country. It has become rare in these quiet days in the academy that your average white, middle-class audience can indulge in such ecstasies of liberal shame, and they were clearly grateful to Professor Baker for an opportunity to abandon themselves to it.

Of course, presentations like those of Professors Showalter and Baker put any respondent at a tremendous rhetorical disadvantage. Anything resembling dissent risked being excoriated as a sexist or racist attack on the voices of freedom. This Professor Holquist must have realized, for when it came time for him to respond he contented himself with a few apologetic mumblings about how "political considerations" had kept black studies from becoming institutionalized as successfully as gender studies. But Professor Hartman did venture a few tentative criticisms. Noting that both presentations exhibited a strong utopian element, he began by remarking the high pitch of his colleagues' rhetoric; he even made bold to ask whether their rhetoric wasn't sometimes "stronger than their concepts." The end they envisioned was "generous," he hastily added; but he had to admit that on the "conceptual level" he was "perplexed, even disconcerted."

Though he would seem to have long since given up serious criticism for modish intellectual esoterica, Professor Hartman's remarks reminded one that he has done brilliant and lasting work, especially in the field of English Romantic poetry; and one was reminded, too, that he was without doubt the most distinguished scholar to participate in the symposium. What worried him was the possibility that the essentially political programs outlined by his colleagues would compromise the freedom and independence of the university, jeopardizing disinterested scholarship. Recognizing that the university is in many respects a place apart, he gently urged caution lest overt political imperatives be allowed to determine the character of university life. He seems, alas, to have underestimated both the extent to which the political infiltration of intellectual life was the frankly acknowledged goal of his more radical colleagues and the enormous strides which that infiltration has already made.

VI Bourgeois plots and other pedagogical matters

Although it began quietly, the third session of the Yale symposium on Literary Theory and the Curriculum ended by showing just how frankly acknowledged such political imperatives could be. It was entitled "The Institution of Criticism: What Should We Be Teaching, and Teaching Future Teachers to Teach?" and included Gerald Graff (then teaching at Northwestern University, now at the University of Chicago) and Margaret Ferguson (then at Columbia University) as the session's main speakers; Neil Hertz of Johns Hopkins University and Peter Brooks responded.

Professor Graff's presentation, "What Should We Be Teaching When There's No 'We'?" was by far the most practical paper in the symposium. Whatever one thought of his ideas, it was clear that he had devoted some considerable time to thinking about the problems of the classroom. In his view, the basic problem was that though the "we" of the academy is far more inclusive now than it used to be, there is no agreement on first principles and hence no consensus about what should be taught, or how. His solution was simply to dispense with the ideal of consensus and adopt a model of conflict. We don't need a consensus, he told us, to carry on work in the academy; we can agree to disagree and—as he has put it again and again in subsequent symposia and papers—"teach the conflict."

In some respects, Professor Graff's proposals were

reminiscent of the teaching of John Dewey. He tended, for example, to downplay "content" in favor of process. If many students are going to fail to understand much of what they read anyway, Professor Graff argued (and given the hermetic quality of contemporary academic criticism, who can blame them?), then the content of what they read "hardly matters." What does matter, according to Professor Graff, is the way reading feeds into students' experience and engages their interest.

Turning to some practical applications of this insight, he suggested that one might experiment with "teacher swapping" (not to be confused with team teaching), an innovation in which one teacher teaches a course for, say, five weeks, after which another comes in and begins by asking what the first teacher said, probing his presuppositions and prejudices. Despite certain attractive elements in Professor Graff's proposal, in the end it is a prescription for confusion, guaranteed to muddle young minds. If, as he acknowledged, students often have trouble even assimilating what they read, simply providing them with a diet of conflicting arcane theories is not going to help matters. But the real problem with Professor Graff's vision—as with the progressive ideas from which it derives—is that it ends up purchasing the illusion of pluralistic concord at the price of intellectual content. It never seems to occur to Professor Graff that some intellectual positions might be truer or more worthy of transmission than others. Lecturing us about how important it is to keep the discussion going among ideological adversaries, he neglects to ask himself whether cultivating ideologies ("teaching the conflicts") is the proper business of the university. If it "hardly matters" what students read, it will "hardly matter" what they know or believe.

But Professor Graff appeared as a beacon of moderation and sanity in comparison with his successor, Margaret Ferguson. Though delivered in measured, even demure, tones, her paper on "Teaching and/as Reproduction" was easily the most radical presentation of the symposium. Her thesis was that in liberal bourgeois society teaching must be seen primarily as a means by which the ruling class perpetuates or "reproduces" inequitable class relations. In one sense, certainly, Professor Ferguson is quite right that schools are "sites for social reproduction." That is a main reason that civilized cultures have always put such stock in education. The problem today, however, is not that our schools "reproduce" the culture and values that support them, but that they are doing the job so poorly.

Yet to hear Professor Ferguson tell it, things are bad indeed in the particular capitalist bourgeois society that she has the misfortune to inhabit and work in. She began by questioning the appropriateness of the word "should" in the title of the session: given the enormous constraints that the university supposedly places on "thought and action," what sense does it make to ask what we *should* be teaching when the question of what we *can* be teaching is so pressing? And isn't it problematic, she asked her colleagues, to see ourselves primarily as critics or teachers and only secondarily, if at all, as state functionaries or employees of a major corporation?

But think about it. What is so compromising about being an employee of the state or a corporation, even a "major corporation"? At what point did Leftist attitudes so infiltrate everyday language that working for the Post Office or General Foods, let alone a "major corporation" like Columbia University, should *ipso facto* seem to carry with it a moral taint? Are we to believe that the citizens of a socialist country are spiritually or physically freer from state control than their counterparts in Western democracies? Odd then, isn't it, that they are rushing the world over to embrace the principles of Western liberal democratic societies? And what dire constraints does Professor Ferguson imagine the university imposes upon the "thought and action" of its employees? One could not help noticing that this tenured radical appeared remarkably unconstrained that afternoon.

That Professor Ferguson's paper should be littered with such contradictions should not surprise us. They represent the standard operating equipment of intellectual Marxists, who are always ready to trump mere empirical evidence with the charge of "false consciousness" or bad faith—reserving to themselves the determination of what is to count as genuine insight and authenticity. Hence it was only to be expected that Professor Ferguson should describe "capitalist social relations" as "monolithic" and then, by virtue of her criticism, arrogate to herself a place outside that allegedly monolithic totality. And it was simply business as usual that she should rail against the liberal tradition and its ideal of "pluralist accommodation," even though it was only in a society governed precisely by that spirit of "pluralist accommodation" that criticism of the sort she propounded would be tolerated.

But in order to get the full flavor of Professor Ferguson's *Weltanschauung*, let us look for a moment at the book that provided her with the inspiration and title for her paper, *Reproduction in Education and Society*, by the French Marxist sociologists Pierre Bourdieu and Jean-Claude Passeron. A work of aggressive impenetrability, *Reproduction in Education and Society* advances the thesis that education in bourgeois societies has the "social function of reproducing the class relations, by ensuring the hereditary transmission of cultural capital." The book consists of a series of highly contentious propositions about social life and education dressed up and elaborated in the abstract, pedantic argot favored by certain academic Marxists. Near the beginning of the book, for example, Messrs. Bourdieu and Passeron inform us that *"All* PEDAGOGIC ACTION (PA) *is, objectively, symbolic violence insofar as it is the imposition of a cultural arbitrary by an arbitrary power."* Their use of the term "objectively" here—recalling as it does an older tradition of "scientific" Marxist analysis—is a touch especially worth savoring. And later on, they confide that the corrupted ethos of the bourgeoisie reveals itself in its very language. Hence they distinguish between "bourgeois language," which is said to tend to "abstraction, formalism, intellectualism and euphemistic moderation," and "working class language," which

> manifests itself in the tendency to move from particular case to particular case, from illustration to parable, or to shun the bombast of fine words and the turgidity of grand emotions, through banter, rudeness and ribaldry, manners of being and doing characteristic of classes who are never fully given the social conditions for the severance between objective denotation and subjective connotation.[*]

All this is the sheerest quackery, of course, though it does

[*] Pierre Bourdieu and Jean-Claude Passeron, *Reproduction in Education and Society*, edited by Richard Nice, with a foreward by Tom Bottomore, SAGE Studies in Social and Educational Change,

inspire the droll question whether its authors believe they have achieved anything like the stylistic frankness they claim to admire in "working class language."

Like her mentors, Professor Ferguson displayed a thoroughgoing animus toward the Western democratic tradition. Invoking the Italian Marxist Antonio Gramsci, she castigated the "ideology" of free will propagated by Western bourgeois societies. And on a lighter note, she indulged in ridiculing the authors of an article that appeared in *Commentary* magazine for suggesting that traditional liberal academics attempted "to promote intellectual openness and tolerance through an honest reading of the West's achievements."* Naturally, this provoked considerable mirth in the audience, for who in the academy still believes in either the West's achievements or its honesty?

After Professor Ferguson's performance, the responses could hardly help seeming anticlimactic. Neil Hertz maundered on about education as a process of "unmasking" and the desirability of opening up the university "to as many modes of self-dramatization as possible," while Peter Brooks took the occasion to pillory Secretary Bennett for his "reactionary" and "sclerotic" views about education. Reflecting on the title of the session, Professor Brooks noted that he understood "us" to mean "we who are not nostalgic for the old consensus." Even the formal proceedings of the symposium, with its round of speakers

---

Volume 5 (Silver Spring: SAGE Publications, 1977), *seriatim*, pages 199, 5, 116.

* Stephen H. Balch and Herbert I. London, "The Tenured Left," *Commentary*, Oct. 1986, page 50.

didactically addressing an audience from a podium, was too formal and "too canonical" for his taste. Perhaps he would have preferred a series of spontaneous improvisations?

The discussion that followed, however, proved quite lively. Two exchanges in particular seem worth remarking. In one of the symposium's rare moments of dissension, Professor Graff rose to challenge Professor Ferguson's presentation. Though he assured the audience that he considered himself "on the Left," he nevertheless felt that Professor Ferguson had given a distorted picture of the situation in the American academy. Compared to what, he asked, may we complain that our universities are sites of "ideological reproduction"? Ah, yes: "Compared to what?" The question marked the day's single burst of common sense. Where else, Professor Graff asked, would one find the ideas of Marx, Foucault, Althusser, and Professor Ferguson's other heroes taken seriously except in the university? Where else would her presentation not only be encouraged but actually listened to and (one assumes) paid for?

Obviously infuriated by her colleague's impertinence, Professor Ferguson responded but did not really reply to these questions. Instead, she pointed out that success in the university, especially for women and minorities, comes at a tremendous psychic cost. She confided that she herself had had to internalize a code of decorum and manners to succeed in the academy; almost sadly, she assured the audience that she was not going to stand up and swear at us—or at Professor Graff—much as she might want to at the moment; part of the price of being there on the podium was being trained not to do such things. And in case we didn't get it the first time around, she reminded us that she regarded the real problems in the academy as political problems: questions about the canon or pedagogy or education in general were merely fronts for political issues. Not surprisingly, Professor Ferguson's confession was greeted by a loud round of applause.

Professor Graff replied by asking Professor Ferguson what she proposed to do with the many people in the academy who happened not to agree with her? No one, he observed, had addressed himself to that rather elementary question. Nor was anyone going to. Sensing that the moment was ripe, Professor Baker intervened from his place in the audience to charge that Professor Hartman's contribution to the symposium had been a "conservative, possibly racist response." Moreover, he declaimed, Professor Hartman had indulged in "an extraordinary valorization of the university," implying as he did that the life of the mind was a delicate thing that the university ought to take care to protect from the crass exigencies of society at large. This, too, got a rousing round of applause from an audience apparently disgusted with the the whole idea of "valorizing the university," even if they were only too happy to inhabit its protected purlieus. And poor Professor Hartman: "Conservative"! "Racist"! One wondered which epithet stung worse. He made some effort to respond, but it soon became clear that nothing as feckless as a reasoned reply could influence the course of opinion in a room so charged with overheated rhetoric.

VII The Stanford debacle

What is particularly depressing about such spectacles is the thought that, far from being atypical, they represent the dominant current of opinion in our most prestigious institutions of higher education. Yale, Harvard, Princeton, Johns Hopkins, Columbia, Brown—the company represented is nothing if not renowned. And of course such institutions serve as models for their less prestigious brethren, so that what is chic at Harvard one semester is sure to be aped at the state school or aspiring liberal arts college down the road the next. Nor should one think such antics as were on display at Yale and in the pages of *Salmagundi* are confined to the realm of theory, that they are battles waged only in the pages of obscure academic journals and from the podiums of academic conferences. Indeed, one of the defining cases involving canon revision—the dropping of the Western culture requirement at Stanford University in the spring of 1988—showed how resolutely the debate has moved out of theory and into practice.

The controversy at Stanford dates back to April, 1986, when members of the Black Student Union complained that the requirement of a year-long course for freshmen in Western culture was racist, sexist, and failed to address the needs of minority students or women. It is even reported that one critic of the course declared that it is "not just racist education, it is the education of racists." Racism is a subject to which we shall return. But it is worth noting here that at Stanford "racism" is something that apparently is only a problem when directed against certain pre-selected groups. How else can one understand the letter written in June, 1988 to the Stanford student newspaper by the president of the Black Student Union, which began by explaining that "It is an unfortunate fact of life that most students at Stanford are white, middle class, privileged, sheltered and apathetic" and went on to confide that "I do not like most white people"? Just imagine the uproar that would have ensued if the student newspaper had printed that same letter with the adjective "white" changed to "black."* In any event, these charges and instances of racism provide the appropriate context in which to appreciate one of the most dramatic and telling moments in the controversy: the spectacle of the Rev. Jesse Jackson marching with five-hundred students at Stanford chanting "Hey hey, ho ho, Western culture's got to go."

For many observers, the Rev. Jackson's sentiments seemed to sum up the issue with all possible clarity. The question was how Stanford, itself a glittering product of Western culture, would respond. The answer came at the end of March, 1988, when the Faculty Senate voted 39–4 to abandon its required course in Western culture. Part of the Stanford curriculum since 1980, the Western culture requirement was to be gradually replaced with a new cluster of courses called "Culture, Ideas, Values," a name designed to preserve a hint of civilization in its initials—it is known as "CIV" for short—but without the offending adjective, "Western." It should be noted that, like its successor, the Western culture requirement did not stipulate that all students take the same course. Rather, students were free to choose among eight year-long courses with titles like "Great Works," "Values, Technology, Science

* Reprinted in "Stanford Documents," assembled by Sidney Hook, in *Partisan Review*, Fall 1988, *seriatim*, pages 662, 664.

and Society," "Philosophy," and "Humanities." Unlike the courses in the "Culture, Ideas, Values" program, however, the eight courses in the Western culture program were all built around a "core list" of sixteen acknowledged masterpieces of Western culture, including selections from the Bible, Homer, Plato, Augustine, and Dante.

Abandoning even that slender basis of commonality in the one required humanities course at the university is disturbing enough. Even more disturbing is the patently political rationale for the change. According to the faculty plan for the program, all the courses in the "Culture, Ideas, Values" program must include "works by women, minorities and persons of color" and at least one work each quarter must address issues of race, sex, or class. As with Professor Showalter and the Yale Bulletin entry for Women's Studies, it is not said whether any of the works must address issues of literary merit, aesthetic excellence, philosophical sophistication, or historical importance. Such criteria presumably belong to the "racist" and "sexist" heritage of Western culture that Stanford is endeavoring to dispense with. But Donald Kennedy, the university's president, nonetheless proclaimed the change "a substantial improvement."*

Not everyone agreed. Kennedy found his supporters, to be sure, but then-Secretary of Education William Bennett, for example, publicly castigated the change as education by "intimidation." And numerous editorials, reports, and letters in major newspapers across the country regarded

---

* "Stanford Alters Western Culture Course," in *The New York Times*, 2 April 1988.

the scuttling of the required course in Western culture with dismay. In an effort to counter the negative publicity, the administration did everything it could to downplay the significance of the change: What was all the fuss about? Stanford wasn't throwing out Western culture *tout court*, it was merely opening up the curriculum in the name of "diversity" (which has since become a favorite code word) and pluralism. In letters addressed to Stanford "friends," parents, alumni, and other potential sources of financial support, administrative officials from the president on down affirmed that Stanford was still a citadel of liberal learning, that—far from being a step backward—the "modification" (as the official university documents liked to put it) of the Western culture requirement represented a victory for reason, culture, and tolerance.

Charles Junkerman, the assistant dean of undergraduate studies, was somewhat franker—perhaps inadvertently so—in a letter he wrote to *The Wall Street Journal* defending Stanford's new course. Fifty years ago, Dean Junkerman wrote, John Locke might have had something to tell us about the question "What is social justice?" But now "it may be that someone like Frantz Fanon, a black Algerian psychoanalyst, will get us closer to the answer we need."*

So John Locke, one of the chief philosophical sources of political liberalism and perhaps the single greatest philosophical influence on the Constitution of the United States, is to be scrapped in favor of Frantz Fanon. And who was Frantz Fanon? The short, evasive, answer is that Fanon was a French-educated psychiatrist from Mar-

* *The Wall Street Journal*, January 6, 1989.

tinique. But he is not remembered for his contributions to psychiatry, as Assistant Dean Junkerman's epithet may imply, but for his politics, for what Professor Fox-Genovese called his theory of "purging violence." What the good assistant dean was thinking of—but did not say—was that Fanon was stationed in Algeria during the French-Algerian war, was radicalized and became a leader of the Algerian National Front, and delivered himself in the early Sixties of a revolutionary screed entitled *The Wretched of the Earth*. One of the most widely available editions of this book in English comes with a predictably admiring preface by Jean-Paul Sartre, then in one of his most politically radical phases. *The Wretched of the Earth* is essentially a pep talk for Third World revolutionaries committed to achieving "decolonialization" through the systematic application of violence. "Have the courage to read this book," Sartre advises: "it will make you ashamed, and shame, as Marx said, is a revolutionary sentiment."

Here is a small sample of what Frantz Fanon, the man whom Assistant Dean Junkerman hopes might "get us closer to the answer we need" regarding the question of social justice, has to say about Western culture in the first section of his book, "Concerning Violence": "When the native hears a speech about Western culture he pulls out his knife—or at least makes sure it is within reach."* Of course, the primary allusion in this passage is to the statement, variously attributed to Goering and other Nazi party members, that "When I hear the word culture, I

---

* Frantz Fanon, *The Wretched of the Earth*, preface by Jean-Paul Sartre, translated by Constance Farrington (New York: Grove Press, 1963), page 43.

reach for my gun." It is worth keeping that allusion in mind as one ponders Fanon's message. For it must not be forgotten that Fanon's book, though cast in the passionately aggrieved rhetoric of political redress, was written as an incitement to murder. It might also be mentioned that though Fanon's main object of attack is Europe, he does not entirely neglect the United States. "Two centuries ago, a former European colony decided to catch up with Europe," he writes near the end of his book. "It succeeded so well that the United States of America became a monster, in which the taints, the sickness, and the inhumanity of Europe have grown to appalling dimensions."* Edifying, is it not, especially when considered as a replacement for John Locke in a required course for freshmen at Stanford?

Assistant Dean Junkerman was also a co-signatory, together with the dean of undergraduate studies, of a mollifying letter addressed to parents of Stanford students. "Unfortunately," they wrote, "outside the immediate campus there has been a good deal of misunderstanding about the changes that were made . . . . Rest assured that our faculty will develop academically challenging and responsible tracks for the new CIV Program. Indeed, one very impressive new track, entitled 'Europe and the Americas,' is already under development. . . ."†

Let us take a brief look at what this "impressive new track" on Europe and the Americas, first taught in the fall

---

* *Ibid.*, page 313.

† "The Process and the Product: The Inside Story on the Western Culture Debate," a letter sent by Dean of Undergraduate Studies Thomas Wasow and Assistant Dean of Undergraduate Studies Charles Junkerman in the fall of 1988.

of 1988, offers students. Since faculty is still required to assign some classics, in the first section of the course, entitled "Conventions of Selfhood," students are required to read a portion of St. Augustine's *Confessions*. That is in a class called "The Body and the 'Deep' Interior Self." But things get going a few days later with a class devoted to the subject "Multicultural Selves in the Navaho Country," for which students are assigned the film *The Story of a Navaho Family, 1938–1986*. (This is one of several required films for the course.)

Our visit with the Navahos is followed the next week by a class called "Our Bodies, Our Sheep, Our Cosmos, Ourselves," with reading from *Son of Old Man Hat* by Left Handed. Naturally, there is the obligatory reading from Karl Marx later in the course. And then, under the rubric "Making Other Cultural Selves," a class devoted to "Labor, Gender, and Self in the Philippine Uplands," for which the reading is from—are you ready?—*Genesis* and *Revelations*. Perhaps the Bible is hard to come by out in Palo Alto, since this assignment, alone among the assignments for this course, is followed by the parenthetical notation, "to be distributed." And lest one think that Assistant Dean Junkerman had bandied about Frantz Fanon's name merely as a hypothetical instance, rest assured, as he might say, that Fanon occupies an honored place in Stanford's new "Europe and the Americas" course. The section on "Forging Revolutionary Selves" begins with a class called "Violence and the Self" and generous readings from *The Wretched of the Earth*.

There are several things that must be said about this curricular debacle at Stanford. First, as President Donald Kennedy noted in a soothing letter of February 15, 1988 to Stanford friends, "the primary voices for change have been the faculty's." He meant by this admission to reassure Stanford's benefactors that charges of "intimidation" by students had been exaggerated. And, notwithstanding the agitation by members of the Black Student Union and others, he was undoubtedly right: the faculty was in the end to blame for the demise of the Western culture course at Stanford. But of course this is more, not less, troubling, because it means that the elite body of the Faculty Senate at Stanford—those men and women entrusted with helping to set educational policy at one of our greatest universities—willingly, nay, eagerly, voted 39–4 against preserving even a minimally traditional educational requirement. Now, instead of an introduction to masterpieces, students at Stanford are getting Frantz Fanon, the movies, and "Our Bodies, Our Sheep, Our Cosmos, Ourselves."

VIII   The triumph of Left Eclecticism

Like most of the reflections in the *Salmagundi* colloquy and the symposium at Yale, the demise of the Western culture requirement at Stanford underscores the predominance in the academy of what the literary critic Frederick Crews has aptly dubbed "Left Eclecticism." As Professor Crews explains, Left Eclecticism is not identical to Marxism, exactly, but represents any of a wide variety of anti-establishment modes of thought from structuralism and post-structuralism, deconstruction, and Lacanian analysis to feminist, homosexual, black, and other patently political forms of "criticism." At the heart of Left Eclecticism, writes Professor Crews, is an understanding, ultimately borrowed from the Marxist ethos, that analytic and theoretic discourse is to be judged primarily by the radicalism of its stance. The schools of thought thus favored make sharply divergent claims, yet all of them set themselves against allegedly repressive Western institutions and practices. In dealing with a given painting, novel, or piece of architecture, especially one dating from the capitalist era, they do not aim primarily to show the work's character or governing idea. The goal is rather to subdue the work through aggressive demystification—for example, by positing its socioeconomic determinants and ideological implications, scanning it for any encouraging signs of subversion, and then judging the result against an ideal of total freedom.*

Taken together, the *Salmagundi* collection, the Yale symposium on the canon, and Stanford's abandonment of its Western culture requirement provide a small but valuable inventory of the sort of thing Professor Crews has in mind. While there is much more to be said about the influence of Left Eclecticism in the academy, at this point I wish only to underscore the goal that Professor Crews identifies of subduing the work "through aggressive demystification." For it is often in the name of radical demystification—of skepticism raised to the highest power—that the assault on the traditional goals of higher education proceeds. The idea is, of course, that by shedding inherited beliefs, traditions, and prejudices one thereby frees oneself for more genuine insight. It rarely occurs to these champions of disillusionment that demys-

* Frederick Crews, *Skeptical Engagements* (New York: Oxford University Press, 1986), pages 138–139.

tification consistently pursued results in its own particularly sterile forms of remystification. In fact, what we have witnessed is what the Australian philosopher David Stove described as "the frivolous elevation of 'the critical attitude' into a categorical imperative." The principal result, Stove noted, has been "to fortify millions of ignorant graduates and undergraduates in the belief, to which they are already too firmly wedded by other causes, that the adversary posture is all, and that intellectual life consists in 'directionless quibble.'"*

That so many of the teachers and scholars we have discussed are apparently prepared to jettison the intellectual principles and, indeed, the moral grounding that have nourished and given meaning to their disciplines is a deeply foreboding sign. And the ominousness of the current situation is only compounded when we realize that many of these same men and women now hold positions of considerable power and influence in the colleges and universities that are charged with educating our youth. The cynicism, devotion to shallow intellectual fashion, and unthinking importation of politics into the humanities that these educators display make it easy to wonder, with Allan Bloom, whether "there is either the wherewithal or the energy within the university to constitute or reconstitute the idea of an educated human being and establish a liberal education again."† One must believe that such energy and wherewithal does or could exist. But the radical ethos prevailing in the academy means that their achievement is not only ever more precarious, but also ever more urgent.

---

* David Stove, *Scientific Irrationalism: Origins of a Postmodern Cult* (New Brunswick: Transaction Publishers, 2001), page 185.

† *The Closing of the American Mind*, page 380.

CHAPTER TWO

Speaking Against the Humanities

I The academy strikes back

THE ASSAULT on the canon has been one of the most publicly controversial elements in the recent debate over the future of the humanities in this country. But that assault must be understood in the context of the enormous changes that have taken place over the last four decades in the academic understanding of the nature and goals of liberal arts education. Many of these changes—the demand that the curriculum be recast to accommodate racial, sexual, or ethnic sensitivities, for example—are overtly political. Other changes—the attack on the ideal of disinterested scholarship, for example, or the rise of deconstruction and its postmodernist progeny—also rest partly on political presuppositions, though often in ways that are not immediately apparent.

Perhaps the best way to begin to appreciate the extent of these changes is to consider the academy's response to its critics. A telling introduction to this subject is the brief

65

report issued by the American Council of Learned Societies entitled *Speaking for the Humanities.** A slender thirty-eight pages, this pamphlet was written jointly by seven prominent academics—including one dean and six directors of humanities centers—and was endorsed by an additional twenty-one professors from across the country.† It is intended partly as a position paper or manifesto, outlining what has come to be the established academic view of the humanities. It is also intended as a response to critics of the academy such as Allan Bloom, William Bennett, and Lynne V. Cheney, who succeeded Secretary Bennett as director of the National Endowment for the Humanities and whose report on the state of the humanities‡ takes up where

* George Levine, *et al.*, *Speaking for the Humanities*, ACLS Occasional Paper, No. 7, 1989.

† The authors are Peter Brooks, whom we met in the last chapter; Jonathan Culler, Professor of English and Comparative Literature and Director of the Society for the Humanities at Cornell University; George Levine, Professor of English and Director of the Center for the Critical Analysis of Contemporary Culture at Rutgers University, who also undertook to orchestrate the writing and editing of the pamphlet; Marjorie Garber, Professor of English and Director of the Center for Literary and Cultural Studies at Harvard; E. Ann Kaplan, Professor of English and Director of the Humanities Institute at the State University of New York at Stony Brook; and Catharine R. Stimpson, then Professor of English and Dean of the Graduate School at Rutgers, and now, after stints as president of the Modern Language Association and head of the MacArthur Foundation, a dean at New York University.

‡ Lynne V. Cheney, *Humanities in America: A Report to the President, the Congress, and the American People* (Washington: The National Endowment for the Humanities, 1988).

Secretary Bennett's *To Reclaim a Legacy* left off in criticizing the way that the academy has dealt with the humanities.

The charges that *Speaking for the Humanities* attempts to answer fall roughly into two categories. There is, first, the question of what we might call the statistical health of the humanities. In *To Reclaim a Legacy*, for example, we read that since 1970 the number of students majoring in the humanities has declined by about half, by nearly two-thirds in the case of history, that fewer than half of all colleges and universities require foreign language study for the bachelor's degree—down from ninety percent in 1966—and that a student can now be graduated from seventy-five percent of our colleges and universities without having studied European history. Similarly, *Humanities in America* reports that between 1966 and 1986—a time when the number of bachelor's degrees awarded in this country increased by eighty-eight percent—the number of bachelor's degrees awarded in the humanities declined by thirty-three percent. It also reports that one can be graduated from eighty percent of our four-year colleges without taking a course in the history of Western civilization, from more than eighty percent of our institutions of higher education without taking a course in American history, and from sixty-two percent without taking a course in philosophy. According to these and other reports,* then, in the past few decades American education has suffered a wholesale flight from the humanities.

* See for example the statistical appendix to *What's Happened to the Humanities?*, a collection of essays edited by Alvin Kernan (Princeton: Princeton University Press, 1999).

Speaking for the Humanities responds, in essence, with the time-honored two-step known as backing and filling. It goes something like this: Yes, there has been a nationwide decline in humanities enrollments, but it is not the fault of the way the humanities are being taught; no, there wasn't such a big decline in enrollments after all, and even if there was, people like Secretary Bennett and Lynne Cheney don't understand its real significance; OK, there was a precipitous decline in humanities enrollments, but it was because economics suddenly became such a popular subject—again, not our fault; well, possibly there was a decline in humanities enrollments at some institutions, but the number of English majors at Rutgers University did not decline during the last two decades and at Harvard the number of students majoring in the humanities "actually" rose.

One need not be a statistician (or a psychologist) to realize that the authors of *Speaking for the Humanities* are merely temporizing. Nor are they convincing in their responses to the second, more substantive, category of charges: that the humanities have become over-specialized and needlessly obscure, that they have repudiated the ideal of disinterested scholarship in order to pursue various politicized educational agendas, and that they have often abandoned the study of the great works of the Western tradition in order to lavish attention on material that is secondary, trivial, or of dubious intellectual importance.

Once again we find the authors of *Speaking for the Humanities* indulging in a good deal of the old two-step: The humanities have not become over-specialized, or if they have it's because "the problems are almost always more complicated than the popular interpretation allows"

and, what's more, "to be specialized is not to be trivial"*
We are told, too, that the humanities have not simply given
up the ideal of disinterested scholarship, or if they have it's
because 1) there are no such things as disinterestedness or
objectivity anyway, or 2) if there are such things, they
aren't all they have been cracked up to be. (Take your
pick.) Besides, why worry about boring things like objectivity, disinterestedness, or facts when "the humanities are
better conceived as fields of exploration and critique rather
than materials for transmission," that is to say, when the
intellectual and moral substance of the humanistic tradition is regarded as material for free play ("exploration")
rather than a precious legacy worthy of preservation. We
also discover that the humanities have not become more
politicized, they have simply woken up to the fact that
"everything is political." Nor, apparently, have the humanities given up great works, they've merely expanded
the definition of what counts as great. And so on.

Although it is written in the sanitized prose that group
authorship imposes, *Speaking for the Humanities* is a
disturbing document on any number of levels. For one
thing, it exhibits an extraordinary contempt for the non-
academic public. Consider only the assertion that
"professionalization makes thought possible"—as if those
who are not professionals are therefore incapable of
thought. Indeed, this statement reveals a great deal about
the patently self-serving spirit that informs *Speaking for
the Humanities*. Its authors concede that many unenlightened people seem "frightened" that recent develop-

---

* Unless otherwise noted, quotations in this section are from *Speaking for the Humanities*, pages 4–16.

ments in the humanities will "subvert the moral order." But their response is to retreat to the platitude that "to live with uncertainty is one of the conditions of great art." The implication of course is that our beleaguered humanists have the rare courage to withstand the existential uncertainties of great art and that therefore the public must indulge them. What they don't say is that everything in their cultivation of specialization and attitude of professionalization conspires against the preservation of great art, tending instead to transform art into fodder for pedantic academic commentary.

In the same vein, they explain that it

> is precisely because the teachers of the humanities take their subject seriously that they become specialists, allow themselves to be professionals rather than amateurs— belle lettrists who unselfconsciously sustain traditional hierarchies, traditional social and cultural exclusions, assuming that their audience is both universal and homogenous.

In other words, only your professional academic, equipped with a Ph.D. and preferably with tenure, is canny enough to escape bondage to naive and intellectually crippling assumptions about social and cultural power. No mere Mencken or Orwell or Auden could do it, you see, because, as amateurs and belle lettrists, they were just too unaware of "traditional hierarchies" to tell us anything of much value. As the English critic John Gross has noted apropos this passage,

> at the very least, the attitudes enshrined in *Speaking for the Humanities* hold out the threat of an academic closed

shop. But there is something in them that goes deeper than that, there is a hostility not merely towards the freelance, but towards the free response. For in spite of its apparent variety, a great deal of critical theory is coercive, designed to enforce approved social and political attitudes (roughly speaking, any attitude that rejects "traditional hierarchies"). The belittling of the *belle lettrist*, the person who writes as he pleases, is at bottom a demand for ideological conformity.*

In addition to the arrogance that *Speaking for the Humanities* communicates, there is the problem of its underlying conception of what constitutes a liberal arts education. At the same time that the distinguished authors of this pamphlet are busy telling us that everything is just fine in the academy, that the criticism launched by Secretary Bennett and others regarding over-specialization "is badly off the mark," they also confide that

> developments in modern thought . . . have made us alert to what is left out when "the best that has been thought and written" is selected or when discussion focuses on "man." We have learned to ask whether universalist claims do not in fact promote as a norm the concerns of a particular group and set aside as partial or limited those of other groups.

The measured tone of the prose ("developments in modern thought," etc.) conceal a deep if somewhat evasive dis-

---

* John Gross, *The Rise and Fall of the Man of Letters: English Literary Life Since 1800*, revised edition (Chicago: Ivan R. Dee, 1991), page 330.

regard for the substance of the humanities as traditionally conceived. Perhaps the first question one wants to ask is what "developments" are the authors of this pamphlet thinking of? They imply that they have some sort of evidence for the highly contentious propositions that they put forth: that humanistic education should *not* be concerned with the best that has been thought and written, for example, or that the aspiration of the humanities to speak to the concerns of all men and women is only a cover for one group's interests. But in fact the only "development" they could point to is the rise of a politicized view of education that requires the redefinition of the curriculum along the lines specified by the "gender, class, and race" lobby or the various postmodern relativists championing one or another version of intellectual nihilism.

It is also worth noting how much *Speaking for the Humanities* gives away in its contemptuous dismissal of higher education as an effort to acquaint students with "the best that has been thought and written." The phrase, of course, is a nod to Matthew Arnold, the Victorian poet, critic, and man of letters. Arnold had looked to the preservation and transmission of the best that had been thought and written as a means of rescuing culture from anarchy in a democratic society. And, indeed, that a liberal arts education sought the best was one reason college was once referred to as "higher" education: it was "higher" in the sense not only of providing more education but also in the sense of providing a deeper acquaintance with the formative ideas and values of our culture. These days, however, at a time when such "value judgments" are looked upon with suspicion and all comparisons of quality are considered invidious, Matthew Arnold and everything he stood for are rejected as elitist.

In fact, *Speaking for the Humanities* really speaks for this attitude of rejecting what the humanities have traditionally stood for. In this respect, however, it is no different from many other developments in the academy today. One thinks especially of the rapid growth of academic programs devoted to the study of popular culture. It must be understood that, whatever legitimate interest the academic study of popular culture may hold, the study of pop culture has been pursued primarily as a means of attacking the traditional academic concentration on objects of high culture. This can be seen in any number of modish academic movements, but is perhaps most completely exemplified by the movement called Cultural Studies. The latest and most important academic effort to resuscitate Marxist analysis and liberate the humanities from an "elitist" concern with high culture, Cultural Studies had its origin in Britain but has quickly gained an important following in this country. Its adherents are especially numerous at colleges and universities with interdisciplinary humanities centers, which provide a natural roost for Cultural Studies. Richard Johnson, one of the founders of Cultural Studies in Britain, put the chief issue bluntly in what is generally considered the charter document for the movement, "What Is Cultural Studies Anyway?" "Analysts [i.e., teachers] need to abandon once and for all," he writes, "both of the two main models of the critical reader: the primarily evaluative reading (is this a good/bad text?) and the aspiration to text-analysis as an 'objective science.'"*

* Richard Johnson, "What Is Cultural Studies Anyway?," *Social Text: Theory / Culture / Ideology*, Winter 1986/7, pages 38–80; this quotation, page 74.

What are the implications of this effort to jettison both readings that are "primarily evaluative" and the goal of objectivity? One implication is that the highest achievements of civilization are somehow off limits or inaccessible to certain groups on the grounds that they are not of the appropriate sex, ethnic heritage, or race. It's as if the teachings of Plato, because he was a white European male, were therefore necessarily unintelligible to Chinese women or black men. Indeed, it is important to recognize how deeply exclusionary—one might even say racist and sexist—are the suppositions that stand behind the emancipationist rhetoric one finds scattered throughout *Speaking for the Humanities* and other contemporary academic credos. As is often the case, rhetoric promising greater openness, diversity, and pluralism actually helps to perpetuate the most stringent intellectual conformity.

It is also important to note that the "critique" of what it pleases the authors of this pamphlet to refer to as "the positivist ideal of objectivity and disinterest" is not a critique at all but simply a generalized animus against the notions that reality is not an invention and that the human mind is capable of apprehending truths that exist apart from the perturbations of subjective fancy. If one wanted to characterize the epistemological foundations of this animus, probably the most generous word one could propose would be *adolescent*—after all, what could be more adolescent than this spirit of contempt blended as it is with an almost comic self-absorption?

The political implications are even more forbidding. For behind any cavalier dismissal of truth lies a disdain for empirical reality that can easily be enlisted by tyranny. This was underscored by the influential literary critic and scholar Tzvetan Todorov in his review of *Speaking for the*

Humanities. Taking issue with the authors' dismissal of "objectivity and disinterest"—a dismissal that is based, they proudly remind us, on "the consensus of most of the dominant theories"—Todorov notes how "awkwardly reminiscent" it is of the torturer O'Brien's terrifying speech in George Orwell's *1984*: "You believe that reality is something objective, external, existing in its own right. . . . But I tell you, Winston, that reality is not external. Reality exists in the human mind and nowhere else." As Winston discovered, it was not advantageous to dispute this idea.* There are many other disturbing things about *Speaking for the Humanities*. Some, like the anachronistic "alternative" readings the authors offer, would be downright funny if one didn't know they were being taken seriously and perpetuated as "developments in modern thought." Thus, for example, we discover that *The Tempest* is being widely read as an allegory about imperialist conquest: Caliban is the exploited native, you see, and Prospero the evil imperialistic European. Similarly, *Paradise Lost* is presented as a problem text for feminists because Milton portrays Adam as being "for God only" but Eve as being merely for God in Adam. If such interpretations were critical bagatelles, admired more for their ingenuity than their insight, there would be no need for concern. But in fact they are taken very seriously and, indeed, provide models for a whole range of ideological attacks on the humanities. What a reading of *The Tempest* as an imperialist drama and a reading of *Paradise Lost* as a feminist tragedy have in common is an eagerness to subordinate literature to an extraneous

* Quoted in Tzvetan Todorov, "Crimes Against Humanities," *The New Republic*, July 3, 1989, pages 26–30.

political agenda, the agenda of Third World racial concerns on the one hand and feminist restitution on the other. In both cases, what threatens to be lost is not only the integrity of the individual text—bad enough though that is—but the whole idea of literature as a distinctive realm of expression and experience with its own concerns, values, and goals. No one would deny that literature is often about politics; but that is a far cry from maintaining, as do the authors of *Speaking for the Humanities*, that the *essence* of literature is politics.

Equally disturbing is the extent to which *Speaking for the Humanities* is a kind of position paper for that newly refurbished academic entity, the interdisciplinary humanities center. As the authors note, at the time of their writing there were already some three hundred such centers at campuses scattered around the country. Generously funded by universities, corporations, and government agencies such as the National Endowment for the Humanities, these centers have increasingly become—to use a word much in vogue—"sites" of enormous institutional power and prestige. The authors of *Speaking for the Humanities* place great stock in the promise of this relatively new institution. Yet paradoxically, it is by no means clear that the rise of the humanities center is a beneficent development for the study of the humanities. Far from seeking to preserve the intellectual and moral integrity of the humanities, in recent years such centers have typically become the favored homes of every new radical academic movement, from the New Historicism and Cultural Studies to Queer Theory and Postcolonial Studies.

Moreover, existing as they do on the margins of the traditional academic disciplines, such academic enclaves are typically dedicated to the goal of what Thomas Short referred to as "breaking the disciplines." Thus it is that one often hears talk of "post-disciplinary" studies and programs that seek to transcend the traditional divisions between academic subjects so that professors trained in English can pretend to be philosophers, philosophers can pretend to be literary critics, and everyone can absorb large doses of sociology in order to overcome the ingrained habit of regarding any academic subject as worthy of study in its own right. *Speaking for the Humanities* is full of praise for both the idea of academic specialization and the proliferation of interdisciplinary humanities centers. But nowhere do its authors mention that one of the most often declared ambitions of the new interdisciplinary movements is to undermine the intellectual and institutional prestige of traditional specialized scholarly work—"blurring," as the one-time philosopher Richard Rorty put it, "the literature-philosophy distinction and promoting the idea of a seamless, undifferentiated 'general text.'"

II Rocking around the clock

Let us now turn to look briefly at the sort of thing at least some of the authors of *Speaking for the Humanities* regard as worthy objects of attention for humanistic study. In many respects, the pamphlet owes its genesis to one of its authors, Professor E. Ann Kaplan from the State University of New York at Stony Brook. It was she who first went to the ACLS to suggest that it sponsor a meeting of directors of humanities centers, and it was out of the meetings that followed that the "need" for an institutional response to recent criticisms of the academy was articulated. There is a great deal in *Speaking for the Humanities* about the sanctity of new "research" being undertaken by contemporary humanists, whose work may be too specialized and "professional" to be intelligible to the general educated reader, of course, but who are nonetheless avidly pursuing important "developments in modern thought."

What sort of research does Professor Kaplan herself pursue? Her specialty seems to be Hollywood movies— she has written several books on the subject—though she has also branched out into the promising field of rock videos. More specifically, her book *Rocking Around the Clock: Music Television, Postmodernism, & Consumer Culture** is an investigation of MTV with special reference to the rock videos of the pop singer Madonna—"the female star," Professor Kaplan tells us, "who perhaps more than any other embodies the new postmodernist feminist heroine." In *Rocking Around the Clock*, Professor Kaplan enumerates the five types of rock video she has discerned in the course of her painstaking research into MTV and provides recondite analyses of such landmark works of art as "Smokin' in the Boys' Room" by the rock band Mötley Crüe, "Rebel Yell" by Billy Idol, and John Cougar Mellencamp's "Hurts So Good," which, we discover, "addresses recent interest in sado-masochism on the part of both young men and women."

Not that this book is intended to be a popular account

---

* E. Ann Kaplan, *Rocking Around the Clock: Music Television, Postmodernism, & Consumer Culture* (New York: Methuen, 1987). Unless otherwise noted, quotations in this section are from this volume. See especially pages 31, 89–95, 114–117, 147–148.

of this popular entertainment medium. On the contrary, though Professor Kaplan is not terribly adept at the practice, she does everything she can to jazz up (or perhaps we should say "rock up") her pages with formidable quotations from Lacan, Derrida, Jameson, and other certified academic gurus. For example, in a chapter entitled "Gender Address and the Gaze in MTV," she begins by telling us that "we need particularly to explore how far theories of the 'male gaze' apply to watching television," confides the exciting news that "the plethora of gender positions on [MTV] is arguably linked to the heterogeneity of current sex roles and to an imaginary [*sic*] constructed out of a world in which all traditional categories, boundaries, and institutions are being questioned," and concludes that "the romantic video functions in the pre-symbolic dyadic terrain between the illusory merging with the mother and the phallicism that follows the mirror phase."

Naturally, Professor Kaplan also takes every opportunity to introduce a dollop of politically correct persiflage. Early on in the book, for example, we are told that "the racist aspect of MTV . . . reflects aspects of Reagan's America." And near the end of the volume, she muses that

> one could see the effacing in MTV of old boundaries between high and low culture, between past, present, and future, and between previously distinct art forms as an exhilarating move toward a heteroglossia that calls into question moribund pieties of a now archaic humanism. . . . The creativity and energy of rock videos could represent a refusal to be co-opted into the liberalism that has brought America to its present crisis.

The chief merit of Professor Kaplan's "analyses" are as graphic specimen documents bearing witness to cultural decadence. Who would have thought it possible that a woman entrusted with teaching college English and directing a humanities center at a major university would make her scholarly reputation writing about "Smokin' in the Boys' Room," the rock videos of Madonna, and so forth? And do take note of Professor Kaplan's diction: "moribund pieties," "archaic humanism," "the liberalism that has brought America to its present crisis." One would never know that the real crisis concerns the fact that words like "humanism" and "liberalism"—to say nothing of "objectivity," "disinterestedness," and "truth" —have been drained of meaning and are now regarded, precisely, as "moribund" by men and women whose lives were once devoted to the ideals those words named. In one of the most excoriated sections of *The Closing of the American Mind*, Allan Bloom discusses what he believes to be the baneful effects rock music has had on the imaginations of students. Many people found his conclusions extreme. "I believe," Bloom wrote, that rock music "ruins the imagination of young people and makes it very difficult for them to have a passionate relationship to the art and thought that are the substance of liberal education." A perusal of *Rocking Around the Clock* makes Bloom's judgment seem like an understatement.

Professor Kaplan's book raises another issue as well. While her performance, bedizened as it is with snippets of Lacanian analysis, is more pretentious than many such expositions, in its basic approach and effort to

* *The Closing of the American Mind*, page 79.

academicize popular culture *Rocking Around the Clock* is by no means exceptional. At campuses around the country, and especially in interdisciplinary programs and centers around the country, we have for some time now been witnessing an aggressive effort to erase the qualitative distinction between high culture and popular culture. As the critic John Simon noted apropos a collection of essays by Susan Sontag, "nothing succeeds better than highbrow endorsement of lowbrow tastes."* And this effort, so dear to radical chic intellectuals in the 1960s, has now become commonplace in the academy, where the degraded and demotic world of pop culture has been embraced wholesale.

Professor Kaplan's lucubrations also suggest the extent to which literary scholars and other humanists have gleefully sought to introduce the methods, concerns, and subject matter of the social sciences into the humanities. More and more, courses in literature seem like amateur exercises in sociological or anthropological sermonizing. Professor Kaplan's book is merely one of this large and growing genre. We are now at a point almost diametrically opposed to the ideal envisioned by Matthew Arnold. Instead of perpetuating the best that has been thought and said, our new humanists assure each other and their students that "best" is a socially relative term and that, at bottom, one might just as well study the "text" of "Smokin' in the Boys' Room" as bother reading Wallace Stevens, let alone someone as fusty as Matthew Arnold.

---

* John Simon, *The Sheep from the Goats: Selected Literary Essays* (New York: Weidenfeld & Nicolson, 1989), page 24.

III The eclipse of the self

The attack by the academy on fundamental terms and distinctions takes several forms. At the same time that the Professor Kaplans of the profession are busy watching MTV and complaining about "the liberalism that has brought America to its present crisis," others are employing more conventional academic tools in an effort to cast doubt on the values and aspiration of traditional humanistic inquiry. A striking example of the latter appeared in 1986, when Stanford University Press published *Reconstructing Individualism: Autonomy, Individuality, and the Self in Western Thought,** a collection of essays drawn from papers presented at a conference of the same title that had been held at Stanford two years previously. Including contributions by such formidable scholars as the art historian Michael Fried, the philosophers Stanley Cavell, Martha C. Nussbaum, and Ian Hacking, the sociologist Niklas Luhmann, the historian Natalie Zemon Davis, the literary critics John Frecero and Stephen Greenblatt, and others of similar academic repute, the volume may be taken as a "state of the art" interdisciplinary report on recent academic thinking about individualism. And because the notion of individualism has traditionally occupied a central place in the humanities, we may also look to *Reconstructing Individualism* for

---

* *Reconstructing Individualism: Autonomy, Individuality, and the Self in Western Thought,* edited by Thomas C. Heller, Morton Sosna, David E. Wellbery, *et al.* (Stanford: Stanford University Press, 1987). Unless otherwise noted, quotations in this section are from this volume. See especially pages 1–2, 16, 35–49, 86–99, 110–116, 197, 337.

further insight into the way the more advanced precincts of contemporary academic speculation has "reconstructed" the goals and values of humanistic education.

It has become practically axiomatic in the academy that one cannot invoke so jaded a notion as "individualism" without an elaborate garland of reservations, qualifications, and caveats. Just as Professor Kaplan unself-consciously referred to an "archaic humanism," so any academic discussion of the subject of individualism has to be undertaken with the clear understanding that one is dealing with tainted goods. As we have seen, the very idea that there is something special about the individual is likely to be taken as a "RED FLAG" by progressive academics for whom individualism is tantamount to racism. Because individualism is widely recognized as one of the bedrocks of Western liberal thought and society, no as it were self-respecting (not to say individualistic) academic would dream of taking it "straight," of dealing with it on its own terms as an idea that continues to have a profound claim on us morally and intellectually. "Individualism" in this sense is only slightly less disreputable in the academy these days than that ultimate term of abuse, "bourgeois."

Accordingly, we read in the introduction to *Reconstructing Individualism* that the "animating assumption" of the conference and the volume of essays it inspired was that "the concept of the individual, which has played such a central role in the formation of the post-Renaissance world, needs to be rethought in the wake of the severe criticisms which have been directed against it" over the course of the last century. "Developments in the material and social realms," we read, "such as industrialization and the emergence of mass society" have rendered the individual "problematic," have even "altered the ontological foundations of individual identity." By now, having been subjected to the "deconstructive" scrutiny of such critics as Marx, Nietzsche, and Freud— to say nothing of the legions of academics who carry on in their name today—individualism can be made academically palatable only if it is suitably "reconstructed." While the particulars of this envisioned "reconstruction" are never really set forth, it is nonetheless clear that most of these essays are to be seen primarily as attempts to explore alternative, "reconstructed" versions of individualism—"postcultural" versions, perhaps (to employ a word brandished by one of the essays): versions of individualism sophisticated enough to dispense with anything so embarrassing as particular individuals. "At the volume's close," the introduction cheerfully concludes, "the figure of the individual has not been discredited or dissolved so much as displaced and transposed."

Perhaps. But it must be said that most of the efforts at "displacement" and "transposition" collected here also do what they can to discredit the "figure of the individual." In "Toward a Relational Individualism: The Mediation of the Self Through Psychoanalysis," for example, Nancy Julia Chodorow assures us that "psychoanalysis radically undermines notions about autonomy, individual choice, will, responsibility, and rationality, showing that we do not control our lives in the most fundamental sense." Let's think about this for a moment. In what sense has psychoanalysis really *undermined* the ideas of will, choice, responsibility, etc.? After all, did not Professor Chodorow *will* to write this essay? Did she not *choose* to contribute to this volume? Did she not assume the *responsibility* of submitting a manuscript by a certain date? Notwithstanding the voluminous attempts of academic psychoanalysis to convince us that we are creatures of unconscious impulses, do we not in fact bear witness to the cogency and pertinence of these concepts every day?

Among the chief casualties of this brand of criticism are its heroes. Nietzsche has suffered particular indignities at its hands. Typical is Werner Hamacher's long and elliptical essay called " 'Disgregation of the Will': Nietzsche on the Individual and Individuality." Amazingly, he manages to grind all of Nietzsche's trenchant comments on the subject into a murky verbal paste. "The term 'individuality,' " Professor Hamacher tells us, "properly applies only to what transgresses the series of forms and the form of forms (typological knowledge and its objective correlatives), dissociating itself from the rigor mortis of canonical life forms, eluding the subsumptive compulsion to general categories, advancing toward a future that withdraws from every typology and objectification." This is Nietzsche, champion of Dionysus, philosopher of the Anti-Christ? "I shall repeat a hundred times," Nietzsche wrote in *Beyond Good and Evil*, "we really ought to free ourselves from the seduction of words!"* Obviously, there are some things you can't say too often.

To speak of "seduction by words" brings us to one of the main features—one might even say "principles"—of the sort of chic academic criticism that *Reconstructing Individualism* specializes in: the attempt to enliven its cruelly abstract, anemic prose with an obsessive concern

---

* Friedrich Nietzsche, *Beyond Good and Evil* §16, in *The Basic Writings of Nietzsche*, translated with introductions by Walter Kaufmann (New York: Random House, 1966), page 213.

with sex, preferably perverse sex, the more violent the better. To employ one of its favorite terms, we might even say that such criticism—which has become increasingly prominent in the academy—"fetishizes" the erotic. The chief locus of sexual relations is not, of course, between living individuals but within language itself. Perhaps because they have lost interest in particular individuals, these critics of individualism find that language is where the real excitement lies. This makes for some pretty silly speculation, but it does allow one to throw around lots of terms like "phallocratic," "castration," and so on. *Reconstructing Individualism* is full of this sort of thing. Stephen Greenblatt, for example, a celebrated champion of the New Historicism in literary studies, bases his entire article on "Fiction and Friction" on the story of a seventeenth-century French hermaphrodite, the insistence that sexual difference is "unstable and artificial," and a theory about the relation between individualism, "sexual chafing," and "the wantonness of language."

Indeed, recourse to the more extravagant precincts of the erotic seems to have become a kind of ritual gesture, a verbal tic in the academy. One first says something about language—about how everything is really only a corollary of language, etc.—and then one introduces a sexual twist. Paolo Valesio offers a good example in his essay on "The Beautiful Lie" (the "lie" being individualism, of course). Having told us that individualism is "a poetic concern, a concern with linguistic intensification and shaping," he proceeds to note that here, "as in every intensification of reading, not only the link with the process of writing emerges, . . . but the link of both processes with solitary and self-sufficient love—with the softly existential grounding of solipsism, masturbation."

86

Or take Christine Brooke-Rose's essay on "The Dissolution of Character in the Novel." In the midst of the usual litany about the death of character—"character," like "individualism," turns out to be in need of "reconstruction"—we read that "characters are verbal structures; they are like our real-life relationships but have no semblance of a referent. More and more swollen with words, like stray phalluses they wander our minds, cut off from the body of the text." Those phalluses! They crop up everywhere today.

The treatment of sex in such works as *Reconstructing Individualism* highlights one of the great ironies of the whole enterprise: it goes on and on about the importance of reading more carefully, more critically, more openly, and then proceeds to display a quite remarkable obtuseness about the specific works it addresses. Concentrating on some detail of a text, it misses the whole; isolating verbal similarities, it misses the sense.

And, my, what terrible English we encounter here! Many of the essays in *Reconstructing Individualism* occupy a vertiginous hinterland of the mind where words spin themselves out in hopeless, jargon-laden opacity. And it is important to realize that this is precisely the kind of "specialization" and "professionalization" that *Speaking for the Humanities* is at pains to defend. One could open *Reconstructing Individualism* pretty much at random for examples, but Niklas Luhmann's reflections on "The Individuality of the Individual" contain some choice items. "We may, of course, define emotions as the autopoietic immune system of the autopoietic psychic system; but again: is this emotionally adequate?" Anyone care to answer that? "The most important consequence," Professor Luhmann continues a bit later, "might well be that the theory of autopoietic systems seems to bar all ways back to an anthropological conception of man. It precludes, in other words, humanism. [Yet another term, incidentally, that has been singled out for academic "reconstruction"] . . . This means that we have to invent new conceptual artificialities in order to give an account of what we see when we meet somebody who looks and behaves like a human being. How do we know that he is one?" Hard to say, hard to say.

IV Hunting Courbet

All of these faults—deliberately perverse interpretations, verbal obscurity, etc.—are writ large in Michael Fried's contribution to *Reconstructing Individualism*: "Courbet's Metaphysics: A Reading of 'The Quarry.'"* It is indeed an exemplary performance, and it shows that the new approach to the humanities has infiltrated and perverted the traditional methods and concerns of art history as well as literary studies. The announced subject of Professor Fried's essay is Gustave Courbet's 1856 painting *The Quarry*, a hunting scene that depicts a moment of rest after a successful hunt. In the left foreground, we see the vanquished deer hanging from a branch, its head lolling sideways on the ground. To the right, receding into a shadow, the hunter—generally acknowledged to be a

---

* This essay was the germ of Fried's book *Courbet's Realism* (Chicago: The University of Chicago Press, 1990). I discuss Fried's interpretation of Courbet at greater length in my book *The Rape of the Masters: How Political Correctness Sabotages Art* (San Francisco: Encounter Books, 2004), pages 33–54.

self-portrait—leans back dreamily against a tree. Further to the right, the *piqueur*, the master of the hounds, sits in a brilliant slip of light blowing a hunting horn. In the right foreground two dogs, also brightly illuminated, frisk playfully. It is well to supply this simple description at the outset, for as Professor Fried proceeds with his interpretation one's grasp of the particulars of Courbet's painting is likely to become shaky.

Among much else, Professor Fried's interpretation indulges heavily in a second main principle of fashionable academic criticism: namely, the principle that holds that whatever a work (poem, painting, novel, essay, etc.) is ostensibly about, at bottom it is self-referential, being primarily a symbol of the activity of painting or writing. The overt subject of the work may mislead one into supposing that it is really about something else, something quite tangible in one's physical or emotional experience—a hunting scene, for example. But an adroit practitioner of the new academic criticism easily overcomes such "extrinsic" objections. One powerful aid in this task is the word "symbol" and its fashionable variants: "metaphor," "metonymy," "synecdoche," "trope," etc. Like the philosopher's stone, recondite use of these terms can transform the base material of reality into the gold of "intertextuality." Professor Fried provides us with many wonderful examples of the procedure. We do not have to read far into his essay before we are told that the *piqueur* is really

another of Courbet's characteristically displaced and metaphorical representations of the activity, the mental and physical *effort*, of painting. Thus the young man's strange, half-seated pose (with nothing beneath him but his folded jacket) may be taken as evoking the actual posture of the painter-beholder seated before the canvas. The hunting horn, held in his left hand, combines aspects of a paintbrush (I'm thinking of the horn's narrow, tubular neck) and a palette (it's rounded shape) though strictly resembling neither, and of course a horn being blown is also a traditional image of the fame Courbet forever aspired to win by his art.

It's not long, in fact, before Professor Fried can conclude that "all three principals—hunter, roe deer, and *piqueur*—are in different respects figurations of the painter-beholder [Courbet himself]." One only wonders what he has against the dogs: why aren't they, too, "figurations of the painter-beholder"? Isn't their playfulness there in the painting's foreground a symbol of the playful dialogue of the creative mind at work—doubled to represent the simultaneous interplay of the productive and critical faculties, tokens of the artist's awareness of his intractable animality—but you see how it works.

Operating on the principle that if something isn't shown, it is more present than if it is, Professor Fried has no trouble populating the canvas with all manner of objects and significances that Courbet somehow forgot to include. Is there no gun depicted in the painting? No problem: "In place of the missing musket there is the *piqueur*'s hunting horn, previously described as symbolizing the painter's tools (and therefore linking those tools with the absent weapons)." *Therefore*? "Therefore" approximately in the sense of "abracadabra," perhaps. But what about sex? We have seen that no such interpretation can be complete without a dash of the erotic, preferably outlandish; but where in this forest scene could one conjure sex? A tired hunter, self-absorbed *piqueur*, two dogs, and a dead deer may not seem much to work with. Not to worry: "I for one," Professor Fried confides, "am struck by the implied violence of the exposure to the hunter's viewpoint of the dead roe deer's underside, specifically including its genitals."

One has to admire Professor Fried's brass. And his well-developed sense of just how far he can intrude upon the reader's credulity without making concessions to common sense. "The last observation may seem excessive," he allows.

> For one thing, I am attaching considerable significance to a "side" of the roe deer we cannot see as well as to a bodily organ that isn't actually depicted. For another, the hunter isn't looking at the roe deer but faces in a different direction. But I would counter that we are led to imagine the roe deer's genitals or at any rate to be aware of their existence by the exposure to our view of the roe deer's anus, a metonymy for the rest. . . . I would further suggest that, precisely because the roe deer's anus stands for so much we cannot see—not simply the roe deer's genitals and wounded underside but an entire virtual face of the painting—such an effect of equivalence or translatability may be taken as indicating that the first, imaginary point of view is more important, and in the end more "real," than the second.

The imaginary point of view is more important and in the end more real than the point of view discerned with one's eyes: this sums up Professor Fried's method. But wait, there is more. In a long footnote to this passage, he tells us that

My suggestion that *The Quarry* calls attention to the roe deer's undepicted genitals and to their exposure to the hunter or at least to his point of view invites further discussion in terms of the Freudian problem of castration. Now what chiefly characterizes the painting's treatment of these motifs (if I may so describe them) is the absence of any signs of special or excessive affect and in particular of anxiety, which may seem to indicate that for the painter-beholder the implied threat to the roe deer's genitals was simply that, an objective menace, not the expression of a primal insecurity. On the other hand, the absence of affect ought perhaps to be seen as a further expression of the splitting of the painter-beholder into passive hunter and active *piqueur*: that is, it would be a further index of the hunter-painter's manifest passivity, which itself might be described as a sort of castration.

Consider: the roe deer's genitals are undepicted, therefore the painting "invites" discussion in terms of the Freudian notion of castration; the hunter isn't looking at the deer: no matter, the deer's genitals are exposed "at least to his point of view" (i.e., if he only turned his head, he would see them); despite this alleged threat of castration, the hunter displays no special signs of affect or emotion, quite the opposite, in fact—never mind: being passive may itself be described as "a sort of castration" (on which account I suppose that a painting of a man asleep or unconscious or dead would provide an even more dramatic index of preoccupation with castration). Poor Courbet!

Even to raise objections would risk complicity with Professor Fried's undertaking, granting it a measure of credibility it can never have. For the suggestion that *The Quarry* has anything to do with castration—indeed, that it has anything to do with sexual violence period—is ludicrous. If any of the theories of Sigmund Freud has a bearing on the matter, it is not his conjectures about castration anxiety or "displacement" but his method of free association: here at any rate we may have a clue to Professor Fried's own critical method.

Professor Fried's speculations about the hidden sexual current in Courbet's painting are perhaps the most outrageously absurd aspect of his interpretation of *The Quarry*. But in many ways even more absurd—because it touches directly on the core of Courbet's painting—is the end to which Professor Fried's complex hermeneutical apparatus tends. This is summed up in his title: "Courbet's Metaphysics"—probably the drollest piece of unintentional wit in the whole of *Reconstructing Individualism*. Drawing in part upon an obscure work by the obscure nineteenth-century French philosopher Felix Ravaisson, Professor Fried concludes that "the project of Courbet's Realism—of his metaphysics—was above all to represent" the "indemonstrable ideality" of nature. Well, Professor Fried is certainly right that the ideality of Courbet's artistic project is "indemonstrable"; but then untrue propositions do tend to exhibit that inconvenient property. Nevertheless, one cannot help but admire Professor Fried's sly apposition of "realism" and "metaphysics" here, as if these opposing terms really meant more or less the same thing.

Of course the truth is that in the repertoire of Courbet's beliefs, there is nothing that can even remotely be described as a "metaphysics." Indeed, few painters can have been more overtly *anti*-metaphysical than Gustave Courbet. In part, that is what the usual description of him as a "Realist" intends. Courbet himself put the matter with admirable clarity in 1861 in a letter to his students.

I also believe that painting is an essentially CONCRETE art and can only consist of the representation of REAL AND EXISTING objects. It is a completely physical language that has as words all visible objects, and an ABSTRACT object, invisible and non-existent, is not part of painting's domain. Imagination in art consists in knowing how to find the most complete expression of an existing object, but never in imagining or in creating the object itself.*

So much for Professor Fried's contention that the "imaginary point of view is more important, and in the end more 'real,' than the second."

V It's only a game

The Glass Bead Game is a mode of playing with the total contents and values of our culture; it plays with them as, say, in the great age of the arts a painter might have played with the colors on his palette. All the insights, noble thoughts, and works of art that the human race has produced in its creative eras, all that subsequent periods of scholarly study have reduced to concepts and converted into intellectual property—on all this immense body of intellectual values the Glass Bead Game player plays like the organist on an organ.
—Hermann Hesse, *The Glass Bead Game*

Like many of the essays in *Reconstructing Individualism*, Professor Fried's interpretation of Courbet's painting

---

* Letter of December 25, 1861, reprinted in *A Documentary History of Art*, Volume III, selected and edited by Elizabeth Gilmore Holt (New York: Doubleday, 1966), page 352. Courbet's emphasis.

brings considerable erudition and an even more considerable ingenuity to bear upon his subject. We read about Courbet's method of composing a painting by joining separate strips of canvas, are privy to considerations of the evidence of pentimento, and witness the rehearsal of a stunning array of scholarship. But to what end? As in Hesse's Glass Bead Game, the matter at hand is merely the occasion, the raw material for an elaborate interpretive exercise. What we see throughout these essays is an extraordinary amount of learning and analytical talent engaged in what is at bottom a narcissistic game. Whether the occasion be Nietzsche, or St. Augustine, or psychoanalysis, or a tangled account of hermaphroditism in seventeenth-century France, "individualism" is only the theme upon which the players execute their hermeneutical arabesques—not to illuminate the idea but to embellish the pages of their critical text. "The whole secret," as Kierkegaard once put it in an analysis of this sort of aestheticism, "lies in arbitrariness. . . . You consider the whole of existence from this standpoint; let its reality be stranded thereon."* And the fact that the notion of individualism is assumed to be bankrupt only makes the game more piquant. The task then becomes finding a way of "reconstructing" individualism without precisely reinstating or legitimating it; and in this task, at least, it must be said that most of the essays excel.

What Michael Fried has in common with Stephen

---

* Søren Kierkegaard, *Either/Or*, volume I, translated by David F. Swenson and Lillian Marvin Swenson, with revisions and a foreword by Howard A. Johnson (Princeton: Princeton University Press, 1971), page 295.

Greenblatt, Werner Hamacher, and most of the other contributors to this volume is the almost casual cynicism characteristic of an age that, to quote Kierkegaard again, *"leaves everything standing but cunningly empties it of significance."** In itself, the performance of the writers collected in *Reconstructing Individualism* is nothing out of the ordinary. The players are more skilled than many, but in essence it is simply business as usual in the academy these days. Particularly dispiriting is the thought that many of these men and women are among the brightest, most talented scholars in their respective fields. That they should have chosen to abandon anything like a traditional humanistic approach to their subjects and have given themselves up shamelessly to the latest intellectual fashions is an ominous sign of the malaise suffered by the humanities at even our most prestigious institutions. But of course what is most disturbing is the thought that the defiant hermeticism and gratuitous triviality represented by *Reconstructing Individualism* are not only being pursued as "research" by these "humanists," but are also being broadcast as genuine hu-manistic inquiry in the classroom and lecture hall. That constitutes a slander on tradition and a fraud against students.

In order to get a more tangible sense of what humanistic inquiry means in the environment of today's academy, let us return to the Whitney Humanities Center at Yale University to consider some of the presentations that were given at a day-long public symposium in the spring of 1986 on "The Humanities and the Public Interest." The

---

* Søren Kierkegaard, *The Present Age*, translated by Alexander Dru (New York: Harper & Row, 1962), page 42.

purpose of the event, in the words of a university press release, was "to re-examine the traditional association between the study of the humanities and the guardianship of humanistic values in the context of contemporary American society." Peter Brooks, who presided over this event as well, expanded on this in the press release: "The symposium will ask whether the case for the humanities can rest on traditional assumptions, or whether a new rationale is needed if the humanities are to claim a major place in contemporary modes of thought and analysis."

The symposium opened with some introductory remarks by Professor Brooks, who noted that the original impetus for the symposium was his favorite reading material, former Secretary of Education William J. Bennett's report on higher education in the humanities, *To Reclaim a Legacy*. As we have seen, this report defends precisely those "traditional assumptions" of the humanities that Professor Brooks hoped the Yale symposium would question. For himself, Professor Brooks declared his "profound disagreement" with the conclusions and general outlook of Secretary Bennett's report, taking issue especially with what he described as its "intellectual fundamentalism." Professor Brooks's opening remarks were very brief, but they established the tenor for the day's discussion; and since he identified Secretary Bennett's report as the catalyst for the symposium, we may begin by returning to take a closer look at the report's argument.

To Reclaim a Legacy begins by reaffirming the traditional role of the humanities as the chief instrument of our cultural self-definition. Its presiding spirit is Matthew Arnold, whose faith in the ennobling effects of high culture, of "the best that has been thought and said," is patent throughout the report. Elaborating on Arnold's famous phrase, Secretary Bennett describes the humanities as "the best that has been said, thought, written, and otherwise expressed about the human experience." The humanities are important, he writes, because

> they tell us how men and women of our own and other civilizations have grappled with life's enduring, fundamental questions: What is justice? What should be loved? What deserves to be defended? What is courage? What is noble? What is base? . . .
>
> These questions are not simply diversions for intellectuals or playthings for the idle. As a result of the ways in which these questions have been answered, civilizations have emerged, nations have developed, wars have been fought, and people have lived contentedly or miserably.

The real source of the controversy surrounding Secretary Bennett's report lies not so much in such general observations as in his prescriptions for "reclaiming" the legacy he finds threatened and, in the end, in his understanding of the substance and definition of that legacy. In the simplest terms he calls for a reshaping of undergraduate study "based on a clear vision of what constitutes an educated person." In his view, the goal of the humanities should be a "common culture" rooted in the highest ideals and aspirations of the Western tradition.

Nevertheless, it is important to note that, despite accusations to the contrary, Secretary Bennett does not advocate restoration of a previous state of affairs. He insists that the solution to the current crisis in the humanities "is not a return to an earlier time when the classical curriculum was the only curriculum and college was available to only a privileged few." Given the charges of elitism and reaction that his proposals have brought forth, especially from the most elite of our universities, it seems well to emphasize the point. "American higher education today serves far more people . . . than it did a century ago," Secretary Bennett writes.

> Its increased accessibility to women, racial and ethnic minorities, recent immigrants, and students of limited means is a positive accomplishment of which our nation is justly proud . . . . But our eagerness to assert the virtues of pluralism should not allow us to sacrifice the principle that formerly lent substance and continuity to the curriculum, namely, that each college and university should recognize and accept its vital role as a conveyor of the accumulated wisdom of our civilization.

It is of course this final affirmation that has angered Secretary Bennett's opponents. For one thing, who decides what counts as "the accumulated wisdom of our civilization"? In Arnold's terms, why should the humanities be concerned primarily with the *best* that has been thought and said? Does that not exclude a large portion of human experience? And does not that mass of experience deserve "equal time" in our institutions of higher education? Here again, who is to say what counts as "best"? Perhaps the Arnoldian injunction has been interpreted too narrowly, too "ideologically," too exclusively? Furthermore, why should the humanities focus so intently upon the past? Why should they not concern themselves as much with the *creation* as with the *preservation* and *transmission* of culture? Such questions are at the heart of Professor Brooks's "profound disagreement" and charge of "intellectual fundamentalism"—a charge that has been loudly echoed in the academy and that was to be advanced with great zeal that Saturday at Yale's Whitney Humanities Center.

It was not, however, until the second, and most publicized, session, "The Social Mission of the Humanities," that the subject of the humanities and the public interest really came into focus. This session featured a "dialogue" between the late A. Bartlett Giamatti, who had not yet given up the presidency of Yale University to become commissioner of baseball, and Norman Podhoretz, the conservative critic and sometime editor of *Commentary* magazine. Responding to President Giamatti and Mr. Podhoretz were Henry Rosovsky, former dean and professor of social science at Harvard, and Cornel West, a ferociously articulate black radical who was then a professor at the Yale Divinity School and is now (after a stint at Harvard) at Princeton. It was in this session that the real issues facing the humanities in contemporary American society were most clearly set forth.

Mr. Podhoretz spoke first. The humanities, he said, cannot be justified on practical grounds. Because the knowledge and culture they represent are "good in themselves," their ultimate justification is simply their intrinsic value. From this it follows that the humanities cannot directly help us in the formulation of public policy; nor do they yield any particular political position; nor indeed does acquaintance with the humanities necessarily make us morally more upright or more humane—think only of the cultivated Nazi commandants who also savored Mozart. Echoing the sentiments expressed in Secretary Bennett's report, Mr. Podhoretz identified the chief function of the humanities to be the creation of a "common culture."

Central to this view of the humanities is the idea of a more or less generally recognized canon of works that define that common culture and preserve its traditions. Mr. Podhoretz admitted that there will always be disagreement about the composition of the canon at, as it were, its edges; but he claimed that, at least until recently, there has been a widely shared consensus about the core body of works that constitute "the best that has been thought and said."

In one sense, this view of the humanities can be said to be exclusive or "elitist," since it presupposes a rigorously defined notion of what it means to be an educated person. But in another sense, it is deeply democratic for it locates authority not in any class or race or sex, but in a tradition before which all are equal. As Mr. Podhoretz observed, to the extent that the humanities are crucial to the maintenance of civilized life, it is essential that as many people as possible have the opportunity to steep themselves in the great works of the canon: only thus is high culture preserved and transmitted. Furthermore, as the transmitter of the canon, of what Mr. Podhoretz described as our "intellectual patrimony," the humanities have traditionally instilled a sense of the value of the democratic tradition we have inherited. And it is in this respect, he noted, that the humanities *do* have a political dimension, insofar as they rest upon a belief in the value and importance of Western culture and the civilization that gave birth to it.

With the social and political upheaval of the Sixties and early Seventies, Mr. Podhoretz continued, this entire conception of the humanities came under radical assault. Not only the idea of a common culture founded upon a recognized canon of great works, but the very notion of a politically autonomous realm of culture was dismissed as naïve, ethnocentric, or somehow repressive. Even the fundamental belief in the value of Western culture and civilization—the value, that is to say, of the whole humanistic enterprise—was undermined. And while it is true that the more extreme manifestations of this revolt have disappeared, Mr. Podhoretz maintained that the radical attitudes espoused in the Sixties and Seventies live on in attenuated form in the academy—even, or rather especially, in the humanistic disciplines, in the values and assumptions that typically inform the teaching and study of the humanities. For the most part, he said, a study of the humanities now tends at best to encourage a feeling of "mild contempt" for culture as traditionally defined and at worst to inspire outright hatred of our civilization and everything it stands for. And because of this sedimented radicalism in the academy, the humanities, however much they may still add to an individual's enlightenment and culture, no longer really contribute to the common good.

Mr. Podhoretz's diagnosis was met with great hostility. I overheard the idea of a "common culture," for example, variously described as "moribund," "imperialistic," and "fascist." It was also considered to be "sexist," I gathered, judging from the knowing looks that his use of the phrase "intellectual patrimony" occasioned. President Giamatti began by telling us that he found Mr. Podhoretz's talk "internally contradictory," for is there not a contradiction between asserting the essentially private nature of the humanities and then lamenting that they no longer conduce to the commonweal? In fact, though, President Giamatti's charge depended upon distorting Mr. Podhoretz's description of the humanities. It is one thing to say that the humanities cannot be justified on instrumental grounds, as Mr. Podhoretz did, quite another to say that

they are a private affair entirely without social consequence, which no one but President Giamatti thought to
propose.

The president of Yale University, who at one time was
known as a scholar of Renaissance literature, also came
out strongly against the idea of a canon. Instead, he
thought that the humanities should encourage "modes of
thinking that would discipline the imagination without
pretending to direct it"—the idea being, I suppose, that it
doesn't much matter what one learns so long as one
learns something. President Giamatti even claimed that
this was the "Greek view" of education. Perhaps he
meant the view current in contemporary Greece; certainly,
the idea that education should seek "to discipline the imagination without pretending to direct it" is completely
foreign to the classical ideal of *paideia*, of formative
education, as well as to the teachings of Plato and Aristotle. One thinks, for example, of the quite definite ideas
that Plato expressed about what should and should not
be taught in his discussion of education in the third book
of *The Republic*. But leaving the Greek view of education
to one side, President Giamatti's reservations about the
importance of the canon do help us understand his
central charge against Mr. Podhoretz: that his view of the
humanities is "solipsistic" and "spiritually selfish." Basically, President Giamatti presented Mr. Podhoretz as an
elitist who wanted to keep culture for himself. But the
real difference between them was that Mr. Podhoretz
wanted the *substance* of the humanities to be as widely
available as possible, whereas President Giamatti was
happy with what we might call universal schooling—the
substance, the content, of what was taught was for him
incidental.

If nothing else, President Giamatti exemplified the strategy that Henry Rosovsky, the session's first respondent, identified as the prime imperative for academic administrators—"Be vague." Professor Rosovsky went on to suggest that the hallmark of the humanities was "an eternal dissatisfaction," that the humanities ought in fact to "engender a kind of dissatisfaction," and hence that they "should not be conservative." Against Mr. Podhoretz's vision of a "common culture," Professor Rosovsky sided with President Giamatti in questioning the desirability of adhering to a canon and in extolling as an alternative to this the ideal of a "multi-culture" nourished by disparate sources and traditions. It is worth noting that the phrase "multi-culture" and its variants have become code words for an approach to the humanities that is in effect *anti*-cultural—at least anti-high-cultural. Part of the rhetoric of "pluralism" and "diversity," the elevation of "multicultural" experience cloaks the abandonment of traditional humanistic culture. It belongs with prattle about the humanities instilling "dissatisfaction" and the desirability of undermining the traditional canon. Such sentiments are heard everywhere in the academy today, but it did seem odd coming from the lips of a man who in the early Seventies, when he was a dean at Harvard, had been a staunch supporter of the canon and one of the chief architects of Harvard's now dismantled core curriculum. In 1974, faced with the prospect of curricular anarchy, Professor Rosovsky publicly deplored the loss of "an older community of beliefs and values";* now he looks to the

---

* Quoted in Gilbert Allardyce, "The Rise and Fall of the Western Civilization Course," *American Historical Review*, June 1982, pages 696–697.

loss of those beliefs and values as a prelude to the establishment of a multicultural paradise. *Autres temps, autres moeurs.*

VI Gender, race, and class

But the most articulate, as well as the most histrionic, response to Mr. Podhoretz came from Cornel West. Professor West's performance combined something of Houston Baker's appeal to race with aspects of Margaret Ferguson's generalized discontent with Western liberal society to produce a potent rhetorical effect. Approximating the fervor of a political rally or revival meeting, he clearly won the hearts and minds of the Yale audience. They thrilled to his rhetoric, punctuating his impassioned speech with enthusiastic applause. Professor West warmed up with a few words about "decolonization," "the eclipse of European dominance" in the world, and the disintegration of "white, male, WASP hegemony" in the academy. (I had thought that WASPs were white by definition, but no matter: "white, male, WASP hegemony" has an edifying ring to it.) He pictured the evolution of the humanities in recent years as a reflection of a worldwide struggle for freedom against what it has pleased him to describe elsewhere as "the final fruits of bourgeois humanism: North Atlantic ethnocentrism."*

In Professor West's view, the "collapsing consensus"

* See his "Afterword: The Politics of American Neo-Pragmatism," in *Post-Analytic Philosophy*, edited by Cornel West and John Rajchman (New York: Columbia University Press, 1985), pages 259–275.

that Mr. Podhoretz spoke of tokened not decline but liberation. The Sixties, far from being a debacle, were a "watershed" for the humanities. For one thing, the "onslaught" of popular culture that began then has helped undermine elitist notions of high culture. Then, too, the attention lavished on the history and literature of blacks, women, peasants, and other groups has revealed the traditional canon to be the biased, ethnocentric construction that it is. Hence the "self-contempt" that Mr. Podhoretz said a study of the humanities tended to instill these days is really "a deeper self-critique" that mirrors important changes in the world ("the eclipse of European dominance," etc.), changes that must be recognized and accommodated "if we are not to blow up the planet."

I hasten to add, though, that in criticizing Mr. Podhoretz, Professor West by no means sought to align himself with President Giamatti. On the contrary, he criticized both men for their "lack of historical sense" and their "conservatism." (One notes that in the academy the word "conservative" has degenerated into a term of abuse.) Distinguishing between the "battle-ridden neoconservatism" of Mr. Podhoretz and the "more charming" conservatism of President Giamatti, Professor West wondered whether the "dynamism" championed by President Giamatti didn't at bottom merely represent "the recovery of high-brow classical humanism." He can rest easy on that score.

The real clue to Professor West's view came with his celebration of the incorporation of the New Left into the university. Among other things, he championed the New Left for creating "combat zones" that could challenge the entire ethos of bourgeois humanism that stands behind the humanities as traditionally conceived. And taking issue with Mr. Podhoretz's criticism of the intellectual, moral, and political effects of the New Left, Professor West described writers like Herbert Marcuse and the post-World War II French Marxists as "the best of Western civilization."

It is important to consider Professor West's identification of Herbert Marcuse and the "French Marxists" as representatives of "the best of Western civilization." Just what do these writers and thinkers stand for? What have they contributed to furthering the fundamental principles of the humanities? Consider Louis Althusser, one of the most influential of the French Marxists whom Professor West admires. In an interview that he gave in 1968, this example of the "best of Western civilization" explained that he had come to philosophy through his attempt to "become a Communist militant" during and after World War II. Having finally understood that "philosophy is fundamentally *political*"—more specifically, that it is a tool of "class struggle"—Althusser also realized that "it was not easy to resist the spread of contemporary 'humanist' ideology, and bourgeois ideology's other assaults of Marxism." Being an intellectual, a philosopher, made things especially difficult, he confided: "Proletarians have a 'class instinct' which helps them on the way to proletarian 'class positions.' Intellectuals, on the contrary, have a petty-bourgeois class instinct which fiercely resists this transition."* Most would agree, however, that Althusser succeeded rather well in overcoming the specified

---

* Louis Althusser, "Philosophy as a Revolutionary Weapon," reprinted in *Lenin and Philosophy and Other Essays*, translated by Ben Brewster (New York: Monthly Review Press, 1971), pages 11–22.

resistance, even if he finally fell prey to "contemporary humanist ideology" when he confessed to murdering his wife in a fit of insanity in 1980.

Then there is Marcuse. One could turn to any number of his works for an introduction to his view of the value of the humanities—to the "Political Preface" that he added to the 1966 edition of *Eros and Civilization*, for example, where he calls for a thoroughgoing revolt against "the political machine, the corporate machine, the cultural and educational machine" of "affluent western society."* What he calls for, in short, is a revolt against just those political, social, and intellectual traditions that define the humanistic endeavor. The best précis of Marcuse's thinking about such matters is to be found in his notorious 1965 essay "Repressive Tolerance."† Unable to deny that modern Western democracies offer their citizens an unparalleled degree of personal and political liberty, Marcuse is nevertheless able to denounce the West as essentially "totalitarian" by the simple device of declaring its brand of liberty "repressive" and a product of "false consciousness." (What a versatile tool of obfuscation the notion of "false consciousness" has been, utterly exempt as it is from subservience to mere "empirical reality"!) Indeed, he offers a simple formula for distinguishing between the "repressive tolerance" that expresses itself in the real world in such phenomena as freedom of assembly and the "liberating tolerance" that would seem to occur

* Herbert Marcuse, *Eros and Civilization: A Philosophical Inquiry into Freud* (Boston: Beacon Press, 1966), page xvii.

† Reprinted in *A Critique of Pure Tolerance*, by Robert Paul Wolff, *et al.* (Boston: Beacon Press, 1969), pages 81–123.

chiefly in his imagination: "Liberating tolerance," he writes, "would mean intolerance against movements from the Right, and toleration of movements from the Left."

In brief, then, what Marcuse wants is "not 'equal' but *more* representation of the Left," and he blithely sanctions "extralegal means if the legal ones have proved to be inadequate." In one of the more extraordinary passages of the essay, Marcuse admits that the "extreme suspension of the right of free speech and free assembly is indeed justified only if the whole of society is in extreme danger," but continues immediately to note that

> I maintain that our society is in such an emergency situation . . . . Different opinions and "philosophies" can no longer compete peacefully for adherence and persuasion on rational grounds: the "marketplace of ideas" is organized and delimited by those who determine the national and the individual interest. In this society, for which the ideologists have proclaimed the "end of ideology," the false consciousness has become the general consciousness—from the government down to its last objects.

There is no escape, apparently—unless, that is, one happens to be blessed, as Marcuse apparently believed himself to be, with the privileged insight, what we might call the "true consciousness," that allows one to penetrate such nearly universal mendacity.

It is in the context of such ideas that we must understand the conception of freedom that underlies Professor West's view of the humanities. Like his heroes, Professor West finds the "ideology of pluralism" suspect because it "domesticates" radical thought. And like them, too, he questions the traditional "bourgeois" notion of the citizen as a "bearer of rights." Instead, he lobbies for an idea of citizenship that would incorporate "collective action," that would "undermine the liberal protection of rights" in favor of a more encompassing ideal—an ideal that aspires to nothing less than coercive control of all thought and expression.

We can begin to appreciate some of the practical effects of Professor West's position by considering the controversy over the issue of free speech that is erupting on many campuses today. There have lately been moves by college and university administrations across the country to circumscribe or prohibit speech and behavior that is considered racially or sexually "insensitive." In an important article on the subject, Chester Finn, former assistant secretary of education, adduces numerous examples: a six-page "anti-bias code" replete with stiff penalties for violators recently issued by the University of Wisconsin, or the University of Michigan's prohibition of speech that "stigmatizes or victimizes an individual on the basis of race, ethnicity, religion, sex, sexual orientation, creed, national origin, ancestry, age, marital status, handicap, or"—my favorite item—"Vietnam-era veteran status."* Nor is such legislation limited to state schools. Emory University in Atlanta, the University of Pennsylvania, and Stanford, for example, have all instituted bans on what has come to be called "ethnoviolence." These restrictions on the kinds of things that can be said and talked about apply inside as well as outside the classroom and they have had—in the words of a brief by the Michigan Amer-

* Chester E. Finn, Jr., "The Campus: 'An Island of Repression in a Sea of Freedom,'" *Commentary*, September 1989, pages 17–23.

ican Civil Liberties Union—a "chilling effect on the free expression of ideas" in the university.*

One event that seemed particularly indicative of these pernicious trends against free speech in the academy was a weeklong program of panels and "workshops" that took place at Harvard University under the rubric "AWARE," an acronym that stands for "Actively Working Against Racism and Ethnocentrism." Robert Detlefsen, who reported on the AWARE symposium for *The New Republic*, recounted many extreme positions adopted by participants. A former dean at Dartmouth College, for example, suggested that Dartmouth and Harvard were "genocidal in nature" because of their attitudes toward racial issues. But somehow among the most disturbing things in Detlefsen's article is the account of a talk by a Harvard professor of ichthyology who told the AWARE audience that one should never "introduce any sort of thing that might hurt a group" because "the pain that racial insensitivity can create is more important than a professor's academic freedom."†

We may well want to deplore speech and action that hurts the feelings of others. But what does it mean that the university, traditionally an institution dedicated to the free exchange of ideas, has so blatantly encroached upon that freedom in the name of a certain vision of political rectitude? What does it mean, for example, that Dean Hilda Hernandez-Gravelle, whose Office of Race Relations and Minority Affairs at Harvard originated the AWARE program, called for a ban on "50s" nostalgia

* Quoted in "It's Speech, Not Sex, the Dean Bans Now."

† Robert R. Detlefsen, "White Like Me," *The New Republic*, 10 April 1989, pages 18–21.

parties because racism was rampant in America in the
1950s? Or that Barbara Johnson, a professor of French at
Harvard, should declare at the AWARE symposium that
"professors should have less freedom of expression than
writers and artists, because professors are supposed to be
creating a better world"?

What makes such statements so obnoxious is not
simply the extraordinary aura of superior self-righteous-
ness they exude, as if professors and academic deans have
some special purchase on "creating a better world."
There is also the fundamental constitutional issue that
these anti-harassment policies violate the right to free
speech guaranteed by the First Amendment. As one of the
leaders of the Stanford student government admitted,
"What we are proposing is not completely in line with the
First Amendment. But I'm not sure it should be. We at
Stanford are trying to set a different standard from what
society at large is trying to accomplish."* It is a sobering
irony that what began as an appeal by the Left for "free
speech" at Berkeley in 1964 has ended by an equally fervent appeal by the Left for the imposition of censorship.
A further irony, as Chester Finn has noted, is that at a
time when colleges and universities have given up attempting to act *in loco parentis*, a time when they are
busy installing condom dispensers in dormitories and dis-
tributing "safe sex" kits to freshmen, they should suddenly act to curtail so radically this one aspect of personal
behavior.

The politically motivated origins of this campaign
against unpopular ideas are not hard to discern. Now,

---

* "Drives by Campuses to Curb Race Slurs Pose a Speech Issue," *The
New York Times*, April 25, 1989.

when the student population at many colleges and universities is becoming increasingly conservative, the rise of political correctness is nothing less than an effort by left-leaning faculties and administrations to impose the politics and mind-set of the Sixties by fiat. As Alan Charles Kors has noted,

"harassment policies" at a growing number of universities have used the real need to protect students and employees from sexual and racial abuse as a partisan pretext for . . . "privileging" one particular ideological agenda, and for controlling speech deemed offensive by those designated as victims of American society (including those "victims" about to receive Ivy League degrees!).

Moreover, it is important to note how corrosive unfounded charges of "racism," "sexism," and the like can be. The philosopher Sidney Hook got to the heart of the issue when he observed that

as morally offensive as is the expression of racism wherever it is found, a false charge of racism is equally offensive, perhaps even more so, because the consequences of a false charge of racism enable an authentic racist to conceal his racism by exploiting the loose way the term is used to cover up his actions. The same is true of a false charge of sexism or anti-Semitism. This is the lesson we should all have learned from the days of Senator Joseph McCarthy. Because of his false and irresponsible charges of communism against liberals, socialists, and others among his critics, many communists and agents of communist influence sought to pass themselves off as Jeffersonian democrats or merely idealistic reformers. They would all complain they were victims of red-baiting to prevent criticism and exposure.[*]

It is worth pondering Sidney Hook's remarks as one attempts to digest the professoriate's smug and unending charges of racism, sexism, elitism, and the rest. What Professor Kors wrote about the University of Pennsylvania's attitude can be applied equally to other institutions intent on mandating virtue for their students and faculty: "In short, Penn is a tolerant and diverse community, and if you do not agree with its particular notions of tolerance and diversity, it will gladly re-educate you."

VII   A new rationale for the humanities?

Since the second session of Yale's symposium on the humanities and the public interest had sought to dispose of the traditional rationale for the humanities, it seemed only appropriate that the final session should address itself to the question of formulating a new rationale for its discredited predecessor. The session was moderated by Professor Brooks, and featured presentations by Jonathan Culler, one of the authors of *Speaking for the Humanities* and a professor of English and comparative literature at Cornell University, and Vincent Scully, a popular professor of art history at Yale. Among the respondents to Professors Culler and Scully was the late Carolyn G. Heilbrun, once an influential academic feminist and professor of English at Columbia University.

Anticipating a central argument of *Speaking for the*

---

[*] "Stanford Documents," page 655.

Humanities, Professor Culler began by criticizing the traditional rationale for the humanities as "universalist" and "foundationalist." As we have seen, this is practically *de rigueur* for right-thinking academics. The pretension to be "universalist," he said, was primarily a political consideration: the humanities as traditionally conceived had presumed to speak universally to the human condition, but had in fact represented a narrow "white male" viewpoint. The attempt to be "foundationalist" involves epistemological considerations: the humanities had pretended to provide a foundation for both thought and values, but radical criticism in the last decades had exposed the fictional, and ideologically motivated, ground of that pretense. Professor Culler did not, however, attempt to formulate the new rationale for the humanities that he demanded, but instead offered a list of "divided imperatives" that he thought the humanities ought to heed. It seems that he may be better at deconstruction than construction, however, for the list he offered was vague, even banal—the humanities ought to "assume unity" but also assert the value of other cultures, and so on—though it was full of appropriately combative rhetoric and wonderful-sounding, Nietzschean proclamations like his suggestion that thought really becomes valuable "only when it is extreme." Professor Culler never really specified his own idea of a good college curriculum. But one can bet that it wouldn't be "ethnocentric"—indeed, it's not even clear that it would be anthropocentric, since Professor Culler wondered in passing whether a view of the humanities based exclusively on a study of mankind wouldn't be guilty of "speciesism."

Mercifully, Professor Culler did not pursue this absurdity, though it was taken up by Vincent Scully, who began his talk by suggesting that what we needed was not so much a new rationale for the humanities as a new rationale for "animality." Professor Scully then treated us to a slide show that opened, as such slide shows must, with a picture of the snow shovel Marcel Duchamp presented as a work of art in 1915. What won't be taken as a work of art today! Professor Scully reflected, and then went on to share with his audience a number of other truly novel ideas: that the movies and television have emerged as the dominant style of modern life, for example, or that the artist must be "open-minded, pluralistic, poised for surprise."

Carolyn Heilbrun began her response on a melancholy note, observing that even now, even at a symposium on the humanities at Yale in 1986, she was the only woman on the panel. I, too, was surprised that Professor Brooks could have made this elementary blunder. He must have known that such a discrepancy in numbers would be criticized. He must also have known that the important thing in such situations is not to get the best speakers for the occasion but to assemble a panel with the correct ethnic, social, and sexual mix. Professor Heilbrun went on to note that, though she was also the oldest person on the panel, it was the symposium's youngest representatives, Professors Culler and West, who spoke for her. She, too, believed that college should "teach us to be dissatisfied" and that thought is really valuable only when it is extreme. As the panel's official feminist, she also told us that it is the questions that women can ask about the canon that are the important ones. While she did not specify what these important questions were, one got a pretty good idea of the kind of thing she had in mind when she criticized Professor Scully for presenting Michelangelo's depiction of the creation of man as representative of the human condition. After all, both God and Adam were—well, there's no getting around it: they were male, and how universal can that be?

This session, and the symposium, ended with a few comments and questions. Particularly important were Professor Heilbrun's assertion that our reading of texts is inescapably "ideological," and Professor Brooks's concluding observation that, because the humanities are "inherently subversive," the recent developments in the academy that people like Secretary Bennett and Mr. Podhoretz bemoan ought actually be taken as signs of health. Together, these comments seemed to epitomize the proceedings in New Haven that day, and are worth examining more closely.

The idea that all reading is "ideological" has gained great currency in recent years. Among other things, it implies that weA are imprisoned by our point of view, that our language, our social or ethnic background, or our sex inescapably determine the way we understand things. But are we so imprisoned? Granted that such contingencies *influence* our point of view, do they finally determine it? We shall return to this question in Chapter Six. For the moment, let us merely ask what it might mean to say that "all reading is ideological." It is important to realize that "ideologies" are not simply a set of guiding opinions; rather, as the social philosopher Hannah Arendt pointed out some years ago, they are "isms which to the satisfaction of their adherents can explain everything and every occurrence by deducing it from a single premise." In this sense, Arendt notes, an ideology differs from a simple opinion "in that it claims to possess either the key to history, or the solution for all 'riddles of the universe,' or the intimate knowledge of the hidden universal laws which are supposed to rule nature and man."* Yet it is precisely this sort of distinction that the contention that all reading is ideological dismisses. It dismisses, in other words, the critical distinction *between* a point of view and an ideology, between an individual perspective on the world—which *as* a perspective is open to challenge, accommodation, correction—and an *idée fixe*.

And in this context, since Matthew Arnold has been so consistently castigated by champions of "new rationales" for the humanities, it is worth noting that, in his once celebrated essay on "The Function of Criticism at the Present Time" (1865), Arnold identifies "disinterestedness" as the chief mark of responsible criticism. In describing criticism as "disinterested," Arnold did not mean that it presumes to speak without reference to a particular point of view—though critics of the idea often so caricature it. Rather, he meant a habit of inquiry that keeps "aloof from what is called 'the practical view of things' . . . by steadily refusing to lend itself to any . . . ulterior, political, practical considerations about ideas."† In contemporary terms, we might say that Arnold looked to criticism to provide a bulwark *against* ideology, against interpretations that are subordinated to essentially political interests. The ideal of such disinterested criticism is rejected by many contemporary critics as naïve (or worse), though the criticism that they practice is no more astute than Arnold's but only, alas, more ideological.

* Hannah Arendt, *The Origins of Totalitarianism* (New York: Harcourt Brace Jovanovich, 1973), *seriatim*, pages 468, 159.
† In *The Portable Matthew Arnold*, edited with an introduction by Lionel Trilling (New York: The Viking Press, 1972), page 248.

Arnold is also relevant in considering the oft-voiced contention that education ought to instill "dissatisfaction" or, to use Professor Brooks's more dramatic formulation, that the humanities are "inherently subversive." Such sentiments are so widely shared in fashionable academic circles today that it is almost taken for granted that the function of education is not to impart knowledge but to subvert, to excite "dissatisfaction." Thus it is that *Speaking for the Humanities* assures us that "the humanities are better conceived as fields of exploration and critique rather than materials for transmission." Behind this idea is a deep suspicion of authority, a suspicion that would have us collapse another critical distinction: the distinction between authority and authoritarianism. Yet it is a good question whether the humanities can survive in any recognizable form without accepting the authority of tradition. It is indeed for this reason that, in "The Literary Influence of Academies," Arnold praised the willing "deference to a standard higher than one's own habitual standard in intellectual matters" as the result of a "sensitiveness of intelligence."* And thus it is, too, that Hannah Arendt suggested that "conservatism, in the sense of conservation, is of the essence of the educational activity, whose task is always to cherish and protect something." "The real difficulty in modern education," Arendt wrote,

> lies in the fact that, despite all the fashionable talk about a new conservatism [Arendt was writing in 1958], even that minimum of conservation and the conserving attitude without which education is simply not possible is in our

* *Ibid.*, page 273.

119

time extraordinarily hard to achieve. . . . The crisis of authority in education is most closely connected with the crisis of tradition, that is with the crisis in our attitude toward the realm of the past . . . . The problem of education in the modern world lies in the fact that by its very nature it cannot forego either authority or tradition, and yet it must proceed in a world that is neither structured by authority nor held together by tradition.[*]

"Neither structured by authority nor held together by tradition"—in the end, this would seem to describe the goal of the "new rationale" for the humanities envisioned at Yale and elsewhere. And of course the real casualties are the students and junior faculty, who often haven't the foggiest notion of the value of the tradition they have been taught to disparage. The senior faculty at least are generally old enough to recognize what it is they are abandoning. Champions of the "new rationale" like to pretend that they are merely thinking more critically than the tradition had allowed. In fact, though, they have often degenerated from the rigors of criticism to a rootless and sharply politicized nihilism. The influence and prestige of the academy have made proponents of these new rationales important cultural forces in and out of the academy; a closer look at a representative sample of their language and guiding ideas will give us fuller appreciation of what is at stake when tradition and authority are rechristened as the enemies rather than the preservers of culture.

[*] Hannah Arendt, "The Crisis in Education," reprinted in *Between Past and Future: Eight Exercises in Political Thought* (New York: Penguin, 1978), *seriatim*, pages 192–193, 195.

CHAPTER THREE

The *October* Syndrome

I Through a glass eye, darkly

F EW THINGS have contributed more to the debasement of contemporary intellectual and cultural life than the honored place now accorded to deliberate obscurity. Deconstruction and semiology, structuralism and post-structuralism: these and kindred obfuscatory theories imported from the Continent continue to be favored staples in much of what passes for intellectual discourse today. Not that this is surprising. "Obscurity," as the historian Keith Windschuttle has noted, is "a clever way to generate a following"—not least because many people mistakenly assume that obscure writing indicates deep thinking.* Combined with the unexamined assumption that the realm of high culture—indeed, that the very *idea* of high culture—is irredeemably tainted by political interests, this triumph of opacity has largely succeeded in transforming

---

* *The Killing of History,* page 6.

serious discussion of art, literature, and culture into a congeries of hermetic language games.

In our academic journals, university classrooms, and even in our museums' exhibition catalogues, arcane, pseudo-philosophical jargon and radical sentiment compete to forestall genuine engagement with aesthetic or intellectual issues. Alas, only the radical sentiment receives clear and frank expression. As we have seen, even as clarity and intelligibility are spurned as simple-minded, the traditional ideal of disinterested scholarship is bluntly dismissed as a cover for class or ethnic privilege and Western culture itself is pilloried as a bastion of unacknowledged sexist and imperialistic attitudes. Given this intellectual climate, it is hardly surprising that criticism should degenerate into a species of cynicism for which nothing is properly understood until it is exposed as corrupt, duplicitous, or hypocritical. Nor is it surprising that the ideal of art or literature as a relatively autonomous endeavor—an endeavor, that is to say, which is free from direct political imperatives—should be ridiculed as a fantasy perpetrated by the entrenched and parochial interests of bourgeois taste. Today, while criticism—or what generally goes under the more impressive-sounding name of "critical theory"—pursues its polysyllabic hunt for suppressed political motives, many artists and writers have likewise adapted themselves to the prevailing ethos and have more and more come to see themselves primarily as purveyors of politically correct attitudes and politically approved notions of social enlightenment.

There can be little doubt that the primary source of these evils is the academy. For it is precisely the predominance of aggressively opaque rhetoric and political posturing in the humanities departments of our colleges and universities that has validated and, as it were, underwritten the proliferation of such practices. In seeking to understand the origin of this cultural debacle, however, one must not underestimate the role played by those multitudinous and influential props of university life: academic journals devoted, at least ostensibly, to the arts and the humanities. *Diacritics, Critical Inquiry, Tel Quel, New Literary History, Representations, Social Text, Yale French Studies*: these are a few of the more influential academic organs peddling politicized obscurantism. It is in the pages of such journals that the latest personalities, chic theories, and critical vocabularies are auditioned and, if found acceptable, are trotted out over and over again until they become verbal tics, part of the atmosphere of academic exchange and requisite equipment for any graduate student or assistant professor with his eye on the grail of tenure. Lacan, Jameson, Benjamin, Barthes, Derrida, de Man, Bataille, Althusser, Foucault—these and a few other names from the current pantheon are scattered like confetti through their pages; "logocentric," "phallocentric," "imperialist," "aura," "strategy," "marginalization," "text," "signifier"—these are some of the more attractive terms that one finds repeated *ad nauseam.*

This is not to suggest that these journals—and their number, be assured, is legion—are all of a piece. Each has its own identifying wrinkle, its distinctive editorial "personality." Yet while none is in any sense popular or widely read, some few have emerged as peculiarly influential and representative of the spirit of politicized obscurantism under which our cultural life labors. Of these representative few, none is more political, more opaque, or more influential in certain "advanced" circles than the quarterly *October*. So consummately does *October* epitomize these qualities, and so successful has it been in combining fashionable academic jargon with radical political ideology, that one is tempted to single it out as a specimen case. The publication of *October: The First Decade, 1976–1986** provides a good opportunity to consider the magazine in some detail, to catalogue its salient features, and to discuss some of its recurrent themes. The more closely one examines its contribution to current intellectual and artistic debate, the more one is tempted to regard *October* not simply as a magazine but as a *syndrome*, a set of symptoms typifying a somewhat amorphous but nonetheless unmistakably prevalent malaise affecting intellectual life in and out of the academy.

II The *October* syndrome

Started in the spring of 1976, *October* soon established itself as a cynosure of approved opinions in the confusing firmament of advanced literary and artistic taste. In many respects, the *October* syndrome was already in full flower in the inaugural issue. Here readers were treated to a tortuous lead essay by the much revered Michel Foucault on Magritte's famous drawing *"Ceci n'est pas une pipe."* (Surrealism and semiotics: what a perfect combination with which to begin *October*!) Among other delicacies

---

* *October: The First Decade, 1976–1986*, edited by Annette Michelson, Rosalind Krauss, Douglas Crimp, and Joan Copjec (Cambridge: MIT Press, 1987). Unless otherwise noted, quotations in this chapter are from this volume.

included in that first issue was an essay by Rosalind Krauss on the video "art" of Vito Acconci, Lynda Benglis, and others. A sample sentence: "One could say that if the reflexiveness of modernist art is a *dédoublement* or doubling back in order to locate the object (and thus the objective conditions of one's experience), the mirror-reflection of absolute feedback is a process of bracketing out the object." Really? There were also some notes on filmmaking by Hollis Frampton ("The mode we call reading entails a correct extrapolation of the axiomatic substructure from the artist's immediately apprehensible tradition," etc.) and the first part of a three-part essay by Jeremy Gilbert-Rolfe and John Johnston that pretended to discover thematic similarities between Thomas Pynchon's novel *Gravity's Rainbow* and Robert Smithson's massive "earth work," *Spiral Jetty.* "In *Gravity's Rainbow,*" we read in that essay, "digression becomes the whole through an approach to writing which, again as in Cézanne, unifies all data by insisting on a model which substitutes redistribution for climax."*

October's influence and distinctive character owe much to two of its founding editors, Rosalind Krauss—the well-known art critic and professor of art history at Columbia University—and Annette Michelson—the veteran critic and professor of "cinema studies" at New York University. (The other founding editor, the critic and painter Jeremy Gilbert-Rolfe, left the magazine after three issues.) Professor Krauss, especially, has been a moving force in the world of academic art criticism. The recipient of many academic honors, her extraordinarily hermetic writings as well as her teaching and editorial proclivities

---

* *October,* Spring 1976, *seriatim,* pages 57, 106, 58.

have exerted a great influence on contemporary academic art criticism, helping to shape the substance and style of the work of many students and younger art critics.*

In the introductory note to their first issue, the editors reveal that the journal was named partly in "celebration" of the heyday of the Russian avant garde that was inaugurated by the Bolshevik Revolution of October, 1917, partly in commemoration of Sergei Eisenstein's 1928 film *October* (better known as *Ten Days That Shook the World*), which itself was made to commemorate that wonderful event. Indeed, in bringing *October* to the world, they hoped to replicate and abet for our own time that fusion of avant-garde art and revolutionary politics that has been one of the abiding dreams of certain utopian Marxists for much of this century. Despite a promise to include work that is "at times idealist" as well as work that is "materialist," they frankly acknowledged that *October* was inspired by a commitment to the Marxist dictum that art and culture are essentially reflections of economic processes. "*October*'s strong theoretical emphasis will be mediated by its consideration of present artistic practice," the editors assure us. "It is our conviction that this is possible only within a sustained awareness of the economic and social bases of that practice, of the material conditions of its origins and processes, and of their intensely problematic nature at this particular time."

The *October* syndrome not only involves a loving embrace of cultural Marxism (it embodies in the purest

* See "Feeling Sorry for Rosalind Krauss," in my book *Art's Prospect: The Challenge of Tradition in an Age of Celebrity* (Chicago: Ivan R. Dee, 2003), pages 72–83.

form imaginable what Frederick Crews identified as Left Eclecticism), but also, as a kind of corollary, a violent attack on middle-class culture and society, especially in its American varieties. The phrase "intensely problematic at this particular time" already points in that direction, for what the editors mean to imply is that contemporary artistic practice in America is crippled by being insufficiently "aware" of its "social and economic bases." And that's only the beginning. It is a prominent feature of the *October* syndrome that, whenever possible, the discussion of art or ideas should be extended to include an indictment of Western capitalist society. Again, the editors' note for their inaugural issue provides a preliminary taste of the procedure. " 'October', " they write,

> is a reference which remains, for us, more than exemplary; it is instructive. For us, the argument regarding Socialist Realism is nonexistent. Art begins and ends with a recognition of its conventions. We will not contribute to that social critique which, swamped by its own disingenuousness, gives credence to such an object of repression as a mural about the war in Vietnam, painted by a white liberal resident in New York, a war fought for the most part by ghetto residents commanded by elements drawn from the southern lower-middle-class.

The contention that "art begins and ends with a recognition of its conventions" is something we shall have occasion to consider more closely below; it, too, is an essential feature of the *October* syndrome. (As indeed is the description of a work of art as "an object of repression" and the blithe rejection of the controversy over Socialist Realism, as if that Stalinist interdiction of art were some negligible disturbance in an otherwise glorious cultural and social renaissance.) But the editors' concluding observation is one especially worth pausing over. "Elements drawn from the southern lower-middle-class"? One wonders what these connoisseurs of contempt would have said had they discovered such snobbery and class prejudice in, say, the writings of other white liberal residents of New York.

In any event, *October: The First Decade* provides an even more glaring showcase for the *October* syndrome. The opacity, the radical pronouncements, the obsession with violence and perverse sexuality, the assumption that art should be primarily a form of political activism: it's all vividly displayed in this collection of two dozen pieces. Consisting of essays, mostly, *October: The First Decade* also includes interviews, portfolios of photographs, translations of historical documents, and a translation of a long poem about sex and language by the German writer Peter Handke. Its contents are arranged under six categories: The Index, Historical Materialism, Critique of Institutions, Psychoanalysis, Rhetoric, and The Body. The tenor of the volume can be gleaned by sampling the titles of its contributions: "The Index of the Absent Wound (Monograph on a Stain)," "Mimicry and Legendary Psychasthenia," "From Faktura to Factography," "The Judgment Seat of Photography," "Of Mimicry and Man: The Ambivalence of Colonial Discourse," and "On the Eve of the Future: The Reasonable Facsimile and the Philosophical Toy." Speaking of "The Index," one could have wished that the editors or the MIT Press had seen fit to provide the book with one—and that they had provided some identifying material on the contributors.

Before turning to the particular works anthologized

here, we must sample the prefatory remarks supplied by the editors. Alluding once again to Eisenstein's film *October* and to the revolutionary ethos of the Russian avant garde after 1917 as the magazine's inspiration, they declare that "*October* is emblematic for us of a specific historical moment in which artistic practice joined with critical theory in the project of social construction." In other words—though of course they never put it like this—the term "October" commended itself because of its association with a moment in which art was enlisted in the service of Communist ideology and propaganda. In this context—the context of an "artistic practice" joining with "critical theory in the project of social construction"—they note that the legend appearing on the cover of every issue of the magazine, "Art | Theory | Criticism | Politics," expresses the "conjunction" they seek to realize in the material they publish. A more truthful advertisement for the contents of *October* would be "Art = Theory = Criticism = Politics."

Like so many people affected by the *October* syndrome these days, the editors of *October* look especially to Russian Constructivism as a model in their struggle against the depredations and superficialities of contemporary Western culture. The deliberate blurring of the boundary between aesthetics and politics, the intoxication of succumbing to vanguard revolutionary sentiment, the rejection of cultural activities not amenable to the cause of the socialist renovation of society: all this recommended the atmosphere surrounding Constructivism to the editors of *October*. Unfortunately, that golden revolutionary moment was difficult to sustain. After one of their frequent assurances that their fondness for post-Revolutionary Russia is not colored by "nostalgia" (a prime bourgeois vice, nostalgia), the editors explain that "we wished to claim that the unfinished, analytic project of construc-tivism—aborted by the consolidation of the Stalinist bur-eaucracy, distorted by the recuperation of the Soviet avant garde into the mainstream of Western idealist aes-thetics—was required for a consideration of the aesthetic practices of our own time."

Please note the argument: Constructivism was both "aborted by the consolidation of the Stalinist bureaucracy" as well as "distorted" by being assimilated "into the mainstream of Western idealist aesthetics." Let's leave to one side the dubious claim that the achievements of Russian Constructivism—think only of artists like Malevich and Rodchenko—can be said to have been "distorted" by being assimilated to the idealist tradition of Western art. For our understanding of the *October* syndrome, the important thing is the principle that any criticism of Stalinism or totalitarianism must be ritually followed up with a criticism of the United States or West-ern culture or capitalist (actually, I believe the required phrase is "late capitalist") society.

One of the central appeals of the *October* syndrome, the feature that perhaps more than any other assures its contemporary relevance, is its contention that the art and activist politics of the 1960s and early 1970s marked an exuberant reflowering of the kind of revolutionary spirit that enlivened the Constructivist movement in the early years of the Bolshevik Revolution. "The 1960s," we are told, "had witnessed . . . extraordinary developments in the visual and temporal arts: in painting, sculpture, dance, performance, and film." But in order to under-stand and perpetuate these "extraordinary develop-ments," we are now urged to resuscitate "the kind of critical theory" that burgeoned in the former Soviet Union sixty or seventy years ago. Precisely this is the task that the editors of *October* set for themselves. Continuing "the unfinished project of the 1960s" has not, one gathers, been an easy task. For one thing, just when the "extraordinary developments" of the Sixties and Seventies were beginning to get going, bang, a period of reaction set in. Then, too, the dazzling, promiscuous display of new styles and pseudo-styles that marked the period has been misunderstood by others. "We did not see this juncture as that of the vaunted 'death of the avant-garde' and a new 'pluralism.' We saw it rather as that of late capitalism, a time of continued struggle to radicalize cultural practices, and of the marginalization of those attempts through the revival of traditional artistic and discursive tendencies."

In the face of this nefarious attempt to exclude ("marginalize") certain artistic practices and to revive "traditional artistic and discursive tendencies"—such "tendencies," that is to say, as easel painting, figure drawing, and writing intelligible prose—the editors of *October* considered their work on the magazine to be "the necessary response to what was *once again* a consolidation of reactionary forces within both the political and cultural spheres" (my emphasis). "Once again"? The previous "consolidation of reactionary forces," remember, referred to Stalinism; this time it refers to . . . well, to American society under the leadership of Jimmy Carter and Ronald Reagan.

In order to appreciate just how bad things are under the jackboot of American democracy in the late twentieth century, one need only attend to the plaintive cry of the editors' peroration. It brings together so many of the

political features of the *October* syndrome that it is worth
quoting at some length. "We in New York," they write,

saw our community forced out of the SoHo they had
helped to create, forced in turn to collaborate in the evic-
tion of even more marginal populations from the Lower
East Side, as the creation of a new art district was con-
scripted as a wedge for real-estate development . . . . We
saw, at the same time, the very artistic experimentation
that we had associated with the SoHo community abandoned in favor of the production of luxury objects for
consumption and investment, often now by multinational
corporations. . . . [W]e watched in dismay as art institutions resurrected the claims of disinterestedness. . . .

Our attention also had to be directed toward the
operations within these institutions [the artist's studio, the
gallery and museum, the corporate patron, the discipline
of art history] of a system of privilege that rewarded the
masculine and ignored the rest, that addressed itself to a
male subject that it took as adequate indicator of the
universal. A radical ignorance with respect to sexual difference had to be confronted. Women had to be written
into historical and contemporary cultural practices as
producers and as addressees. This task would entail,
however, more than a simple retrieval of women from
neglected historical archives or the support of contemporary women's work. It would also entail a reconception
of the scotoma that kept women from sight not as an impediment to be removed but as a process of vision itself.

So many complaints in so little space! SoHo became
expensive; the fledgling galleries of New York's Lower
East Side were dupes of the real estate developers; some

of the young artists of the Sixties grew up and began making money (and, what is worse, selling their art not only to corporations but, evil of evils, to *multinational* corporations—Margaret Ferguson, where are you?); some museums repudiated the politicization of art and attempted once more to deal with art "disinterestedly," i.e., as art instead of as a form of political activism; and so on. Obviously we are dealing with a late-capitalist plot of terrifying dimensions.

But while we are on the subject of abandoning "experimentation" in "the SoHo community . . . in favor of the production of luxury objects for consumption and investment," perhaps we should reacquaint ourselves with the beginning of Janet Malcolm's 1986 profile of Ingrid Sischy in *The New Yorker.* Sischy was then the editor of *Artforum,* a journal with fewer scholarly pretensions than *October,* but no less a dispenser of opaque politicized cant about art and culture. Malcolm's article dilates not only on Sischy's career at *Artforum* but the whole super-chic downtown art scene. With unerring journalistic instinct, she opened her article by recounting a visit to Rosalind Krauss. "Rosalind Krauss's loft, on Greene Street," Malcolm began,

> is one of the most beautiful living places in New York. Its beauty has a dark, forceful, willful character. Each piece of furniture and every object of use or decoration has evidently had to pass a severe test before being admitted into this disdainfully interesting room—a long, mildly begloomed rectangle with tall windows at either end, a *sachlich* white kitchen area in the center, a study, and a sleeping balcony. An arrangement of geometric dark-blue armchairs around a coffee table forms the loft's sitting

room, also furnished with, among other rarities, an an-
tique armchair on splayed, carved feet and upholstered in
a dark William Morris fabric; an assertive all-black Mini-
malist shaped-felt piece; a strange black-and-white photograph of ocean water; and a gold owl-shaped Art Deco
clock.*

Could it be that even Rosalind Krauss has been "con-
scripted as a wedge for real-estate development"? Or is
this merely an illustration of the old adage that living well
is the best revenge?

III   Rats, capitalism, and other artistic phenomena

Unfortunately, a full appreciation of the *October* syndrome requires that one consider more than these rather
programmatic statements about *October*'s predecessors
and aspirations. One must also examine some of its chief
arguments, recurrent themes, and stylistic habits. Perhaps
the single most important contention advanced by the
October set is the idea that "art begins and ends with a
recognition of its conventions." No doubt this statement
is susceptible to a variety of interpretations. But when
considered as part of the *October* syndrome, it means
that our chief interest in art should not be in the art itself—in whatever special perception of beauty or sudden
insight it might be capable of communicating—but rather
in the "strategies" (to use that indispensable critical term)
that the art employs to question its own formal and social

* Janet Malcolm, "Ingrid Sischy," *The New Yorker*, October 20,
1986, page 49.

presuppositions. In this sense, art becomes a kind of *meta-art*, art whose chief concern is with its social, economic, and conceptual presuppositions, just as criticism becomes meta-criticism, criticism that is concerned more with its own methodology than with the aesthetic substance of art.

Douglas Crimp provides a sterling example of one aspect of this procedure in his essay "The Art of Exhibition." Discussing the Documenta Exhibition of 1982, Mr. Crimp expresses his outrage that credence is given to an idealizing view of art, a view of art that values art for its aesthetic or even its spiritual qualities. (As Professor Krauss put it in another *October* essay, one not included in this volume, "by now we find it indescribably embarrassing to mention *art* and *spirit* in the same sentence.")* For his part, Mr. Crimp combats the idealization of art by reminding his readers of the large number of homeless people in New York City and the large number of rats found in a lot next to his apartment building. This provides an occasion to castigate former Mayor Koch ("the most reactionary mayor in New York's recent history," etc.) and, of course, ex-President Reagan, and to praise artists like Christy Rupp, who specializes in producing images of attacking rats, and Jenny Holzer, whose "art" consists of slogans pasted on city walls, engraved on stone benches, or immortalized in the flashing lights of electronic signboards.

Both artists, Mr. Crimp assures us, stand outside the nasty, inequitable system of established galleries and museums, and both produce "works manufactured cheap

---

* Rosalind E. Krauss, *The Originality of the Avant-Garde and Other Modernist Myths* (Cambridge: MIT Press, 1985), page 13.

and sold cheap, quite unlike the paintings and sculptures within museum buildings." Well, Mr. Crimp is surely correct that their works are "quite unlike" the paintings and sculptures one *used* to find in museums. I wonder, though, if he has been following Miss Holzer's career lately—since, for example, she was selected by a panel of distinguished museum directors and curators to represent the United States at the 1990 Venice Biennale (the first woman so honored), since her photograph appeared on the front page of *The New York Times*, since her electronic signboards have been fetching (at last count) between $30,000 and $50,000 apiece? "Protect Me From What I Want," "Abuse of Power Should Come as No Surprise": these are some of the artistic masterpieces that have made Miss Holzer famous. She calls them "mock clichés," but I believe she is altogether too modest: they are the real thing, and one only wonders how well she— or her champion Mr. Crimp—feels she is doing at resisting the depredations of museums "whose real but disguised condition is that of the international market for art, dominated increasingly by corporate speculation"?

There is a good deal about "corporate speculation" and real estate in the *October* reader. Instead of an examination of the *art* of the New York's Lower East Side, for example, we find an essay about the social and economic effects of the gentrification of the area. And instead of an examination of the artist's studio as a place where art is made, we find a dissection of the studio as the "material presupposition" of art "production." In "The Function of the Studio," we learn that "analysis of the art system must inevitably be carried on in terms of the studio as the *unique space* of production and the museum as the *unique space* of exposition. Both must be

investigated as customs, the ossifying customs of art."
Why, you might ask, are the customs (presumably, the
author means "conventions") of art necessarily "ossifying"? We are never told, but we do discover that "the
studio is a place of multiple activities: production,
storage, and finally, if all goes well, distribution. It is a
kind of commercial depot." Yes, sure, an artist wants to
sell his works. But what is of permanent interest about an
artist's studio is precisely what *distinguishes* it from a
"commercial depot." And about that side of studio life,
the aesthetic side, *October* has nothing to say.

The large-scale shift away from a concern with the aesthetic substance of art helps explain a number of salient
features of the *October* syndrome, not least its obsession
with photography and film. (There are more pieces
devoted to photography and film in *October: The First
Decade* than to any other medium.) The favored place
accorded to photography and film in certain critical and
artistic circles today is a complex subject well worth
meditating on. Professor Kaplan has shown us that even
trash like MTV rock videos can serve as grist for the academic grinder. Professor Krauss, who has not yet supplied
us with an interpretation of rock video, tends to prefer
"avant-garde" videos and photography, in which she
finds a deeper (and, I daresay, darker) sexual charge than
most of us could have ever imagined. For example, in
another of her *October* essays that does not appear in this
reader, she meditates on the "phallicism" implicit in two
photographs: a self-portrait by Florence Henri and Man
Ray's "Monument to de Sade," a photograph of a
woman's buttocks upon which is superimposed the outline of an inverted cross. But more remarkable than the

discovery of "phallicism" where it exists only by dint of ingenious hermeneutical imputation are the conclusions that Professor Krauss draws from her discovery. For the phallicism that is said to be implicit "in the whole photographic enterprise of framing and thereby capturing a subject. . . can be generalized way beyond the specifics of sexual imagery to a structural logic."* Among much else, then, Professor Krauss would have us believe that photography is itself an act of sexual conquest, that composing an object in the viewfinder and clicking the shutter are somehow analogous to sexual intercourse.

The attraction of film, video, and photography for those cynical about the claims of traditional art and infatuated with the exhibitionism and surface glitter of "performance art" goes beyond Professor Krauss's rather specialized taste, however. The important thing to grasp is that the appeal of these fashionable art forms has little to do with any specifically *aesthetic* or *artistic* potential they may have. On the contrary, the chief appeal of photography, film, and video is that their "mechanical reproducibility" (to adapt a phrase from Walter Benjamin's adored essay "The Work of Art in the Age of Mechanical Reproduction") promises to demystify both the work of art as a uniquely valuable object and the artist as a uniquely talented, individual sensibility. In other words, one reason photography and film are so highly touted by the *October* set is because they promise to reduce art and artistic creation to the status of an industrialized process. As Professor Krauss puts it in "Notes on the Index: Seventies Art in America," photography "demands that the work be viewed as a deliberate short-circuiting of

* *The Originality of the Avant-Garde*, page 91.

issues of style. Countermanding the artist's possible formal intervention in creating the work is the overwhelming physical presence of the original object."

A similar set of concerns motivate Benjamin H. D. Buchloh's lugubrious essay "From Faktura to Factography." Mr. Buchloh begins by criticizing the founding director of the Museum of Modern Art, Alfred H. Barr,* for being blind to the true revolutionary content of Soviet avant-garde "production," especially photography. (This, by the way, is another tic that the *October* syndrome has inherited from the rhetoric of Marxism and Russian Constructivism: instead of speaking of making or, heaven forfend, of *creating* art, one speaks of artistic or cultural "production.") Never mind that Alfred Barr did more than any other single individual to bring the art of the Soviet avant garde, including the art of photomontage that Mr. Buchloh so admires, to the attention of the American public: his unforgivable mistake was to view it as . . . yes, as *art*, not as a form of political propaganda. In Mr. Buchloh's view, the real value of the avant-garde photography that emerged from Constructivism was that it "had deliberately and systematically disassociated itself" from the framework of modernism "in order to lay the foundations of an art production that would correspond to the needs of a newly industrialized collective society." Hence, what's so wonderful about a certain species of avant-garde

---

* It is worth noting that *October* devoted a large part of its Winter 1978 issue to the diary Barr kept while traveling in the Soviet Union in 1927 and 1928. Thus, while *October* is prepared to honor Barr as a kind of pilgrim to the anointed land, in they end they criticize him for failing to understand the true—i.e., the Marxist—cultural and political significance of his own experience.

photography is that it allows one to forget about art and get on with the business of "social production."

Mr. Buchloh's essay is also useful as yet another example of how the *October* syndrome requires that every mention of totalitarianism implicates Western capitalism and the United States in the general infamy. He begins by lamenting that El Lissitzky and Walter Benjamin's "media optimism" "prevented them from recognizing that the attempt to create conditions of a simultaneous collective reception for the new audiences of the industrialized state would very soon issue into the preparation of an arsenal of totalitarian, Stalinist propaganda in the former Soviet Union. What is worse," Mr. Buchloh continues,

> it would deliver the aesthetics and technology of propaganda to the Italian Fascist and German Nazi regimes. And only a little later we see the immediate consequences of Lissitzky's new montage techniques and photofrescoes in their successful adaptation for the ideological needs of American politics and the campaigns for the acceleration of capitalist development through consumption. *Thus, what in Lissitzky's hands had been a tool of instruction, political education, and the raising of consciousness was rapidly transformed into an instrument for prescribing the silence of conformity and obedience.* (My emphasis.)

That is, the adoption of montage and kindred techniques in America has been used to prescribe "the silence of conformity and obedience." And if the message was not clear enough the first time around, Mr. Buchloh recapitulates his main point in his concluding sentence: "at the cross-section of politically emancipatory productivist aesthetics and the transformation of modernist montage aesthetics into an instrument of mass education and enlightenment, we find not only its imminent transformation into totalitarian propaganda, but also its successful adaptation for the needs of the ideological apparatus of the culture industry of Western capitalism." No doubt we must be grateful to the courageous Mr. Buchloh for breaking the silence and conformity prescribed by the "needs of the ideological apparatus of the culture industry of Western capitalism." But then shouldn't he and his colleagues at *October* be grateful to such organs of "the ideological apparatus of the culture industry" as the National Endowment for the Arts and the New York State Council on the Arts, both of which have been longtime supporters of *October*? Perhaps a future issue of the magazine will be devoted to explaining why *October* deigns to avail itself of funds from government agencies representing a political system they consistently vilify.

IV   Gender, race, and class, redux

The contributions of Messrs. Crimp, Buchloh, *et alii*, provide good examples of one side—what we might call the old-time anti-capitalist side—of the *October* syndrome. But while that certainly helps account for *October*'s cachet in the academy and among "advanced" artistic circles, it is by no means the whole story of its charms. Equally important is the more "philosophical" and "cultural" side of the *October* syndrome, a side for which Professor Krauss certainly sets the tone but which has attracted a number of able imitators.

Of course no such collection as this would be complete

without a large measure of feminist rhetoric. One finds it scattered throughout the volume, but the most amusing —though perhaps also the most frightening—instance is provided by Mary Ann Doane in her essay on feminist filmmaking, "Woman's Stake: Filming the Female Body." Complaining that "Cinematic images of woman [note the singular] have been so consistently oppressive and repressive that the very idea of a feminist filmmaking practice seems an impossibility," Miss Doane proceeds to explore the ways in which a self-respecting feminist might go about the business of making films. It's a tough job. For one thing, since in Miss Doane's view "the essence of femininity is most frequently attached to the natural body as an immediate indicator of sexual difference, it is this body which must be refused."

Yes, it is difficult to film women—or Woman—without a body. Or is it? Miss Doane assures us that "The body is always a function of discourse," so perhaps one could fill up the screen with words? But the real problem, one gathers, is that the very mechanical process of making films is a threat to a woman's sexuality. As Miss Doane explains, "A machine for the production of images and sounds, the cinema generates and guarantees pleasure by a corroboration of the spectators's identity. Because that identity is bound up with that of the voyeur and fetishist, because it requires for its support the attributes of the 'noncastrated,' the potential for illusory mastery of the signifier, it is not accessible to the female spectator, who, in buying her ticket, must deny her sex." Miss Doane notwithstanding, it does seem odd that a journal that has, shall we say, "fetishized" photography and film should publish an essay proclaiming a trip to the movies as something so fraught with ideological danger.

The cultural side of the *October* syndrome is not confined to feminism, however. For sheer pretension, one of my favorite pieces was Georges Didi-Huberman's essay on the Shroud of Turin, "The Index of the Absent Wound (Monograph on a Stain)." "What we need," muses Mr. Didi-Huberman, "is a concept of figurative *Aufhebung.*"

> We would have to consider the dichotomy of its field and its means, and how they deploy a dialectical mimesis as initiation of absolute knowledge; how it attempts to transform sensible space and to begin a movement (Hegel would have said automovement) in the direction of certitude, figural certitude. An absolute seeing that would transcend the scansion of seeing and of knowing; an absolutely reflexive representation. . . .
>
> We have to look at this stain again, but this time with the "foresight" of such figural certainty in mind, or its "phantasm," its *phantasia* in the Hegelian sense; for Hegel considered *Phantasie* an *Aufhebung*, and spoke of the movement of truth as a delirium of absolute translucidity.

Lest the reader be puzzled by this, Mr. Didi-Huberman obligingly supplies an explanatory reference: "Cf. Georg Wilhelm Friedrich Hegel, *The Phenomenology of Spirit.*" The translator and publication data are listed, but no page number for this nearly- 600-page book. Students of Hegel will perhaps hazard that Mr. Didi-Huberman had in mind the passage from the preface to the *Phenomenology* where Hegel speaks of "the true" being "the bacchanalian whirl in which no member is not drunk."* But

* G. W. F. Hegel, *The Phenomenology of Spirit,* translated by A. V. Miller (Oxford: Oxford University Press, 1977), page 27.

who knows? Mr. Didi-Huberman, at least, is never troubled to say.

This sort of thing is standard practice in the pages of *October*. As in so much academic writing these days, arcane references and wild generalizations are thrown around wholesale. One soon realizes that the footnote to Lacan, the invocation of Foucault, of Freud, of Benjamin, the entire (dare one say it?) superstructure of "scholarship" erected in these essays is intended not to further knowledge but to dazzle the reader. Why, for example, does Joel Fineman feel called upon to parade the first line of *The Iliad*, unidentified and untranslated, as an epigraph to his essay on "The Structure of Allegorical Desire"? How many of his readers will be able to read the Greek? Not many, of course, but that is perhaps just as well since the line is slightly miscited, as indeed are several of the Greek words with which Mr. Fineman decorates his essay.

Or consider as a final example Homi Bhabha's "Of Mimicry and Man: The Ambivalence of Colonial Discourse," an essay that, we are told, was first presented in 1983 at the Modern Language Association. Warming up with some reasonably benign reflections on "the discourse of post-Enlightenment English colonialism," and so on, Mr. Bhabha—who has since emerged as an academic superstar in the pseudo-discipline of "post-colonial studies"—quickly gets down to business: "Within that conflictual economy of colonial discourse which Edward Said describes as the tension between the synchronic panoptical vision of domination—the demand for identity, stasis—and the counter-pressure of the diachrony of history—change, difference—mimicry represents an *ironic* compromise. If I may adapt Samuel Weber's formulation of the marginalizing vision of castration, . . ."—but, no, let's leave *that* formulation to one side and continue with some of Mr. Bhabha's concluding remarks.

> In the ambivalent world of the "not quite/not white," on the margins of metropolitan desire, the *founding objects* of the Western world become the erratic, eccentric, accidental *objets trouvés* of the colonial discourse—the part-objects of presence. It is then that the body and the book loose [*sic*] their representational authority. Black skin splits under the racist gaze, displaced into signs of bestiality, genitalia, grotesquerie, which reveal the phobic myth of the undifferentiated whole white body.[*]

There is something terribly pathetic about this sort of display, composed as it is of nothing but clichés and phrases echoing the likes of Melanie Klein, Edward Said, Roland Barthes, and our old friend Frantz Fanon—though whether Mr. Bhabha is fully aware of his sources is unclear. Indeed, the cruelly ironical thing about this essay on mimicry and colonialism is that it is itself nothing but a poor mimicry of the clotted academic rhetoric that passes for scholarship in our universities and journals. That this rubbish should be presented as a "paper" at the Modern Language Association is a somber reminder how far that venerable organization has degenerated in recent years.

There are many choice tidbits that I have left out of ac-

---

[*] I discuss Homi Bhabha at great length in "The Perfect Academic," *National Review* Volume 53, Issue 20, 15 October 2001, pages 56–58.

count here. But readers who find their appetites whetted can turn to the *October* reader to relish such marvels as Georges Bataille's discussion of the Aztec practice of human sacrifice ("Death, for the Aztecs, was nothing," Bataille tells us) or Maria-Antonietta Macciocchi's meditations on the murder of the filmmaker Pier Paolo Pasolini. In Macciocchi's piece, "Pasolini: Murder of a Dissident," we learn that "the death of the opposition sexualizes intensely the life of an entire society, from the dark bowels of fascism to the violence whose language is expressed . . . by the deadly call to aphasia. Is the social link paranoiac?" Who can say?

V What does it all mean?

Although *October* is often opaque and unintelligible, it is not utterly bereft of sense. If one has sufficient patience, something resembling a consecutive argument can often be wrested from the tangled, jargon-ridden prose favored by its contributors. It is difficult, at any rate, to mistake *October*'s enemies.

On the cultural side, one chief target of the *October* set's scorn is the legacy of modernist art and modernist criticism. The emphasis upon individual creativity, the seriousness with which art and indeed the entire realm of high culture was regarded, the faith in the spiritually en-riching potential of art, even, or rather, especially, in a secular age—all this is fundamental to the modernist ethos. And it is all systematically castigated by the writers and editors of *October*.

At bottom, the *October* set's rebellion against moder-nism is the rebellion of the disappointed enthusiast. Like so many others, the editors and contributors to *October* had once seen modernism as a handmaiden of radical politics. The problem is that modernism's affirmation of individuality and high culture, its efforts to reinvigorate rather than destroy the claims of tradition, turned out to be thoroughly incompatible with the dream of radical social transformation. Yet it was precisely upon that dream that modernism's credentials as "avant garde" had to a large extent depended. When it became clear that modernism was not acting to realize that dream, it had to be stripped of its avant-garde status and exposed as an agent of reaction. Thus at the end of her essay "The Originality of the Avant-Garde," Professor Krauss argues that "the historical period that the avant garde shared with modernism is over," and urges upon us "a demythologizing criticism and a truly postmodernist art, both of them acting now to void the basic propositions of modernism, to liquidate them by exposing their fictitious condition."*

When one turns to political matters—matters, I mean, involving elected officials, government policies, and the like (since everything is regarded as political by the *October* set, the distinction is important)—the *October* syndrome obviously tends to be about as direct, but unfortunately about as unconvincing, as the harangues of a soapbox preacher. Western bourgeois society, individualism, capitalism, high art: these are its enemies. Its ideals are radical socialism and anything that works to subvert the existing cultural and political order. Reading through so many pages of *October* brought to mind a remark made years ago by the distinguished English intellectual historian Basil Willey. Discussing the work of

* *The Originality of the Avant-Garde,* page 170.

Sir Thomas Browne, Willey observed that Browne's literary style "was the incarnation of his sensibility."* Style, indeed, is often the incarnation of sensibility. And reflecting on the style of the *October* syndrome—on its opacity, its humorlessness, its pretension, its utter disregard for common sense—one cannot help concluding that, like so many manifestations of academic life today, it is a sensibility for which art and culture exist and have value only as appendages to political ideology.

Of course, it is part of the syndrome that *October* exemplifies that the realm of politics, like everything else, exists primarily as a cerebral phenomenon. In order to appreciate what happens when this essentially abstract, academic radicalism intersects with politics in the everyday sense of the term, let us turn to the strange case of the Belgian-born literary critic and deconstructionist Paul de Man.

* Basil Willey, *The Seventeenth Century Background: The Thought of the Age in Relation to Religion and Poetry* (London: Chatto & Windus, 1950), page 46.

CHAPTER FOUR

The Case of Paul de Man

I Excuses, excuses

> *It is no longer certain that language, as excuse, exists because of a prior guilt but just as possible that since language, as a machine, performs anyway, we have to produce guilt .. . in order to make the excuse meaningful. Excuses generate the very guilt they exonerate.*
>
> —Paul de Man, *Allegories of Reading*

DECEMBER 1, 1987 was an unpleasant day for academic literary critics bewitched by the tenets of deconstruction. That morning, *The New York Times* reported that a young Belgian scholar named Ortwin de Graef had recently discovered that in the early nineteen-forties—at the very moment when Hitler's power was at its zenith and his conquest of Europe seemed assured—the celebrated literary deconstructionist Paul de Man was busy writing articles and reviews, at least one of which was patently anti-Semitic, for Belgian newspapers supporting the Nazi cause. Understandably, the news sent shock waves through the academic literary community. Perhaps the most damaging of de Man's articles appeared in the collaborationist newspaper *Le Soir* on March 4, 1941, under the title "The Jews in Contemporary Literature." "There would not have been grounds for much hope for the future of our civilization," de Man wrote,

> if it had allowed itself to be invaded without resistance by an alien force. In preserving—despite the Semitic meddling into all aspects of European life—its originality and character intact, it has shown that its nature was essentially healthy. Moreover, one thus sees that a solution to the Jewish question that envisions the creation of a Jewish colony isolated from Europe would not involve deplorable consequences for the literary life of the West. It would lose, all told, a few personalities of mediocre value and would continue, as in the past, to develop according to its own great evolutionary laws. *

In other articles he explained that after the fall of France

---

* Paul de Man, *Wartime Journalism, 1939–1943*, edited by Werner Hamacher, Neil Hertz, and Thomas Keenan (Lincoln: University of Nebraska Press, 1989), page 45. This facsimile collection of de Man's wartime writings in French and English translations of his wartime writings in Dutch was hastily cobbled together in an effort to mollify the public outcry that followed the revelation of de Man's connection with Nazi newspapers. Translations from the French are mine.

"the German conquerors were more praiseworthy, just, and humane than the French were in 1918"; he assured readers that "the fascist regime [in Italy] leaves the poet completely free to seek his source of inspiration wherever he wants"; and he praised "the totalitarian regime" [Germany this time] for having overcome the "vague anarchy" of bourgeois French society, replacing it with "definite obligations and duties to which everyone must adapt his talents."* He also found occasion to extol "the present war" as "the beginning of a revolution that aims to reorganize Europe in a more equitable fashion" and to observe that

> the war will only bring about a more intimate union of two things that have always been close, the Hitlerian soul and the German soul, until they have been made one single and unique power. This is an important phenomenon, because it means that one cannot judge the fact of Hitler without judging at the same time the fact of Germany and that the future of Europe can be envisioned only within the framework of the possibilities and needs of the German spirit. It is not a matter only of a series of reforms but the definite emancipation of a people which finds itself called upon to exercise, in its turn, a hegemony in Europe.†

What does the strange case of Paul de Man tell us about the way politics has corrupted the humanities?

* *Ibid.*, *seriatim*, pages 66 (April 12–14, 1941), 32 (February 18, 1941), and 159 (October 28, 1941).

† *Ibid.*, *seriatim*, pages 138 (August 26, 1941) and 159 (October 28, 1941).

Even more than Professor de Man's own behavior, the academy's response to these articles—subsequent digging revealed that there were nearly two hundred—and to de Man's later failure to acknowledge his activities was predictably evasive and temporizing. While the popular press, from *Newsweek* to *The Nation* and *The Village Voice*, condemned de Man, literary academics, with a few notable exceptions, closed ranks and began manufacturing excuses. Already in October, 1987, when the news of de Graef's discovery had begun to leak out, a summit meeting of about twenty deconstructionists—including, *ex officio*, as it were, J. Hillis Miller and Jacques Derrida—convened in Tuscaloosa, Alabama, to examine copies of the offending articles and decide on a policy of what many writers have subsequently called "damage control."

One early example of the procedure was given by Christopher Norris—himself a prominent second-rung deconstructionist who made his reputation championing de Man—in a long and tortuous examination for *The London Review of Books* early in 1988.* Professor Norris offers numerous possible extenuations of de Man's behavior: that the articles in question had been "mined for passages" by de Man's enemies to show him in a bad light, that he was under political pressure to write the articles, etc. But Professor Norris's chief point seems to be that de Man's early brush with totalitarianism was a kind of learning experience that helped make his post-war writing a model of skeptical rigor.

This in fact was a theme often repeated by academics

---

* Christopher Norris, "Paul de Man's Past," *The London Review of Books*, February 4, 1988, pages 7–11.

who weighed in to defend their idol. The famed Jonathan Culler, for example, explained in an article for *The Chronicle of Higher Education* that the discovery of de Man's wartime writings "adds a new dimension to his later writings" and then goes on to tell us that de Man's later critiques now appear "as a critique of ideas and underlying fascism and their deadly quest for unity and the elimination of difference."* In Professor Culler's view, this somehow implies that deconstruction, being deeply skeptical of language, emerges as a formidable opponent of Nazism and totalitarianism. Presumably it follows that de Man, though he wrote anti-Semitic articles for collaborationist newspapers, is an exemplary anti-Nazi, after all. Obviously, deconstruction is a wonderful thing to have on your side.

Among the early responses, at least, the first prize for mystification must go to Jacques Derrida's extraordinary sixty-page eulogy-cum-jeremiad, which appeared in the academic quarterly *Critical Inquiry.* It begins as follows:

Unable to respond to the questions, to all the questions, I will ask myself instead *whether responding is possible* and what that would mean in such a situation. And I will risk in turn several questions *prior to* the definition of a *responsibility.* But is it not an act to assume in theory the concept of responsibility? One's own as well as the responsibility to which one believes one ought to summon others?

* Jonathan Culler, "It's Time to Set the Record Straight About Paul de Man and His Wartime Articles for a Pro-Fascist Newspaper," *The Chronicle of Higher Education,* July 13, 1988, Section 2, page B1.

153

And Derrida more or less concludes with this exercise in wistfulness:

> As for the accused himself, he is dead. He is in ashes, he has neither the grounds, nor the means, still less the choice or the desire to respond. We are alone with ourselves. We carry his memory and his name in us. We especially carry ethico-political responsibilities for the future. Our actions with regard to what remains to us of de Man will also have the value of an example, whether we like it or not. To judge, to condemn the work or the man on the basis of what was a brief episode, to call for closing, that is to say, at least figuratively, for censuring or burning his books is to reproduce the exterminating gesture against which one accuses de Man of not having armed himself sooner with the necessary vigilance.*

"The exterminating gesture"? What Derrida seems to be saying is that criticizing Paul de Man for writing collaborationist articles is somehow to repeat the savage butchery of the Nazis.

In one way or another, this bizarre idea surfaced often in the academic response to Paul de Man. Another prime example was the invective penned by deconstruction's faithful mascot, J. Hillis Miller, for *The Times Literary Supplement*. Professor Miller explains that de Man "was by no means in these early writings *totally* fascist, antisemitic and collaborationist" (my emphasis). Well, OK. Shall we say then that he was only half fascist, anti-Semi-

---

* Jacques Derrida, "Like the Sound of the Sea Deep Within a Shell: Paul de Man's War," *Critical Inquiry*, 14, Spring 1988, translated by Peggy Kamuf, pages 590–652.

tic, and collaborationist? In any event, what Professor Miller found "most terrifying" about the press treatment of de Man "is the way it repeats the well-known totalitarian procedures of vilification it pretends to deplore."* I suppose this means that to point out that someone has written collaborationist pieces for newspapers under control of a totalitarian government is itself an example of totalitarianism. Professor Miller rather specializes in such paradoxes. "A deconstructionist," he observed in one typical expostulation, "is not a parasite but a parricide. He is a bad son demolishing beyond hope of repair the machine of Western metaphysics."† Gosh. This sort of thing does offer moments of comic relief. Thus we find Professor Miller complaining bitterly that "journalists" (than which no more opprobrious epithet exists in an academic's vocabulary) scrambled the facts when reporting on the de Man affair. The trouble is that Professor Miller had spent the past decade or so of his professional life insisting on the indeterminacy of language, denying that there was any such thing as a fact, etc. Now here he was in the pages of *The Times Literary Supplement* complaining loudly that a mean-spirited press had gotten the facts all wrong. It did seem like poetic justice.

Engaging in expert spin-control, what we might call the Tuscaloosa Committee decided to arrange for the

---

* J. Hillis Miller, *The Times Literary Supplement*, June 17–23 1988, pages 676, 685.

† Quoted in David Lehman, *Signs of the Times: Deconstruction and the Fall of Paul de Man* (New York: Poseidon, 1991), page 41. Lehman's scrupulously researched book is far and away the most complete and devastating account of the de Man affair.

publication of all de Man's wartime journalism and related documents as well as to organize a volume of responses from various academics concerned with the controversy. After many delays, both volumes appeared in 1989. Facsimiles of the one-hundred-and-sixty-nine pieces de Man wrote for *Le Soir* in French and translations of the ten articles he wrote in Dutch for *Het Vlaamische Land* were published along with a few other pieces in the above-mentioned volume edited by Werner Hamacher, Neil Hertz, and Thomas Keenan. This triumvirate also edited a long volume of responses, which includes a chronology of de Man's early years and some forty articles by sundry academics eager to have their say about the early de Man.* This volume includes a small handful of dissenting pieces. But the vast majority, after a bit of preliminary hand-wringing, seems to come down squarely on the side of de Man and against his condemnation by the press.

I say "seems" here because, in typical deconstructivist fashion, many of the essays are models of obscurantist obfuscation. In addition to a revised version of Derrida's classic response, we also have such gems as Timothy Bahti's "Telephonic Crossroads: The Reversal and the Double Cross," Jeffrey S. Libert's "From the Authority of Appropriate (De)form(ation) to —: Toward De Man's Totalitarian Acts," and Andrzej Warminski's "Terrible Reading (preceded by 'Epigraphs')." And lest the reader conclude that such preening titles are mere ornaments to more reasonable responses, consider this typical pas-

* *Responses: On Paul de Man's Wartime Journalism*, edited by Werner Hamacher, Neil Hertz, and Thomas Keenan (Lincoln: University of Nebraska Press, 1989).

sage from Professor Warminski's contribution to the debate:

> A certain self-immolating self-reflection—a self-ironization—takes place here as . . . de Man's [words] about Montherlant say one thing and mean another. But ironies do not end here—indeed, irony, once it begins (and it has always already begun), never just ends, at least not just here. No matter how self-immolating it may be, the act of self-reflection always leaves remainders, traces, ashes—a *reste* or a *restance du texte*, as Derrida might put it, that resists the totalization of any oblivion, that insures a certain memory for every forgetting, even "the most total."
> . . . The only memory for *those* remainders is the same journalistic "memory" of the present, the one that "remembers" only the present and hence has neither past nor future (and hence does not happen, is not an event, is not historical)—or only *the* past and the future of total oblivion.*

Anyone care to parse that?

II The making of a critical genius

In order to understand why the academy should have rallied so vigorously to excuse the wartime journalism of Paul de Man, it is necessary to understand that he was no ordinary college professor. Having come to the United States in 1947 as an unknown translator and journalist after the War, he did graduate work at Harvard in the

* *Responses*, page 386.

early Fifties (part of the time as a Junior Fellow in Harvard's prestigious Society of Fellows) and emerged in the mid-Seventies as one of the most sought-after literary theorists in the country. Indeed, by the time he died, in 1983, at the age of sixty-four, Professor de Man was considered by some to be one of the most brilliant literary critical minds of his generation.

With the possible exception of Jacques Derrida—who deserves credit (if that is the word) for being the chief theoretical architect of deconstruction—Professor de Man did more than anyone to institutionalize the "demythologizing" tenets of deconstruction in the literature departments of American universities. Although he in fact published very little, during his years teaching at Johns Hopkins and, later, as Sterling Professor of the Humanities at Yale University, he inspired colleagues and graduate students alike to abandon the methods of traditional literary criticism for the allegedly more rigorous approach of deconstruction—an approach characterized by doctrinaire skepticism and infatuation with the thought that language is always so compromised by metaphor and ulterior motives that a text never means what it appears to mean. "The relationship between truth and error that prevails in literature cannot be represented genetically," he assures us in one typical passage, "since truth and error exist simultaneously, thus preventing the favoring of one over the other."* Even today, though de Man's reputation is irretrievably tarnished, his teachings and catch-phrases are parroted in departments of English

---

* Paul de Man, *Blindness and Insight: Essays in the Rhetoric of Contemporary Criticism*, second edition, revised (Minneapolis: University of Minnesota Press, 1983), pages 164–165.

and Comparative Literature across the country. While neither the man nor his theories were universally beloved, we have seen that both inspired fierce devotion from the many partisans of deconstruction, who since his death have been at pains to eulogize his personal virtues as a colleague, teacher, and friend as well as to praise his intellectual gifts and scholarly accomplishments.

That this paragon of chic academic achievement should stand revealed as the author of anti-Semitic articles for pro-Nazi publications at the height of Hitler's power has been a major embarrassment for his many epigones. The reason is obvious: the frequently heard charge that deconstruction is essentially nihilistic has now acquired existential support of the most damaging kind. Not that those early anti-Semitic articles exactly *prove* that deconstruction is nihilistic; but it is a rum thing when the patron saint of a literary movement that has so proclaimed itself a champion of freedom is brutally exposed as having trafficked with a political force whose very essence was the denial of freedom.

Judging by the storm of articles and testimonials that have appeared, the ritual of exoneration proceeds roughly as follows: First: yes, it's regrettable that Paul de Man wrote those articles, but, after all, he was very young at the time, only in his early twenties: youth is impetuous and often blinded by Romantic enthusiasms. Second: it's unfortunate that the prominent newspapers *Le Soir*, where the majority of his early journalistic efforts appeared, and *Het Vlaamsche Land* should both have been openly collaborating with the Nazi line—still, de Man was ambitious and naturally seized the opportunity to write for the prestigious papers; besides, only a few of his articles were explicitly anti-Semitic: most were simply reviews or notices of current cultural events. Third: it's true that he wondered in an article that appeared in March, 1941 in *Le Soir* ("The Jews in Contemporary Literature") whether the Jews "polluted" modern literature, and that he envisioned the establishment of a Jewish colony "isolated from Europe"; we must remember, however, that this was not as vicious as much anti-Semitic writing circulating at the time and that, as far as we know now, he stopped writing for *Le Soir* near the end of 1942, before most people knew about the Nazi death camps. Fourth: while it's lamentable that he never acknowledged his deeds—that he went so far as to claim on at least one occasion that he had been part of the "Belgian resistance" to the Nazis during the War—perhaps his difficulty in coming to terms with his own past helps explain his tough-minded resistance to the bewitchments of language later in life. . . . *But, still, besides, however*: The qualifications proceed to infinity, almost transforming guilt into innocence, or at least so numbing the mind that the distinction between guilt and innocence begins to blur—begins, in good deconstructionist fashion, to seem merely *linguistic*, merely rhetorical, a matter utterly divorced from the demands of moral judgment. Or, as Professor de Man himself put it in a much-admired essay on Rousseau, "The main point of the reading has been to show that the resulting predicament is linguistic rather than ontological or hermeneutic."*

---

* Paul de Man, *Allegories of Reading: Figural Language in Rousseau, Nietzsche, Rilke, and Proust* (New Haven: Yale University Press, 1979), page 299.

III Professor Hartman reconstructs de Man

Although the pieces collected in *Responses* provide exacting competition, perhaps the single most extraordinary—if not, finally, the most opaque—attempt at damage control that appeared in the wake of the revelations about Paul de Man's wartime journalistic activities surfaced in the weekly journal of opinion *The New Republic*. Entitled "Blindness and Insight" after the title of Professor de Man's influential 1971 collection of essays,* this exercise in critical legerdemain was written by his former colleague, Geoffrey H. Hartman, the Karl Young Professor of English and Comparative Literature at Yale University, whom we met in Chapter One. Himself a still-glittering cynosure of academic fashion, Professor Hartman is widely admired in advanced literary-critical circles for his work on Wordsworth and other Romantic poets and for his impishly convoluted "theoretical" works. Unfortunately, almost everything about his article in *The New Republic* must give us pause: its place of publication, the identity of its author, and not least its content and implications. But because it is emblematic of the academy's top-drawer treatment of de Man, Professor Hartman's reconstruction of his late colleague is worth pondering in some detail.

For example, what does it mean that *The New Republic*—a journal that under its current ownership has made such a show of castigating anti-Semitism and supporting Jewish causes—should have published an essay

* Geoffrey H. Hartman, "Blindness and Insight," *The New Republic*, March 7, 1988, pages 26–31. Unless otherwise noted, quotations from Geoffrey Hartman are from this article.

that coyly fudges the significance of Professor de Man's collaborationist articles by reinterpreting them from the perspective of his later deconstructionist writings? What does it mean that this task should have been undertaken by Geoffrey Hartman? Certainly, one could hardly ask for a better pedigree for the job of moral damage control that Professor Hartman undertook in this article. In addition to his regular academic appointment, he is also an advisory committee member of the Judaic Studies Program at Yale as well as an advisor to the Video Archive for Holocaust Testimonies at the Yale library. And what does it mean that this man who fled Germany as a child in the late Thirties because (as he put it in a 1985 interview) "of the persecution of the Jews" should now devote his considerable rhetorical skills to arguing that "in the light of what we now know, however, [de Man's] work appears more and more as a deepening reflection on the rhetoric of totalitarianism"? And finally, what does it tell us about the state of contemporary literary criticism that one of its most distinguished practitioners should be so enthralled with the tenets of deconstruction that he should blithely distill one of this century's most rebarbative historical realities into an example of what he at one point calls "linguistic pathos"?

Professor Hartman devotes the first third of his article to a more or less straightforward presentation of the facts, so far as they were then known, of Professor de Man's early journalistic career. His account, I believe, is essentially accurate. But his tone—sorrowful rather than outraged—is decidedly exculpatory, and he does everything he can to mitigate the offense. For example, he speaks of "*an* anti-Semitic piece" and the "one" article that "engaged explicitly with the ideology of anti-Semitism" (my emphasis). But suppose we concede that only one article "explicitly engaged with the ideology of anti-Semitism"—that is, was blatantly anti-Semitic: That still says nothing about the scores of other articles that, simply by virtue of appearing in *Le Soir* in 1940, 1941, and 1942, *implicitly* condoned the Nazi's more explicit brand of anti-Semitism, as well as the policies and programs that were instituted on its behalf.

Professor Hartman admits that his late colleague's "formulations" "show all the marks, and the dangerous implications, of identifying Jews as an alien and unhealthy presence in Western civilization." He admits, too, that given the times, his writings were "more than a theoretical expression of anti-Semitism" (meaning, perhaps, that a merely "theoretical" expression of anti-Semitism isn't such a bad thing?). What he nowhere acknowledges is the explicit relation those writings bore to the regnant political force of the Nazis.

Instead, his basic tack is to console us with the thought that Professor de Man did not behave as badly as he might have done. It is true that Professor de Man envisioned the creation of a "Jewish colony isolated from Europe," but he did not demand the extermination of the Jews; he did hail the rise of National Socialism as the "definite emancipation of a people called upon to exercise, in its turn, a hegemony in Europe," but, according to Professor Hartman, his "relation to fascist ideology was not a simple matter." Moreover, Professor Hartman assures us that, "by the terrible standards of the day," an article like "The Jews in Contemporary Literature" was not really "vulgar anti-Semitic writing" and that it "stands out [from the other collaborationist writings, including those of his uncle, Hendrik de Man] by its refusal to engage directly with political matters." The idea is, I suppose, that simply not descending to the vicious racial slurs of a Goebbels merits commendation.

IV The cult of theory, redux

There is something extraordinarily depressing about the spectacle of a scholar of Professor Hartman's distinction and personal history struggling to find extenuating circumstances for writings undertaken on behalf of an ideology and political movement that were bent on his own destruction. But somehow even more depressing is the *way* in which Professor Hartman chose to go about his task. For where the first third of his article provided us with an overview of Professor de Man's collaborationist writings, the balance of the piece attempts to rehabilitate Professor de Man by viewing those writings through the lens of deconstruction. The result is a sterling—if not a Sterling Professor's—example of vindication through obfuscation.

Perhaps out of deference to the gravity of the subject, Professor Hartman forbears to indulge his penchant for elaborate, punning word-play in this article. But as in most of his other critical writings from the past two decades, he proceeds not so much by argument as by a display of maddeningly imprecise verbal arabesques. Not surprisingly, he begins by defending deconstruction against the charges of its enemies. "Deconstruction is neither nihilistic nor cynical," he writes,

> when it questions whether there exists an arena for testing ideas other than the uncontrollable arena of activist

politics; or when it demonstrates that philosophy and literature express the impasse from which ideas spring, as well as those ideas themselves. . . . What is neglected by de Man's critics, who are in danger of reducing all to biography again, is the intellectual power in his later work, the sheer power of critique, whatever its source, that he deploys against the claims of philosophy and theory.

Leaving the particulars of this passage to one side, how does it answer the charge of nihilism or cynicism? Does it provide us with anything more than an unsupported assertion? And as for the vaunted "intellectual power" of de Man's later work, of what does it really consist? Confining ourselves to Professor Hartman's own examples, we learn that "according to de Man, we are always encountering epistemological instabilities, the incompatibility or disjunction between meaning and intent, or between what is stated and the rhetoric or mode of stating it." Translated out of the forbidding argot, what this seems to mean is that deconstruction helps us realize that there is often a difference between appearance and reality, that language forever falls short of expressing exactly what we mean. But isn't this an insight that any thoughtful high school student should have when reflecting for the first time on the way language works? Professor Hartman is certainly correct when he observes that

Those previously suspicious of deconstruction have seized on the revelations. Their sense of deconstruction as morally unsound and politically evasive seems to stand confirmed. They condemn it as untrustworthy because it seeks to avert the reality, and therefore the culpability, of error. That is how they interpret deconstruction's emphasis on the indeterminacy of meaning, and on the complexity of a medium that seems to "speak" us [*sic*] instead of submitting fully to our control.

"Such a judgment is superficial," Professor Hartman assures us, "and divorces deconstruction from its context in the history of philosophy." Really? One need hardly be a deconstructionist to agree that language refuses to submit "fully to our control." In fact, does anyone who has given language a moment's thought believe that it is a perfectly transparent medium, fully under our control?

Again, Professor Hartman is right that those critical of deconstruction take exception to its "emphasis on the indeterminacy of meaning." But that of course is the central question: Is meaning as expressed in language so indeterminate that we are unable reliably to decipher it? What about Professor Hartman's own assertion that meaning is indeterminate? Would he say that the meaning of that statement, too, is indeterminate?

Like so many deconstructionists, Professor Hartman has rather a dualistic view of the matter. He assumes that if one has not abandoned the belief in the intelligibility of language and adopted the skepticism that deconstruction preaches, one must be a kind of cartoon Cartesian, holding that language is like a pane of glass, rendering up the world without loss or ambiguity. The possibility of a middle ground between nihilistic skepticism and naïve belief seems never to occur to him, perhaps because he has been so deeply impressed by deconstructionist caveats like this question de Man asks about Rousseau's *Confessions*: "How are we to know we are indeed dealing with a *true* confession, since the recognition of guilt implies its exoneration in the name of the same transcendental principle of truth that allowed for the certitude of guilt in the first place?"* How indeed?

And as for deconstruction's "context in the history of philosophy"—well, given Professor Hartman's own intractable hostility to anything resembling philosophical analysis (something that is evidenced again and again in his "theoretical" writings), I am sure that it would be most amusing to have him enlighten us about that. As it is, we must be content with his suggestion that deconstruction takes up "the age-old problem" of the relation of language and meaning and his cryptic allusion to the German neo-Kantian philosopher Ernst Cassirer. Cassirer, we are told, "observed that while language wished to overcome 'the curse of mediacy,' it was itself part of the problem it tried to resolve."

Now I doubt that Professor Hartman could have picked a less appropriate figure than Ernst Cassirer to support his brief for deconstruction. Cassirer, another refugee from Hitler's Reich, would be rolling over in his grave if he knew that his name was invoked to support the radically skeptical contentions of deconstruction. In the foreword to *The Philosophy of Symbolic Forms*, his *magnum opus*, Cassirer reviewed the intellectual climate of the 'Teens and early Twenties, warning that "at times, language seemed to be becoming the principal weapon of skepticism rather than a vehicle of philosophical knowledge"—a remark that stands up rather well as a characterization of deconstruction *avant la lettre*. As he put it later in the same volume, "skepticism seeks to expose the nullity of knowledge and language—but what it ultimately demonstrates is the nullity of the *standard* by

---

* *Allegories of Reading*, page 280.

which it measures them."* That is to say, radical skepticism exposes the nullity of the standard of absolute transparency: the standard that deconstructionists falsely impute to anyone who continues to believe in the possibility of stable meanings and the intelligibility of language.

The point is that philosophical analysis is little more than intellectual window-dressing for Professor Hartman. In fact, given his view of language, it is *necessarily* little more than intellectual window-dressing for the simple reason that he denies the power of language to communicate effectively through concepts. It has long been clear that Professor Hartman regards "concept" as a highly suspect term, implying as it does that thought can meaningfully transcend the particularities of language and rhetoric. This suspicion of philosophy and of the cogency of rational analysis is among the chief reasons that he values deconstruction so highly. For deconstruction provides a handy way of appearing to transform philosophy into a species of literature, reducing concepts to so many rhetorical "tropes" and viewing the whole notion of truth as an unstable fictional construct.

It is in this sense that Professor Hartman can offer deconstruction as a defender of the imagination and literature against the supposedly unimaginative depredations of philosophy and science. "Deconstruction is," he explains,

* Ernst Cassirer, *The Philosophy of Symbolic Forms*, Volume I: "Language," translated by Ralph Manheim, preface and introduction by Charles W. Hendel (New Haven: Yale University Press, 1955), *seriatim*, pages 70, 188.

a defense of literature. It shows, by close reading, (1) that there are no dead metaphors, (2) that literature is often more self-aware than those who attack it, (3) that literary texts contain significant tensions that can be disclosed, but not resolved, by analysis. Any mode of analysis, therefore, that sees the text as an organic unity, or uses it for a totalizing purpose (as when the right or the left speaks for history), is blind, and the text itself will subvert or "deconstruct" such closures.

There is a great deal that one might say about this passage, which blends the highly questionable with the portentously trite. The idea that there are no dead metaphors can be refuted by anyone who ever uttered the phrase "that depends" and bothered to consider its etymology. The metaphorical sense of something "hanging down" is indeed "dead" in most everyday uses of the word "depends." I'm not sure what it means to speak of literature *itself* as being "more self-aware than those who attack it"; no doubt Professor Hartman means to remind us that he has read Heidegger's orphic remarks about "language speaking."

But if Professor Hartman is suggesting that many who repudiate the complex charms of literature are philistines, who would disagree? And as for the contention that "literary texts contain significant tensions that can be disclosed, but not resolved, by analysis," here I should think it all depends on what one means by "resolved." In one sense, certainly, it is a statement with which scarcely a single literate individual would disagree. But the real point of this passage is that deconstruction is superior to other modes of interpretation because it provides especially "close readings" of texts, readings that reveal nasty things like the "totalizing" impulses of authors, i.e., their desire for unity and sense.

But one wonders: is deconstruction better at "close reading" than traditional literary analysis? Let us consider an example of close reading that Professor Hartman cites in his apology for Professor de Man.

> It is indeed hard to associate the young journalist (aged 21) with the distinguished theorist (aged 47) who wrote so critically, and so effectively, against Husserl's *The Crisis of European Humanity and Philosophy*. De Man accused Husserl of blindly privileging Western civilization ("European supremacy") at the very time (1935) that Europe "was about to destroy itself as center in the name of an unwarranted claim to be the center." But of de Man, too, it can now be said that "as a European it seems that [he] escaped from the necessary self-criticism that is prior to all philosophical truth about the self."

First of all, one might well ask why Professor Hartman bothered to introduce Professor de Man's discussion of this late lecture by the philosopher Edmund Husserl. One reason that springs to mind is that it gives him the opportunity to speak of "blindly privileging Western civilization," a charge that is as common (one might almost say obligatory) among fashionable academics these days as the diction is deplorable. But then how "effective" is Professor de Man's own criticism? It is odd, to say the least, that he should charge Husserl with illegitimately "privileging" Western civilization when the main point of the lecture in question was to criticize the "mistaken rationalism" or "objectivism" that in Husserl's view had precipitated a major crisis in Western values—a crisis that he could see unfolding around him in 1935 with the ascension of Hitler and institution of Nazi ideas throughout German society. (Indeed, Husserl, as a Jew, was just then being ostracized from the academic community at Freiburg where he had taught for many years.)

One notes, too, that in the essay to which Professor Hartman refers, Professor de Man archly remarks that "why this geographical expansion [of philosophical reflection] should have chosen to stop, once and forever, at the Atlantic Ocean and the Caucasus, Husserl does not say." But Husserl does not say for the simple reason that he never suggests that the spirit of scientific rationality that he discusses in "Philosophy and the Crisis of European Man" (as the lecture is usually translated) *is* bounded "once and forever" by the Atlantic Ocean and the Caucasus.

Quite the contrary. Near the beginning of the lecture, he notes that in invoking the spiritual image of Europe he "does not mean Europe geographically, as it appears on maps, as though European man were to be in this way confined to the circle of those who live in this territory. In the spiritual sense it is clear that to Europe belong the English dominions, the United States, etc., but not, however, the Eskimos or Indians of the country fairs, or the Gypsies, who are constantly wandering about Europe. Clearly the title Europe designates the unity of a spiritual life and a creative activity—with all its aims, interests, cares, and troubles."*

It is a small point, to be sure, but it gives one a good indication of the kind of "close reading"—that is, inaccurate

---

* Edmund Husserl, "Philosophy and the Crisis of European Man," in *Phenomenology and the Crisis of Philosophy*, translated by Quentin Lauer (New York: Harper & Row, 1965), page 155.

and tendentious reading—one can expect from our premier deconstructionists.

V The linguistic nature of the predicament

Of course, Professor Hartman did not treat the readers of *The New Republic* to the *longueurs* of deconstruction simply to provide them with another example of the theory at work. His exposition of the putative virtues of deconstruction was part and parcel of his effort at reconstructing Professor de Man in the face of his early journalistic career. "The discovery of these early articles must make a difference in the way we read the later de Man," Professor Hartman admits.

> The new disclosures imbed a biographical fact in our consciousness, a fact that tends to devour all other considerations; it does not spare the later achievement, whose intellectual power we continue to feel. One crucial and hurtful problem is that de Man did not address his past. We do not have his thoughts. Did he avoid confessions . . . and instead work out his totalitarian temptations in a purely intellectual and impersonal manner?

Leaving aside the euphemistic circumlocutions ("imbed a biographical fact in our consciousness," and so on), we may begin by considering the subterfuge contained in Professor Hartman's concluding question—as if the issue were a problem for psychotherapy: "working out" a "totalitarian temptation." More basically, one might ask: how does Professor Hartman handle the troubling fact that his subject never owned up to his past? That in the one semi-official acknowledgement Professor de Man made of his past—a letter he wrote to the Harvard Society of Fellows in 1955 in response to rumors about his wartime activities—he fudged the extent of his association with *Le Soir*, complaining that "I hear now that I am being accused of collaboration. In 1940 and 1941 I wrote some literary articles in the newspaper "le Soir" and, like most of the other contributors, I stopped doing so when nazi [*sic*] thought-control did no longer allow freedom of statement. During the rest of the occupation, I did what was the duty of any decent person."* Not surprisingly, Professor Hartman handles all this by deconstructing it: "It is possible to link the intellectual strength of the later work to what is excluded by it, to what, in surging back, threatens to diminish its authority. . . . But the postwar writing may constitute an avowal of error, a kind of repudiation in its very methodology of a philosophy of reading."

What this jewel of opacity would appear to mean is that the critical power of deconstruction provides Professor de Man with an intellectually sophisticated substitute for any mere straightforward "avowal of error." The implication is that in the intellectual empyrean inhabited by Professors de Man, Hartman, and company, one can dispense with anything so pedestrian as a frank admission of guilt. After all, has not Professor de Man assured us that "excuses generate the very guilt they exonerate"? But what Professor Hartman's peroration really reveals is how the deconstructionist habit of intellectualizing reality results in a deviousness that willingly forsakes the most basic moral distinctions in its pursuit of ever more clever

* *Responses*, page 476.

rhetorical constructs. As Professor Hartman explains it, "Even to say, quite simply, 'I was young, I made a mistake, I've changed my mind' remains blind if it overlooks the narrative shape of this or any confession." "Narrative shape"? Reading Professor Hartman's exegesis, it is easy to forget that we are not talking about Keats's "To Autumn" but a collection of reviews and articles that appeared in pro-Nazi publications. To invoke the "narrative shape" of confession is not to render the issue any clearer or more morally compelling, but merely to insinuate a new element of intellectualized mendacity into the discussion.

And this—the application of ever more sophistical layers of intellectualized mendacity—is what is finally most troubling about Professor Hartman's essay. While he began with Paul de Man's numerous contributions to collaborationist newspapers, by his second or third page Professor Hartman has transformed the entire discussion into a debate about language. "De Man always asks us to look beyond natural experience or its mimesis to a specifically linguistic dilemma. He claims that the relation between meaning and language is not in our subjective control, perhaps not even human." The idea being— what? That since we are to look beyond "natural experience" to a "linguistic dilemma" and since language is reputedly not under our control we are not responsible for the blunders and evil we perpetrate in the realm of "natural experience"? Does it mean that we are henceforth relieved of the obligation to speak and write straightforwardly about such blunders?

In order to get the full flavor of Professor Hartman's style of thought, it is worth quoting a couple of longish bits of his exposition. "There is no compensation for the failure of action in the perfection of art," he writes, musing on the relation between art and action in Professor de Man's later writings.

> The fields of critical philosophy, literary theory, and history have an interlinguistic, not an extralinguistic, correlative; they are secondary in relation to the original, which is itself a previous text. They reveal an essential failure of disarticulation, which was already there in the original. "They kill the original, by discovering that the original was already dead. They read the original from the perspective of pure language [*reine Sprache*], a language that would be entirely freed of the illusion of meaning."

"Interlinguistic," you understand, not "extralinguistic": in other words, in Professor Hartman's view, neither philosophy, nor literary theory, nor even history refers to the real world (i.e., has an "extralinguistic correlative"). How comforting to know that the atrocities we read about are merely literary phenomena, referring not to the sufferings of real people, real "originals," but only to "a previous text"!

Professor Hartman then goes on to tell us that

> This talk of killing the original, and of essential failure, is strong stuff. Knowing today about the writings of the young de Man, it is not possible to evade them as merely a biographical reference point: the early writing *is* an "original" to which the later writing reacts. De Man's method of reading implies that the relation between late and early is interlinguistic only, that the position he had abandoned, one that proved to be a failure and perhaps culpably blind, is not to be used to explain his eventual

method; but the biographical disclosure may hurt de Man's intelligibility. Though his method insists on excluding the biographical ("extralinguistic") reference, I do not believe that we can read him without identifying the "original" in his case as the mediated and compromised idiom of his early, journalistic writings.

> The earlier self is not off the hook, but the emphasis shifts to the way language operates. The later self acknowledges an error, yet it does not attribute it to an earlier self, . . . because that would perpetuate its blindness to the linguistic nature of the predicament.

"The linguistic nature of the predicament"? This is the culmination of Professor Hartman's extraordinary display? What happened to the concern about racisim that was so loudly voiced at the Yale conference we examined, at Stanford, and elsewhere? Is collusion with racist forces acceptable if it is later papered over with a suitably radical veneer of critical obfuscation? Furthermore, what does it mean to describe Professor de Man's "predicament" as "linguistic"? If nothing else, it is to suggest that the historical reality of his involvement with *Le Soir* and the other fascist papers was at bottom a kind of linguistic, not a moral, lapse. And note, too, Professor Hartman's conjecture that "the biographical disclosure may hurt de Man's intelligibility" when what is a stake is not his "intelligibility" (which remains untouched by the disclosure of his early writings) but his character. It is symptomatic of the real blindness of deconstruction—and of the many literary academics who continue to embrace it—that it should fail to have any insight whatsoever into this fundamental distinction. De Man's critic David Lehman summed it up neatly in *Signs of the Times*:

The de Man revelations brought his disciples to the edge
of the abyss that they claim to seek—and they flinched,
retreating to the safety of their illusions. In their briefs for
de Man, they have provided a dossier of proof that deconstruction is not a value-free science but a program that
promotes a reckless disregard of the truth and a propen-
sity for hero-worship.*

How troubling it is, then, that the tenets, methods, and
governing spirit of deconstruction should be expanding
beyond their original home in departments of literature
and making great inroads into other, even the most pragmatic, disciplines. In order to get a sense of just how far
this process of expansion has gone, let us turn next to
consider an important example of how deconstruction
has installed itself in a discipline and trade that—or so
one might have thought—would be constitutionally resistant to such an airy brand of abstract skepticism.

---

* *Signs of the Times*, page 267.

CHAPTER FIVE

Deconstruction Comes to Architecture

1 The disease spreads

The dream has become a kind of nightmare.
—Mark Wigley, *Deconstructivist Architecture*

IN HIS description of what he calls Left Eclecticism, Frederick Crews speaks of "a given painting, novel, or piece of architecture" being susceptible to the "aggressive demystification" that is now passed off as criticism in the academy. Novels and poems, of course, are prime candidates for the demystifying mystifications of deconstructionists, post-structuralists, and the like. And we have seen that even the paintings of Courbet can be scanned, as Professor Crews put it, "for any signs of subversion." But architecture? Surely architecture, that most public and undeniably *material* of the arts, must be exempt from the misty, politicized attacks of academic critical theory?

178

The answer, unfortunately, is no. Even architecture has fallen prey to the opaque and ideologically charged academicization that has triumphed in other fields. No less a spokesman for the academic vanguard than Jacques Derrida has from time to time turned his attention to architecture. In various essays and even collaborations with architects, he has seduced many students and practitioners of the craft with his hermetic word-play and warnings that architecture is the last stronghold of Western metaphysics and logocentrism.* No doubt it had to happen sooner or later. The tenets, attitudes, and techniques of deconstruction have long since metastasized from their home in departments of English and Comparative Literature and have invaded virtually every branch of intellectual and artistic endeavor. Neither the theory nor practice of architecture has proved to be immune. Indeed, the current situation in certain advanced precincts of architectural education provides a splendid example of the way in which Left Eclecticism has spread throughout the humanities, infecting even so stable and straightforward (or so one would have thought) a discipline as architecture.

Now it is obvious to anyone interested in contemporary architecture that the last twenty-five years have been a time of tremendous ferment, energy, and—above all—confusion for the profession. While a handful of star architects continue to bask in glamour and celebrity, there is widespread suspicion that the profession as a whole is in disarray. The carousel of architectural "styles" that one has seen whiz past with dizzying rapidity, the succession

---

* See especially "Point de la folie—maintenant l'architecture," in *Psyche. Inventions de l'autre* (Paris: Galilee, 1987), pages 477–493.

of pretentious, aggressively mediocre buildings that litter our cities' skylines, the plethora of arcane theories advanced to "explain" every conceivable species of architectural practice—all this has left the world of architecture a bit stunned and uncertain where to turn for direction. The confident rise of postmodernism in the Seventies and early Eighties has been succeeded by a period of doubt and reassessment. Not that there is much indication that the paraphernalia of postmodernism are losing popularity. On the contrary, postmodernist grandiosity remains the order of the day among most corporate clients and ambitious homebuilders hoping to make an architectural "statement." But neither architects, nor their clients, nor the public at large seems quite so sure these days that the answer to the failings of modernist architecture is to be found in skyscrapers bedizened with Chippendale tops and pastel façades or in houses decked out with pseudo-Palladian windows and other bits of pretentious historicist ornamentation.

The resulting atmosphere is one of frenetic indecision. Amidst talk of the death of postmodernism and speculation about the next wave of architectural fashion, vanguard spokesmen for the profession seem deeply divided: apologetic and querulous by turns, longing to proselytize yet lacking a compelling vision of the future. The entire radical agenda of Left Eclecticism has promptly established itself in the resulting vacuum. One thinks, for example, of such manifestations as the journal *Zone*, an erratically published collection of neo-Marxist and poststructuralist meditations on architecture and urban design. But more troubling than such radical ephemera is the extent to which many "mainstream" institutions of architectural education have embraced the ethos of Left

Eclecticism. Three events from the late 1980s—a symposium on architectural education at Princeton University, a debate sponsored by the Parsons School of Design in New York City, and The Museum of Modern Art's exhibition of deconstructivist architecture—offered a good sampling of how far this corruption of architectural education has proceeded in elite architectural circles. Taken together with a handful of books published by some of the participants at those events, they may be said to epitomize the increasingly politicized spirit of contemporary architecture.

II The cult of theory: a primer for architects

Let us begin with "Architecture and Education: The Past Twenty-Five Years and Assumptions for the Future," a day-long symposium sponsored by the Princeton School of Architecture in the spring of 1988. Convened to honor Princeton's premier postmodernist architect, Michael Graves, on the occasion of his twenty-fifth year teaching at the university, the symposium drew an enthusiastic audience of several hundred students, faculty, and interested outsiders, who all crowded into Princeton's elegant McCosh Hall to witness the proceedings. One has not heard quite so much about Mr. Graves lately. But the man who brought us The Portland (Oregon) Public Service Building, the Humana building in Louisville, Kentucky, the proposal to expand the Whitney Museum of American Art in New York City, and sundry other delights (an exhibition of drawings and models by Mr. Graves was on view next door to remind us of his contributions to architecture) continues to occupy a secure place in the upper echelons of his profession. And as like is attracted to like, it was not surprising that the symposium's participants included other such luminaries from the academic world as Peter Eisenman, Robert Venturi, Robert A. M. Stern, Alan Colquhoun, and Frank Gehry.

The festivities began with some brief remarks by Robert Maxwell, then dean of the School of Architecture. Looking back over the changes that had taken place in architectural education during the last twenty-five years, he spoke enthusiastically about the stewardship of his predecessor, Robert Geddes, made some obligatory criticisms of modernist architecture, and praised what he called the "semiotic revolution" in architecture—that university-born revolution that encourages us to treat architecture as a kind of "text" to be deciphered and that went hand and hand with the flowering of postmodernism. As Dean Maxwell rightly noted, the application of semiotics to architecture began in the Sixties and was given a tremendous boost by *Learning from Las Vegas*, Robert Venturi's notorious 1972 manifesto glorifying the semantic richness of the urban strip. Venturi "crossed semiotics with communications and produced postmodernism," Dean Maxwell told us with undisguised pride.

Despite this revolution, however, the good dean also assured us that education at Princeton's School of Architecture had not changed nearly so much as had the practice of architecture over the last quarter century. At Princeton, there was still an "unchanging emphasis on history and theory and a continuing search for a dialogue that will give meaning to practice." An "unchanging" emphasis, it should be noted, that nevertheless has brought with it all manner of "semiotic" innovations, including the newest wrinkle in architectural theory, "deconstructivism." This barbarous neologism—which derives from the more familiar barbarism "deconstruction"—denotes a theory and practice of architecture motivated largely by various ideas and catch-phrases appropriated from chic literary theory. One thus sees architects obsessed with language, rejecting traditional aesthetic values like clarity, order, and harmony, and designing buildings that seek to undermine or "deconstruct" such conventional "prejudices" as the desire for comfort, stability, and commodiousness. Hence it turns out that the great thing about the pluralistic ethos that Dean Maxwell extolled at Princeton is that it can embrace a theory that is utterly at odds with everything traditional architectural pedagogy taught and yet somehow, miraculously, remain "unchanged."

Though his remarks were generously laced with the good-humored, self-congratulatory platitudes that academic administrators are expected to emit on such occasions, Dean Maxwell did obliquely touch upon two points that have come to be absolutely central to most contemporary academic thinking about architecture and that were much in evidence at Princeton that day: 1) the contention that modernist architecture was a social and artistic failure that postmodernism has begun to remedy, and 2) the view that architecture is essentially a "narrative" art. One could not be certain that Dean Maxwell appreciated the troubling implications of these ideas, especially the second; one sensed, indeed, that his avuncular, jokey style and what we might call his academic ecumenicism effectively insulate him from having to contemplate the intellectual or artistic consequences of the ideas he routinely bestows his blessing on as dean; but it soon became clear that several of his distinguished colleagues grasped the radical drift of these two ideas with all possible clarity.

Anthony Vidler, for example, who was then teaching history of architecture at Princeton and who made a name for himself in avant-garde architectural circles for his contributions to the chic architecture magazine *Oppositions* (now defunct) in the Seventies, provided us with an astringently academic lecture on the history of architecture and architectural theory in the university. Professor Vidler aimed to show that, once they had been ensconced in the university, the main task of history and theory of architecture was to uncover the "hidden premises" of the profession and to spark students "to interrogate the limits of their own practice." Supported by a *mélange* of quotations from or allusions to writers as various as the architectural historian Colin Rowe, the literary critic Harold Bloom, and the philosophers Charles Sanders Peirce and Michel Foucault, Professor Vidler championed the contemporary role of architectural history in the university because it made students "uncomfortable" and helped them to "think past" the traditional models of architecture (to what?), because it encouraged them to investigate "the politics of discourse" that was entrenched in the profession, and because it led them to question the unfortunate "hegemony" of the reigning educational system. Here again we can see the extent to which fashionable ideas from departments of English and Comparative Literature have seeped into architectural theory: Professor Vidler's talk was hardly more than a tapestry of clichés bemoaning the ideological nature of traditional educational hierarchies and the essentially subversive nature of history and theory.

But while he adhered strictly to the orthodox academic

position that orthodoxy must be questioned and exposed, Professor Vidler's lecture was no match, either in entertainment value or in defiant insouciance, for the contributions of Peter Eisenman, who spoke next and who made it his business to speak often from the floor as the day went on. Now Mr. Eisenman is a curious case. Excepting Philip Johnson and maybe a handful of others, he is as well known and greatly honored as any American architect living. He has taught at Princeton, at Harvard, at Yale, at Cooper Union, and many other institutions; his fame is international: scarcely a panel of American architects is drawn up for a foreign legation in which his name does not figure. And he is one of only seven architects whose work was chosen to appear in Philip Johnson's much publicized and influential exhibition of "Deconstructivist Architecture" at The Museum of Modern Art in the summer of 1988.

But on what does Mr. Eisenman's reputation rest? A founder and for several years the director of the fabled Institute for Architecture and Urban Studies in New York, he was also an editor and guiding force of *Oppositions* for many years, and was consequently in a position to influence the course of intellectual debate about architectural matters. Though recently he seems to have become interested in building again, his roster of built works is quite small. A few houses in the Sixties and Seventies, a fire station, and more recently, a biology center for the University of Frankfurt, a visual arts center for Ohio State University in Columbus, and a convention center, also in Columbus. Even now, not a great deal more. But Mr. Eisenman has something else that has catapulted him into the forefront of architectural celebrity: he is a tireless theorist, and in his use of modish theory he is adamantly, famously, extravagantly obscure. Indeed, judging from the respectful laughter of his audience at Princeton, his audience, expecting him to be unintelligible, want him to be *outrageously* unintelligible—the idea being that if he is going to be obscure he may as well be amusingly so.

And Mr. Eisenman can be quite amusing. There is something of the intellectual *agent provocateur* about him: he delights in stirring up controversy and strife. Accordingly, he began his *ex tempore* remarks with a couple of anecdotes whose main intent would seem to have been to insult his colleagues. The first was mildly obscene and not worth repeating; but the second had a peculiar pertinence to the proceedings at hand and deserves to be recounted. When visiting the zoo in Cambridge, England, Mr. Eisenman told us, he especially liked to see the tea party that the zoo's monkeys staged on Friday afternoons. Dressed up in the appropriate clothes, some would be coaxed to play maid and go through the motions of serving, while others would sit around as master and mistress. There they were, play-acting, chattering away to themselves, Mr. Eisenman observed, "but they never knew what they were saying." This might, he suggested, have some relevance to what was going on that day at Princeton.

He was right. The uncanny aptness of Mr. Eisenman's anecdote was brought home again and again as the day wore on, not least during the course of his own presentation. Beginning with the charge that "we are all nostalgics" and that the symposium itself was an event of "enormous nostalgia"—"nostalgia," remember, is a prime vice in the opinion of the academy these days—he castigated postmodernism's reactionary penchant for adopting historicist ornamentation. He then went on to predict that the generation of students from 1975 to 1985

would usher in a new era of architectural practice, a
"theoretical practice energized by an idea of history." The
rise of such a practice could afford us the first opportunity to articulate a "theory"—as distinct from a mere
history—of modernism, Mr. Eisenman told us. This new
theory of modernism would not traffic in any nostalgia
for the avant garde but, on the contrary, would be

> a theory of the center, that is, a theory which occupies the
> center. I believe only when such a theory of the center is
> articulated will architecture be able to transform itself as
> it always has and as it always will. . . . But the center that
> I am talking about is not a center that can be the center
> that we know is in the past, as a nostalgia for center.
> Rather, this not new but other center will be . . . an inter-
> stitial one—but one with no structure, but one also that
> embraces as periphery in its own centric position. . . . A
> center no longer sustained by nostalgia and no longer
> sustained by univocal discourse.

Of course, Mr. Eisenman was speaking extem-
poraneously; and it's possible that my tape recorder did
not catch every last word; but there is no denying that
this is an expostulation of formidable elusiveness. Nor is
Mr. Eisenman's more considered prose always more intelligible. His opaque verbal shenanigans—what the critic
Charles Jencks has aptly called his "rhetoric machine"—
are in top form in the essay he contributed to *Houses of
Cards*,* for example, a recent book on his architecture

---

* Peter Eisenman, *Houses of Cards*, with essays by Rosalind Krauss,
Peter Eisenman, and Manfredo Tafuri (New York: Oxford University Press, 1988).

that also includes essays by those other masters of impenetrability, Manfredo Tafuri, a Marxist architecture critic, and Rosalind Krauss, the art critic and editor of *October*. In *Houses of Cards*, Mr. Eisenman presents the six houses he designed (of which only four have been built) in the Sixties and Seventies more or less as demonstration pieces to illustrate his theories about narrative architecture and unsettling the traditional meaning of "home." Appropriately, the houses are not named after their owner or location but are bluntly titled House I, House II, and so on. The book gives a good sense of Mr. Eisenman's style of thought, and it is worth taking a detour to consider some of its more memorable highlights.

Noting that the book was assembled from fragments, Mr. Eisenman correctly observes in his preface that "it promises and prohibits access; it directs and meanders." In the three essays collected here, he writes, "as in the house, the ideas transform and decompose. In fact, I ask that the reader augment a traditional reading of this book by also treating the texts and the book as a whole as objects, and by reading the houses, individually and in ensemble, as texts." Presumably to help the reader augment a "traditional reading" of the book, Mr. Eisenman has included numerous sketches, drawings, and photographs of the houses, as well as photographically reproduced copies of some of his rough notes about the houses—ostentatiously crumpled, torn, and patched-together notes, full of emendations and crossings-out. I suppose we are meant to regard these salvaged scraps (if indeed they *are* salvaged scraps and not carefully manufactured mementos) as the leavings of genius. They do contribute to one's regarding the book as an "object" rather than a text, but they do nothing to deepen one's appreciation of the architecture they are meant to comment on. From the bits on "House IV," for example, we learn that

> this work is an attempt to transcend our traditional view of
> designing
> seeing
> understanding
>
> our environment
>
> it is an attempt to alienate the individual from the known way in which he perceives and understand his environment.*

But the notes are nothing compared to Mr. Eisenman's essay. Grandly informing us that "the essence of the act of architecture is the dislocation of an ever-reconstituting metaphysic of architecture," Mr. Eisenman tells us that the six houses that form the subject of his book are all "governed by the intent to define the act of architecture as the dislocation of consequent reconstitution of an ever-accruing metaphysic of architecture." What, you ask, is "an ever-accruing metaphysic of architecture"? Mr. Eisenman never says, but it is clear that he has a special liking for the word "metaphysic." In addition to the "metaphysic of architecture" that he is fond of invoking, we also encounter the "metaphysic of the center," the "metaphysic of the house," even the "metaphysic of dining."†

Concerning the last, for example, we learn that Houses

* *Ibid.*, page 150.
† *Ibid., seriatim*, pages 167, 169, 174, 181.

III and IV explore "an alternative process of making oc-
cupiable form, . . . a process specifically developed to
operate as freely as possible from functional considerations. From a traditional point of view, several columns
'intrude on' and 'disrupt' the living and dining areas as a
result of this process. . . . Nonetheless, these dislocations
. . . have, according to the occupants of the house,
changed the dining experience in a real and, more impor-
tantly, unpredictable fashion." Please note that Mr.
Eisenman does not assert that the occupants claim that
his ill-placed columns have done anything to make "the
dining experience" more *pleasant*. Nor would he want
them to. For one of the main goals of Mr. Eisenman's architecture (and his writing, too, one suspects) is to subvert anything so bourgeois as comfort or intelligibility. As
he puts it, his houses "attempt to have little to do with
the traditional and existing metaphysic of the house, the
physical and psychological gratification associated with
the traditional form of the house, . . . in order to initiate a
search for those possibilities of dwelling that may have
been repressed by that metaphysic."*

In fact, if Mr. Eisenman can be said to have a thesis, it
is the standard academic chestnut that the threat of
modern technology, and especially of nuclear weapons,
has rendered the traditional notion of the home—more,
the traditional notion of man—otiose. "With the scien-
tifically orchestrated horror of Hiroshima and the consciousness of the human brutality of the Holocaust," Mr.
Eisenman gravely intones, "it became impossible for man
to sustain a relationship with any of the dominant cos-
mologies of the past; he could no longer derive his iden-

* *Ibid., seriatim,* pages 169, 172.

tity from a belief in a heroic purpose and future. . . . Man now lives in an *in extremis* condition." The most wonderful thing about this apocalyptic vision (which is much in evidence in architectural theory these days) is that it licenses the most extraordinary claims. For if man now really lives *in extremis*, then of course everything can be questioned, everything overturned, with impunity, not least the traditional "anthropocentric" function of architecture. Here, in one of his clearer passages, is Mr. Eisenman on the notion that one important function of architecture is to provide shelter:

> But as shelter also exists in the mind as an idea, in its metaphysical state architecture is a conceptual reflection on physical presence, an "absence" in a material sense. From this perspective, what was earlier described as a traditional architectural history founded on dominant vectors of truth can also be seen as an ideological effort to screen architecture's intrinsic absence behind an emphasis on its physic [*sic*]. It could be said that this screening is a sign of the endurance of anthropocentrism's privileging of presence and centeredness, even beyond its own crisis.*

If the issue is architecture considered as a "physic," I suppose one could admit that there is something emetic about this passage. But what, finally, is Mr. Eisenman getting at here? Forget about the deconstructivist curlicues and *non sequiturs*—the prattle about the "metaphysical state of architecture," the illogical suggestion that "a conceptual reflection on physical presence" is somehow the same as "an 'absence' in a material sense":

---

* *Ibid., seriatim*, pages 170, 172, 182.

191

all that is simply part of the verbal static that automatically crackles through his speech and writing. And don't be put off by the formidable talk of "dominant vectors of truth" or "privileging of presence and centeredness." It's nonsense, but I'm quite sure that Mr. Eisenman can't help writing it: his prose has always been like this, laden with half-digested ideas and jargon culled from whatever abstruse academic theories happen to be making the rounds. Perhaps it has something to do with those monkeys he studied in Cambridge. But do consider the final sentence, the one suggesting that traditional architectural history is faulty because it blindly indulges in various "anthropocentric" habits. At bottom, it is nothing more than a simple-minded inversion of every tried and true tenet about the function of architecture, an inversion that is finally as ridiculous as it is initially shocking. Immersed in Mr. Eisenman's chatter, it is sometimes easy to forget that architecture is essentially about building habitable buildings, buildings that we live and work in, play and worship in, not that we struggle to decode. There is a great deal more that one could say about Mr. Eisenman's essay. Perhaps most amusing is his admission, near the end of the piece, that his houses were not as radical as he had hoped because they turned out to be "grounded in the very anthropocentric metaphysic that they were intended to contravene."* Too bad! Though in truth I have confidence that Mr. Eisenman's current love affair with the nihilistic presuppositions of deconstruction will prove to be a great aid in expunging anything resembling an "anthropocentric metaphysic" from his architecture and his theorizing.

* *Ibid.*, page 181.

III The dean speaks up

If few of the speakers at Princeton were as radical as Mr. Eisenman, none were as dazzlingly obscurantist. In fact, after Mr. Eisenman's brief presentation, the proceedings were often downright dull until nearly the end of the day. Robert Venturi was perhaps the most disappointing. One naturally expected something engaging from the author of *Complexity and Contradiction in Architecture* (1966), that self-described "gentle manifesto" that has often been credited with inaugurating the turn to postmodernist architecture. But in the event, he did little more than offer a few reminiscences on the deplorable state of architectural education in the 1940s, when the modernism of Gropius was regnant, and laud Princeton for its consistently "non-doctrinaire" approach to education.

Mr. Venturi's presentation was succeeded by a round-table discussion moderated by the art historian Irving Lavin. Rather like Dean Maxwell, Professor Lavin turned out to be one of those liberal academics who treat every new intellectual fashion as an expression of the beneficent spirit of pluralism. Accordingly, and again rather like Dean Maxwell, Professor Lavin appeared to be in favor of everything and against nothing—except, of course, any position that presumed to question the cogency or desirability of those new intellectual fashions, for such questioning betrayed a lamentable lack of the pluralistic spirit. Thus he admitted that the architecture critic Ada Louise Huxtable fell from grace in his eyes when she dared to criticize postmodernism. In Professor Lavin's view, postmodernism is an attempt to reconstruct "the ancient legacy of culture"—a bizarre thought, it is true, since postmodernism is no more concerned with the "ancient legacy of culture" than is *Vogue* magazine. But it was no more bizarre than his later suggestion that one of the truly nifty things about deconstruction was that it might provide a "common ground" between modernism and postmodernism or that it had something to do with "man's eternal search for a noble ideal of harmony, balance, and perfection, or to his equally eternal struggle with irrationality, instability, and chaos." In other words, for Professor Lavin, deconstruction was hardly to be distinguished from classical humanism.

Dean Maxwell moderated a concluding discussion. He began by professing his pluralistic credentials: "I disagree with everybody who has a final answer," he assured us, "and I agree with everybody . . . who believes that constant change is the order of the day." But Mr. Eisenman was having none of this wishy-washy, Heraclitean liberalism. He rose from his place in the audience to expound a bit about deconstruction, the end of Western metaphysics, and to announce that "We are all a bunch of old fogeys holding on to a teetering system." "The only truth today is that we are found with the loss of truth," he told us darkly, as if such second-hand Nietzschean sentiments were a startling revelation.

Despite Mr. Eisenman's plea that we study things "not as truth but as some sort of knowledge that can be opened up and studied," Mr. Colquhoun's insistence that "education is always a matter of inculcating a certain ideology," and so on, it was often easy to forget that this symposium was supposed to deal with the subject of architectural education. It was with considerable interest, then, that one heard a woman from the audience ask the distinguished members of the panel to compare the requirements for architectural education today with the requirements for a degree in engineering, music, and mathematics. It was an unusually intelligent question. A full answer would have had to say something about those aspects of architecture that are akin to art and craft as well as those that are straightforwardly matters of calculation and engineering. A full answer, indeed, would have said a good deal about the hybrid nature of architecture, its functional *and* its aesthetic claims, its sometimes uneasy place between engineering and art. But the question was not deemed serious by Messrs. Maxwell and company. After a brief embarrassed silence, there were a few half-hearted attempts to dismiss the question with ridicule or patronizing obfuscation. Perhaps this means that Dean Maxwell disagrees not only with "everybody who has a final answer," but even those who ask questions that might admit of such answers. It's a wonderful philosophy for an academic dean.

IV   Building castles in the air

Many of the themes that were bandied about at Princeton that day were also on display at a debate on the subject of "Post-modernist Classicism versus Narrative and Deconstruction in Architecture" which was sponsored by the graduate program in architecture and design criticism at the Parsons School of Design in New York City in the winter of 1988. Moderated by Douglas Davis, then an architectural critic for *Newsweek*, the debate was between the architect and architectural critic Charles Jencks and James Wines, an architect and then director of the graduate program in architecture and design criticism at Parsons. Mr. Jencks is best known for his tireless proselytizing on behalf of postmodernism; it was he, in fact, who gave the term currency in the first edition of his book *The Language of Post-Modern Architecture.* Mr. Wines—who first made his reputation as a sculptor in the Sixties—is the founder of SITE, an "architectural and environmental art group" formed in 1970 "for the purpose of exploring new ways to bring a heightened level of communication and psychological content to buildings, interiors, and public spaces."* Although his star has somewhat dimmed, he was for a moment regarded as one of the leading practitioners of deconstructivist architecture or (as he prefers to denominate it) "De-architecture."

Mr. Jencks spoke first and presented himself as the champion of "postmodern classicism," a phenomenon that he describes as the third stage of postmodernism. The first stage of postmodernism, according to his scheme, occurred in the 1960s and was essentially a reaction against the strictures of modernism; the second stage, which the 1970s ushered in, was a period of "pluralism and eclecticism." Now, according to Mr. Jencks, mature postmodernism in painting and sculpture but especially in architecture "has adopted a classical language." In vocabulary somewhat reminiscent of Peter Eisenman (though it's likely that the influence went the other way), Mr. Jencks described the modern secular world as shot through with a "nostalgia for the center." In his view—and here he takes a very different position from Mr. Eisenman—architecture should seek to recover the center for a de-centered world. His prescription for this task is the frankly symbolic architecture of postmodern classicism.

* James Wines, *De-architecture* (New York: Rizzoli, 1988), *seriatim,* pages 108, 110.

This is not to say that postmodern classicism recovers any *actual* center, any binding social, religious, or philosophical order. Rather, in a fashion reminiscent of Hesse's Glass Bead Game, it merely *plays* with the classical symbols of past systems in order to recapture the *aura* or illusion of belonging to a greater whole. Mr. Jencks enumerated various characteristics of postmodern classicism—its supposition that "disharmony is harmony," for example, or the large role that wit and humor play in its concoctions—but his main point, a point that is illustrated in lavish detail in his book on the subject,* was that the deliberately historicizing symbolism employed by postmodern classicism can provide a quasi-spiritual answer to secular man's real spiritual longings for order and meaning. While he distinguishes postmodern classicism from the "decorated sheds" of Robert Venturi—the symbolic ornamentation he has in mind is not just "stuck on" as it is in Venturi's buildings, he tells us—at bottom they amount to two versions of the same thing. Both advocate arbitrarily applied ornamentation, but for Mr. Jencks the arbitrariness is half-concealed under the cloak of an elaborate symbol system and edifying rhetoric.

Mr. Wines began his presentation by noting that he and Mr. Jencks share a concern with the "communicative or public nature of architecture," but that they differed on the "sources" of communication. In many respects, Mr. Wines's position is substantively closer to Mr. Eisenman's than to Mr. Jencks's. Though not nearly as adept at manipulating language to provide camouflage as is Mr.

---

* Charles Jencks, *Towards a Symbolic Architecture: The Thematic House*, with photographs by Richard Bryant (New York: Rizzoli, 1988).

Eisenman, he nevertheless shares many of his basic suppositions about the situation of architecture in the contemporary world. For example, he concurs with Mr.
Eisenman that postmodernism's return to classical
iconography is reactionary and to be avoided, and he indulges in a similar pre-packaged apocalyptic vision: "We
now live in a time of universal melancholy and troubled
dreams, a time of introspection and foreboding choices,"
he writes in his book and credo, *De-architecture*. For Mr.
Wines, too, it would seem that the chief task of architecture today is to dislocate and discommode. As he explains
in his book, "De-architecture is a way of dissecting, shat-
tering, dissolving, inverting, and transforming certain
fixed prejudices about buildings, in the interests of dis-
covering revelations among the fragments."* And both
Messrs. Wines and Eisenman—like so many other architects and critics these days—pretend that *asserting*
something about the aim or meaning of a building is tantamount to *accomplishing* it. But in art, as in life, there is
often a great gap between between assertion and accomplishment. A poorly designed dining room may be
intended to challenge the conventional "metaphysic of
dining" or whatever, but it is really only a poorly
designed dining room; a dilapidated-looking building is
perhaps supposed to challenge our consumeristic
"prejudices," but it is really just another ugly building.

Yet Mr. Wines differs from Mr. Eisenman in his continued adherence to the idea of architecture as an art.
"De-architecture's basic premise," he writes, "is that art,
not design, is the supreme mission of a building, and that
the creative process must be revised to reflect this objec-

---

* *De-architecture, seriatim,* pages 165, 133.

tive."* In fact, looking through his book and considering the work of SITE, it soon becomes clear that, although Mr. Wines has given up the title of sculptor, his ambition has remained essentially sculptural: SITE's installations are basically large environmental sculptures, some of which happen to be more or less habitable.

Probably SITE's best-known architectural works are still the eight showrooms designed for Best Products Company. Under the patronage of Sydney and Frances Lewis, prominent collectors of contemporary art and owners of Best Products, SITE has designed façades incorporating the principles of de-architecture. The "Indeterminate Façade" (1975) showroom in Houston, for example, "appears to be arrested somewhere between construction and demolition" with its pile of brick punched from the top of the building and cascading down onto the entrance canopy. A more radical, and as yet unbuilt, project is the "Highrise of Homes." In Mr. Wines's words, this "visionary and traditional" idea provides "a matrix of housing choices" for city dwellers.† Consisting of a large U-shaped steel and concrete grid eight to fifteen stories tall, the "Highrise of Homes" is meant to provide modules in which individuals could build single family houses in the style of their choice—modern, colonial, Tudor, Greek revival, you name it. The houses on each level, clustered into "villagelike compounds," would have access to a central elevator and core mechanical services. "The Highrise of Homes," Mr. Wines writes, "is based on the premise that people will benefit from the personal affirmation and territorial definition associated with the

---

* *Ibid.*, page 118.

† *Ibid.*, *seriatim*, pages 145, 163.

detached house, even if it is in the compressed environment of a multistory building." In reality, of course, the "Highrise of Homes" would be a grotesque architectural nightmare, as patronizing to its intended clients as it is stylistically meretricious.

There is a great deal more that one might say about Mr. Wines's theories and the work of SITE, but here I will pause only to consider his contention that "rarely have contemporary buildings come close to the kind of sociological and psychological content expressed in, say, a Beckett play, a Magritte painting, or a Chaplin film."* What do Mr. Wines's examples tell us about his conception of architecture? Is the sort of "sociological and psychological content" to which he alludes something we would wish to find embodied in our buildings? Think of it: an office building that reminded one of *Waiting for Godot* or *Endgame*, a home as unsettling as a Magritte painting, a factory as zany as a film by Charlie Chaplin. Does it sound like a wonderful idea? Note that Mr. Wines suggests that this paucity of "sociological and psychological content" is a particular problem for contemporary buildings. Are we then to assume that older buildings possess a greater measure of such "content"? Chartres Cathedral is one of Mr. Wines's favorite architectural monuments from the past; he discusses it at length as an model of "narrative" architecture. Does Chartres, then, "come close to the kind of sociological and psychological content expressed in, say, a Beckett play, a Magritte painting, or a Chaplin film"?

In the end, Mr. Wines emerges as a kind of anemic, half-hearted imitation of someone like Mr. Eisenman; he

---

* *Ibid.*, page 14.

mimics a good deal of radical rhetoric, but his emphasis on communication binds him to a rather traditional humanistic sentiment; and although SITE's projects are among the most arrogant and high-handed I have seen, they do not really express the kind of fundamental challenge to traditional architectural practice that Mr. Eisenman, for example, advocates.

Quite different is the position preached by Mr. Jencks. For where Messrs. Wines and Eisenman are nihilists in the apocalyptic mode, Mr. Jencks is a happy nihilist. Like his colleagues—at least, like Mr. Eisenman—he assumes that the modern secular world has lost any compelling foundation for shared social meaning; but unlike them, he has no scruples about fabricating a false foundation out of promiscuous fragments gathered from the past. Mr. Jencks's basic message seems to be: if we cannot overcome the modern world, at least we can forget it.

The saccharine, archaizing spirit at work in Mr. Jencks's latest version of postmodernism is on full view in his book, *Towards a Symbolic Architecture: The Thematic House.* Beginning with a chapter called "Fables for Our Time," Mr. Jencks advocates "the conscious reassertion of the symbolic programme, the idea that every client and architect should make up an iconographic contract as explicit as their economic one," as "first steps in a new tradition, or perhaps the revival of an old one."* Not surprisingly, words like "fable" and "parable" are prominently featured in his exposition, and he sprinkles his text with lots of fake Latin names, capitalized abstract nouns, and deliberately archaic drawings with legends like "meaning triumphs over time."

---

* *Towards a Symbolic Architecture*, page 9.

After some general considerations about the troubled place of architecture in a secular world, Mr. Jencks reviews three of his own architectural projects, including one that incorporates the texts of Milton's poems *L'Allegro* and *Il Penseroso* as mood-setters and thematic pointers for a house and garden in California. ("Hence loathed Melancholy," indeed!) But the bulk of the book is devoted to an examination of "The Thematic House," Mr. Jencks's extraordinary renovation of an 1840s London townhouse for himself and his family. Beginning with the front door, which sports cleverly stylized initials of each of the family members, the whole house is an elaborate confection of symbolic motifs. The main downstairs rooms are each associated with one or another of the seasons and are decorated accordingly: spring, summer, Indian summer, autumn, and winter; "Winter" boasts a fireplace designed by Michael Graves. Inside the front door, there is a mirrored room that Jencks dubs the Cosmic Oval, in which the two main themes of the house—cosmic time and cultural time—are given preliminary expression in a mural showing, in Mr. Jencks's words, the "evolution of the galaxies after the Big Bang." There is also a portrait frieze painted by William Stok depicting a dozen cultural "paragons," including the Emperor Hadrian, and Thomas Jefferson conversing with . . . Hannah Arendt. (Really, Mr. Jencks can be powerfully, if unintentionally, funny.) In the bathroom on the ground floor—"the Cosmic Loo," in Jencks's terminology—we have a complicated paint scheme with "light greys below, bright multi-colors in the middle and infinite cosmic gloom above, as in Westminster Cathedral."*

---

* *Ibid.*, page 90.

Then there is the central staircase, the Solar Stair, whose spiral is meant to recall "spiral galaxies, DNA, cyclical motion," according to Mr. Jencks. It is also an abstract representation of the solar year: cast in concrete, its fifty-two steps, each of which is inscribed with seven grooves, make a grand total of three hundred and sixty-five "days." *The Black Hole*, a mosaic by Eduardo Paolozzi at the bottom of the stairs, is meant to symbolize cosmic gloom or something, and on and on it goes, every room in the house weighted down with its load of symbols and inscriptions.

As Mr. Jencks himself has pointed out, there has always been a large element of Camp in postmodernist architecture; but with his "Thematic House" and theory of symbolic architecture, Mr. Jencks has gone beyond Camp and pushed postmodernism firmly in the direction of kitsch. The difference is that where the Camp sensibility retains sufficient self-consciousness to play with the sentimentalized products of bad taste, the kitsch sensibility *surrenders* to them and to the sentimentalized version of reality they promise. Hitherto, postmodernist architecture was funny on purpose; with his "Thematic House," Mr. Jencks is only unintentionally so. Though Mr. Jencks occasionally warns the reader about the dangers of aestheticism in the course of his book, his entire presentation is little more than a recipe for an exquisitely aestheticized—and exquisitely expensive—brand of kitsch.

V Philip Johnson's revenge

Between the ironic skepticism of Mr. Eisenman and the cloying sentimentalizations of Mr. Jencks there is not much to choose. It is difficult to say which impulse will assume dominance in architecture. Since sentimentality exercises a seemingly inextinguishable appeal, one might think of betting on Mr. Jencks. But as has often been pointed out, ours is an ironic age, and the appeal of the radical skepticism preached by Mr. Eisenman and others should not be underestimated. The Museum of Modern Art, at any rate, would seem to be backing the latter movement. Its exhibition of "Deconstructivist Architecture" included projects by Messrs. Eisenman, Gehry, and five other architects whose work self-consciously explores architectural disharmony and fragmentariness. Hailed as the successor to Mr. Johnson's path-breaking exhibition of modernist architecture in 1932—long before Mr. Johnson had given up modernism to become the chief impresario of postmodernist chic—it was easily the most talked about architectural event of 1988.

"Deconstructivist Architecture" featured ten recent projects by seven architects. Some of the projects have been built; some are still under construction; some are . . . well, let's call them unbuilt if not unbuildable speculative exercises. Two of the architects included in the exhibition—Peter Eisenman and Frank Gehry—are senior practitioners with international reputations; the other five—Rem Koolhaas from Holland, Zaha M. Hadid from Iraq, Daniel Libeskind from Poland, Bernard Tschumi from Switzerland (now the dean of the Columbia School of Architecture), and the firm of Coop Himmelblau from Vienna—are younger practitioners whose stars are rising.

What brings these very different architects together is not any shared "style" or beliefs about the tasks of architecture. One would be hard pressed, for example, to find instances of contemporary architecture more disparate in style, character, and intention than Frank Gehry's renovation of a suburban house in Santa Monica (completed in three stages, from 1978 to 1988) and the massive highrise apartment-cum-community center and observation tower built by Rem Koolhaas in Rotterdam in 1982. No, "Deconstructivism" is not in this sense a "school" or movement so much as an *attitude*. As Philip Johnson acknowledged in the brief preface he contributed to the catalogue, deconstructivist architecture, lacking the encompassing vision and "messianic fervor" of modernism, "is not a new style." And far from suggesting the rise of a new school of architecture, he writes, the exhibition was simply an attempt to bring together the recent work of a few important architects "that shows a similar approach with very similar forms as an outcome."[*]

The forms in question are said to derive mostly from the art and architecture of Russian Constructivism and Suprematism that flourished in the late 'Teens and early Twenties, notably the abstract paintings of Kasimir Malevich and the sculpture and architecture of Vladimir Tatlin, Aleksandr Rodchenko, and others. As it happens, the connection between Constructivism and the works on view in the exhibition was sometimes quite tenuous.

---

[*] Philip Johnson and Mark Wigley, *Deconstructivist Architecture* (New York: The Museum of Modern Art, 1988), page 7. The reader may also wish to consult *Deconstruction in Architecture*, a special issue of *Architectural Design*, Volume 58, 3/4, 1988, and Christopher Norris and Andrew Benjamin, *What Is Deconstruction?* (New York: St. Martin's Press, 1988). For a critical look at the movmement, see John Silber *Architecture of the Absurd: How "Genius" Disfigured a Practical Art* (New York: Quantuck Lane, 2007).

Generally, it depended on nothing more than fortuitous formal similarities—where, indeed, there was even *that* connection. Nevertheless, a great deal has been made of the influence of the Russian avant garde on the distinctive forms and aesthetic goals of deconstructivism; we saw this already in our examination of the *October* syndrome and it reappeared here, both in the exhibition itself (which attempted to reinforce the connection by beginning with a smorgasbord of Constructivist paintings and sculpture drawn from the museum's collections) and in the catalogue essay.

Yet even more revealing than this alleged precursor is Johnson's observation about the difference between the spirit of modernism and the spirit of deconstructivism. "The contrast is," he writes, appropriating a striking phrase from a younger colleague, "between perfection and violated perfection." Please note the choice of words: the "perfection" he has in mind is not "missed" or "unattained" or "half-realized" but *violated*. The lurid overtones of violence and corruption are intentional; they are, in fact, central to the ethos of deconstructive architecture.

This becomes painfully clear when we turn to the catalogue essay and commentaries on individual projects, which were written by Mark Wigley, associate curator of the exhibition. "Disturb," "torture," "interrogate," "contaminate," "infect": these are the words he favors to explain and to *praise* deconstructivist architecture. In the projects on view in this exhibition, he tells us proudly, the "dream of pure form has been disturbed. Form has become contaminated. The dream has become a kind of nightmare."*

* *Deconstructivist Architecture, passim.*

206

What makes these projects "deconstructive," according to Mr. Wigley, is their ability "to disturb our thinking about form," in particular, their ability to "disturb" or undermine our taken-for-granted suppositions about the values of traditional architectural order and unity. "Architecture is a conservative discipline," he notes sadly near the beginning of his essay: stability, regularity, order, intelligibility, commodiousness—these are prime virtues for traditional architecture. "Deconstructivism" changes all that by the simple expedient of disparaging traditional architectural values and championing their opposites. Nor should we think that critics have a monopoly on the deconstructivist gambit. We have already considered some samples of Mr. Eisenman's meditations on architecture. Here, for example, is Bernard Tschumi, dean of the School of Architecture at Columbia University:

> It might be worthwhile . . . to abandon any notion of post-modern architecture in favor of a post-humanist architecture, one that would stress not only the dispersion of the subject and the force of social regulation, but also the effect of such decentering on the entire notion of a unified, coherent architectural form.*

Isn't it wonderful that a dean of a major school of architecture should be championing a "post-humanist," "decentering" view of architecture that dispenses with the notion of coherent architectural form?

Mr. Wigley denies that deconstructive architecture derives from "the mode of contemporary philosophy known as 'deconstruction,'" but this is obviously disin-

* Quoted in *What Is Deconstruction?*, page 40.

genuous. His own arguments, and those of most of the architects he discusses, are nothing but a congeries of deconstructionist clichés, beginning with the familiar contentions that everything is a kind of text to be deciphered and proceeding to talk of "decentering the center" and breaking down coherent architectural form.

Then, too, the rhetorical *style* of Mr. Wigley's presentation closely mimics the provocative antics of literary deconstruction. "It is," he muses, "as if some kind of parasite has infected the form and distorted it from inside." Hence the projects on view are said to "reopen the wound" that Russian Constructivism had inflicted on the tradition but that had healed during the reign of modernism. We also learn that "perfection is secretly monstrous. Tortured from within, the seemingly perfect form confesses its crime, its imperfection." In one particularly bizarre passage, Mr. Wigley combines this talk of torture and interrogation with psychoanalysis to produce images that border on the surreal: "The deconstructivist puts the pure forms of the architectural tradition on the couch and identifies the symptoms of a repressed impurity. The impurity is drawn to the surface by a combination of gentle coaxing and violent torture: the form is interrogated."* And on and on. To read Mr. Wigley, one would think that architecture was primarily a form of pathology.

The basic idea behind this overcharged verbiage is that deconstructivist architecture undermines modernist architectural theory and practice, and does so not by offering an alternative but by exaggerating and making overt certain tensions that are said to lurk unrecognized in

* *Deconstructivist Architecture*, pages 10–20, *passim*.

modernism. It is in this sense that it can be said to "violate" perfection, subverting it by exposing its inherent (albeit unacknowledged) "corruption" and "contamination," locating "the inherent dilemmas within buildings." Writing about The Peak, Zaha Hadid's 1982 Hong Kong resort, for example, Mr. Wigley says that "the club is stretched between the emptiness of the void and the density of the underground solids, domains normally excluded from modern architecture but found within it by pushing modernism to its limits, forcing it apart. In this way, the pleasure palace, the hedonist resort, is located in the twisted center of modern purity."*

Of course, what deconstructive architecture offers is not so much a critique as a caricature of modernism. For one thing, while it is certainly true that a good deal of modernist architecture strove for an abstract formal perfection, its emphasis on form was anchored by its concern with function. Form, as the slogan goes, was intended to follow function. Moreover, as Wigley notes, what is really at issue are not modernism's pretensions to formal perfection but its support of established culture. "What is being disturbed [by deconstructivist architecture]," he writes, "is a set of deeply entrenched cultural assumptions which underlie a certain view of architecture, assumptions about order, harmony, stability, and unity." That is to say, what is is being "disturbed" is a commitment to the established conventions of Western society and culture, including an allegiance to values like order, harmony, stability, and unity. And this brings us to the deeper—or we should say, the "repressed"?—reason that so much is made of the Russian avant garde by Johnson,

* *Ibid.*, page 68.

Wigley, and company. As we saw in our discussion of the *October* syndrome, the Russian avant garde offers one of the most dramatic instances of the conflation of art and radical politics in recent history, an instance that commends itself as a model for the revolutionary, subversive rhetoric of deconstructive architecture.*

But is it anything more than rhetoric? Discussing Daniel Libeskind's 1987 City Edge project in Berlin, Wigley asserts that by being angled up off the ground, the structure—a mammoth elevated bar—"subverts the logic of the wall." "By dismembering the wall," he continues, "traditional thinking about structure is also broken down."† Something there is, clearly, that doesn't love a wall, and it's name is deconstruction. It is worth pausing to consider these wholly typical statements from Mr. Wigley. In what sense is traditional thinking about structure "broken down" by the eccentricities of this project? How is the "logic of the wall" "subverted"? (What indeed is the "logic" of a wall?) Is such talk anything more than sophistic blather? Mr. Wigley, like so many of his decontructionist confrères, pretends that simply *asserting* something makes it so: as if a couple of quirky, asymmetrical buildings and a dose of obscure theorizing really undermined anything except the credibility of their proponents. In *The Critique of Judgment*, Kant rightly observed that "the main concern" of architecture is "a certain *use* of the artistic object."‡ For deconstructivism

* *Ibid.*, pages 19–20.

† *Ibid.*, page 34.

‡ Immanuel Kant, *Critique of Judgment*, translated with an introduction by Werner S. Pluhar (Indianapolis: Hackett, 1987), page 191.

the main concern of architecture would seem to be to provide an occasion for rhetorical excess.

We thus come to one of the great ironies of deconstructivist theory: although it makes a tremendous show of exposing the obsession with purity and perfection that were ingredients in some forms of modernism, it is itself an architecture that happens mostly in the head, not on the ground. In this respect, too, it resembles deconstructionist literary theory, which in its flights of theory loses sight of anything so mundane as the meaning or quality of the text it is supposedly examining. Similarly, deconstructivist architecture presupposes an exceedingly intellectualized view of architecture—and of the world—and it is precisely such airy intellectualizing that licenses its more outlandish claims. Untethered to anything so pedestrian as everyday experience, the champions of deconstructive architecture can pretend that architecture is really about "interrogating form," subverting "the logic of the wall," etc., not about building appropriate, serviceable, perhaps even beautiful buildings.

This inveterate intellectualism also helps explain deconstructivism's blindness to its own banality. Mr. Wigley writes that deconstructivist architecture "produces a feeling of unease, of disquiet, because it challenges the sense of stable, coherent identity that we associate with pure form." He presents this as if it were some stunningly novel discovery. But the only thing novel about it is the idea that producing the feeling of unease and disquiet should be the aim of architecture. In Geoffrey Scott's classic monograph *The Architecture of Humanism* (1914), for example, the possibility that there might be buildings that "suggest the idea of instability, the idea of collapse, the idea of restriction, and so forth" is readily admitted. And Scott cheerfully proceeds to note that, confronted with such buildings, "every spectator will judge [them] ugly, and experience a certain discomfort from their presence."* But Scott assumed, simple soul that he was, that ugliness and discomfort were serious *faults* in a building, and that no one would willingly choose to design or inhabit a building that inspired such feelings. The deconstructivists teach otherwise. Discomfort and ugliness are their acknowledged stock in trade— except that they speak not of ugliness but of "torturing form" and so on.

The hard truth is that "Deconstructivist Architecture" is approximately ninety-nine parts hype and one part achievement. It is doubtful whether any of the projects included in the Museum of Modern Art exhibition measure up to the subversive ideal identified as the goal of deconstructivism, much as some of them—one thinks especially of Peter Eisenman's contribution—tried. Furthermore, whatever architectural interest the projects on view in that exhibition may claim is completely overshadowed by the lucubrations of Mark Wigley—pedantry set in motion, abetted, and applauded by Philip Johnson. Indeed, a desire for truth in advertising makes one wish that this exhibition had been titled "Philip Johnson's Revenge," for that is what "Deconstructivist Architecture" is finally about. Revenge for what? Above all, perhaps, for being taken seriously. "What good does it do you to believe in good things?" Mr. Johnson asked in an interview in 1965 with that other apostle of cultural

* Geoffrey Scott, *The Architecture of Humanism: A Study in the History of Taste*, with a foreword by Henry Hope Reed (New York: Norton, 1974), pages 157–158.

fashion, Susan Sontag. "It's feudal and futile. I think it much better to be nihilistic and forget all that."*

Indeed. By the time of his death in 2005 at the venerable age of 98, Philip Johnson had long been recognized as the doyen of postmodernist Camp, a man who was never happier than when foisting off on a credulous public ever more outrageous architectural pranks. In the pursuit of this this cynical game, he was aided by the cloudy academic theories and repellent vocabularies that have been corrupting literary studies for years, as well as by a squadron of academic minions from Michael Graves and Peter Eisenman to Mark Wigley and numerous other academic apologists. Mr. Johnson's distinctively postmodernist period—beginning with a skyscraper adorned with a Chippendale top and proceeding to the pretentious, deliberately convoluted projects and theories he gave his blessing to in this exhibition—constitutes a perfectly logical devolution. When put in the context of Mr. Johnson's origins as a disciple of Mies van der Rohe and champion of high modernism, the chronicle assumes the proportions of a farce. In the context of our present examination of the state of the humanities, the spectacle of Mr. Johnson's career and the influential role he played in fostering the subversion of architecture and architectural education by the new academic establishment appear as particularly grotesque and cynical examples of the deformation of contemporary academic culture.

* Quoted in Charles Jencks, *Modern Movements in Architecture* (New York: Doubleday, 1973), page 209.

CHAPTER SIX

The New Sophistry

"You see before you," he began, *"a man who once believed in the possibility of interpretation. That is, I thought that the goal of reading was to establish the meaning of texts."*
—Morris Zapp, in David Lodge's *Small World*

"What I say is that 'just' or 'right' means nothing but what is to the interest of the stronger party."
—Thrasymachus, in Plato's *Republic*

I The academy closes ranks

ONE OF the chief complaints heard from academics beleaguered by the attacks on the academy launched by Allan Bloom, William Bennett, Lynne V. Cheney, and others is that such critics have given a distorted picture of what is going on in the academy. Instead of pondering the admittedly "challenging" (a favorite code-word for impenetrable and/or subversive) work of contemporary scholars, such conservative critics are said to have focused on provocative course titles or radical-sounding statements taken out of context or a few unfortunate incidents that took place on campuses twenty years ago. They have thus, the story goes, given the public—and other potential sources of financial support and succor—the unfortunate impression that the academy today has largely given up its traditional educational aims and has, at the deepest level, become radicalized. This, for example, was one of Barbara Herrnstein Smith's recurrent points in her 1988 presidential address to the Modern Language Association. Deploring the ridicule that has been heaped on the academy in recent years for its pursuit of obscurity, she assured her flock that the "scholarly significance of a piece of published research is not self-evident from its title" and suggested that journalists be "specifically recruited and trained" under the aegis of the MLA in order to encourage them to provide a more accurate, i.e., a more flattering, picture of the profession than has been evident in the press lately.* As we have seen, a similar concern informs *Speaking for the Humanities*, the polemical brochure issued by the American Council of Learned Societies, which declares that "precisely those things now identified as failings in the humanities actually indicate enlivening transformations."

Anyone acquainted with current academic culture knows that all this is sheer temporizing. One need hardly believe that the title of a course or conference paper reveals everything about its contents to recognize that it is perfectly legitimate to ridicule ridiculous titles—of which, as we have seen, there is a seemingly inexhaustible supply.

* Barbara Herrnstein Smith, "Limelight: Reflections on a Public Year." The text of this address was reprinted in the May 1989 issue of the *Publications of the Modern Language Association of America*, Volume 104, Number 3, pages 285–293.

Nevertheless, Professor Smith has a point, and in the interests of thoroughness it is worth taking the time to consider in some detail at least one example of high-level writing in the humanities these days. As many of the comments and proclamations from the academic conferences we have examined suggest, it would not be at all difficult to find influential professors whose scholarly work and pedagogical aims are blatantly political. Nor would it be difficult to produce countless examples of well-regarded work in the humanities that is needlessly obscure, hopelessly trivial, or frankly at odds with the traditional purposes of humanistic study. Finding academic scholars whose work in the humanities is at once intelligible, intellectually sophisticated, *and* regarded by the profession as being at the forefront of its discipline is a more demanding task.

Among the handful of candidates that suggest themselves, perhaps none is a more articulate representative of one aspect of the radical ethos prevailing in the humanities today than the literary critic and polemicist Stanley Fish. Indeed, at a time when the assault on the humanities by deconstruction and other French imports shows signs of giving way to ever more knowing, overtly political forms of rebuke like the New Historicism and Cultural Studies, few figures offer a more canny version of the academy's revolt against its traditional goals than Professor Fish. Not that he is a newcomer to the academic scene. His early book, *Surprised by Sin: The Reader in Paradise Lost* (1967), helped to inaugurate the so-called "reader response" school of literary theory—according to which the meaning of a literary work inheres not in the text but in the interpretive acts of its readers—and instantly established its young author's reputation as a powerful and ingenious critical intelligence.

Professor Fish's later works include a book on the religious poet George Herbert and a study of seventeenth-century literature. But his next professional *tour de force* came in 1980 when he published *Is There a Text in This Class? The Authority of Interpretive Communities.* This influential collection of essays from the 1970s, most of which are exercises in literary theory as distinct from literary criticism, consolidated and extended his reputation as a formidable academic critic. The book continued in an increasingly radical key his project of "dislodging [the text] as the privileged container of meaning"* and, not quite incidentally, it presented to the reading public the figure of an able and fiercely contentious rhetorician whose name has ever since been at the forefront of academic literary controversy.

Having received his Ph.D. from Yale in 1962, Professor Fish taught for several years at the University of California at Berkeley and then at the Johns Hopkins University before going to Duke University in 1985, where was is now not only professor of English *and* professor of law but also executive director of the Duke University Press and associate vice-provost of the university. This impressive battery of titles—he was also chairman of the English department during a crucial period in the 1980s—suggests the heights to which Professor Fish has risen in his career and neatly summarizes his professional accomplishments. The dual appointment to a university

---

* Stanley Fish, *Is There a Text in This Class? The Authority of Interpretive Communities* (Cambridge: Harvard University Press, 1981), page 3.

chair in English and a professorship in law acknowledges Professor Fish's success in his diverse intellectual endeavors. For while he began his career as a scholar of seventeenth-century English literature, he now devotes much of his attention to the law, teaching courses in the Duke Law School and publishing in law reviews as well as in literary journals. *

It must also be understood that his position as chairman of the Duke English department was no merely honorific administrative post. More than any other individual, Professor Fish must be credited—if "credited" is the correct term—with fashioning the contemporary Duke English department. It was largely through his initiatives (backed, as *The Chronicle of Higher Education* reported, by generous amounts of money from the university, which had targeted the English department for "development")† that Duke was transformed in just a few years from a genteel though perhaps unexciting academic conclave into a bastion of every "advanced" and radical trend currently besetting the humanities. Along with providing lavish new offices for the chairman and a select group of professors, the English department in short order acquired a number of professors well known for their antipathy to traditional humanistic study.

In a series of much-publicized and unusually high-paying appointments, the university hired several high-

---

* In 1999, Professor Fish left Duke to become Dean of the College of Liberal Arts and Sciences at the University of Illinois at Chicago. As of this writing, he is Davidson-Kahn Distinguished University Professor of Humanities and a Professor of Law at Florida International University in Miami.

† *The Chronicle of Higher Education*, May 27, 1987, page 12.

profile "critical theorists," including Barbara Herrnstein Smith, Frank Lentricchia (whom an official university publication described as "the 'Dirty Harry' of Critical Theory"),* Annabel Patterson and her husband, Lee Patterson, as well as Professor Fish's wife, Jane Tompkins, a fervent champion of the New Historicism. The university also acquired younger aspirants like Eve Kosofsky Segdwick, an early proponent of "Queer Theory," whose work brings us back to the subject of course titles. According to the English department's description of courses, Professor Sedgwick's 1989 graduate course on "Gender, Sexuality, and Power in Victorian Fiction" focused on, among other things, "female and male homosocial, homosexual, homophobic, and cross-gender relations." Nor, apparently, is this sort of thing out of the ordinary for Professor Sedgwick. At the 1989 meeting of the Modern Language Association, Professor Sedgwick led a special session entitled "The Muse of Masturbation." In addition to Professor Sedgwick's contribution, "Jane Austen and the Masturbating Girl"—a title that instantly won nationwide notoriety—there were papers on "Clitoral Imagery and Masturbation in Emily Dickinson," and "Desublimating the Male Sublime: Autoerotics, Anal Erotics, and Corporeal Violence in Melville and William Burroughs," this last-named by another Duke professor.† Such lurid titles do not tell us everything about the class and presentations in question, perhaps, but they do give us some clue about what to expect. In any event, together with the much-celebrated Marxist

---

* *Duke*, May-June 1988, page 2.

† *Publications of the Modern Language Association*, vol. 104, no. 6, November 1989, page 1028.

critic Fredric Jameson, who (among his other titles) is chairman of Duke's Graduate Program in Literature, this cadre of chic theorists and literary activists has made Duke one of the most influential anti-traditionalist forces in contemporary academic literary studies.

It is another measure of the extent to which Professor Fish has insinuated himself into the imagination of his discipline that he should have served as the model (or so it is widely rumored) for the character Morris Zapp in *Small World*, an hilariously scathing send-up of the high-powered, jet-setting Lit. Crit. world by the English novelist and literature professor David Lodge. Whether or not Mr. Lodge really had Professor Fish in mind when he created Morris Zapp, anyone familiar with Professor Fish's work can easily imagine him defending as his own the quotation from *Small World* that stands at the head of this chapter. (He would endorse Thrasymachus's words, too, as we shall see.) And given his longstanding interest in the subject of "professionalism," one can also imagine him responding as did Morris Zapp when, after delivering a paper entitled "Textuality as Striptease," he is asked by an exasperated colleague, "Then what in God's name *is* the point of it all?" "The point [of literary interpretation], of course," replied Zapp coolly, "is to uphold the institution of academic literary studies. We maintain our position in society by publicly performing a certain ritual, just like any other group of workers in the realm of discourse—lawyers, politicians, journalists."*

* David Lodge, *Small World* (New York: Macmillan, 1984), page 28.

II Learning to play the game

Indeed, the issue of "professionalism"—what an earlier generation might have called "gamesmanship"—goes a long way toward helping one understand the course of Professor Fish's stunning academic career. Rather like the ambitious Zapp, he is wont to insist that teaching literature is a profession like any other, concerned more with self-perpetuation and self-aggrandizement than with the disinterested pursuit of knowledge. In fact, Professor Fish—again like Morris Zapp and so many real-life academics today—denies that the traditional scholarly ideal of disinterestedness is even possible, let alone desirable. He has repeatedly warned his colleagues against the snares of "anti-professionalism," which he defines as "any attitude that enforces a distinction between professional labors on the one hand and the identification and promotion of what is true or valuable on the other."* Such attitudes might be useful as an occasional corrective, Professor Fish admits; in one place he even refers paradoxically to such anti-professionalism as the "conscience" of the profession. But, at bottom, he argues that the attempt to distinguish between mere professional activity and the disinterested pursuit of truth is a mistake that encourages precisely the kind of false idealism that leads one to ask embarrassing questions like "What is the point of studying literature?"

* Stanley Fish, *Doing What Comes Naturally: Change, Rhetoric, and the Practice of Theory in Literary and Legal Studies* (Durham: Duke University Press, 1989), page 215. See also *Professional Correctness: Literary Studies and Political Change* (Oxford: Oxford University Press, 1995).

In accordance with his own precepts, Professor Fish has been nothing if not "professional." One important expression of his professionalism has been his knack of keeping his criticism one short, provocative step ahead of the criticism practiced by the majority of his colleagues. Looking back over the development of his career, one sees that he early on perfected what Jean Cocteau described as the art of knowing just how far to go in going too far. Thus in *Surprised by Sin*, written at a time when the New Criticism, though waning, was still regnant in the academy, Professor Fish made the daring suggestion that the key to the meaning of *Paradise Lost* lay not in Milton's complex text but in the reader's own struggle with that complexity. We are told that, because Milton wanted the experience of struggling with the poem's syntax to mimic the experience of struggling with and facing up to one's own sinfulness, he wrote in a convoluted style that deliberately confused and stymied his readers. Professor Fish suggests that it is only when the reader sees through his confusion, usually at the end of a sentence when he at last comes to the verb, that Milton's intended pattern of moral education—"mistake, correction, instruction"—is fulfilled.[*] In this sense, Professor Fish argues, *Paradise Lost* continually traces "the reader's humiliation and his education."[†]

Of course, it does seem odd that, if this really were Milton's intention, no one had noticed it before Stanley Fish. One would have thought such a lofty moral design would have been more accessible to ordinary mortal scrutiny. But even odder is the caliber of the reader of

---

[*] Stanley Fish, *Surprised by Sin* (Berkeley: University of California Press, 1967), page 42.

[†] *Ibid.*, Preface.

Milton that Professor Fish assumes. While Professor Fish pursued his case with considerable erudition, ingenuity, and even brilliance, the reader he posits is a model of obtuseness. He never wises up to Milton's supposed intentions and is certainly too shallow a fellow to appreciate the argument of *Surprised by Sin*. As the critic Frederick Crews has observed, Professor Fish's "reader" is a straw man, "a dunce—a Charlie Brown who, having had the syntactic football yanked away a hundred times, would keep right on charging it in perfect innocence, never learning to suspend judgment until he arrived at the poet's verb."*

Professor Fish has long since abandoned the reader-response suppositions he argued for in *Surprised by Sin*. But he has continued in his role of intellectual provocateur, sprinkling his work with arguments and asides that seem designed as much to taunt his readers as to enlighten them. Why else would he have blithely described his style of criticism as a "superior fiction," whose very status as fiction relieves him "of the obligation to be right . . . and demands only that I be interesting"? Again, it must be noted that Professor Fish later repudiated this Wildean assertion from the mid-1970s, calling it "the most unfortunate sentence I ever wrote."† (Readers may wish to propose alternative candidates for that honor.) Yet it is difficult to know quite what to make of his retractions. There are so many of them. The truth is that Professor Fish has made a speciality of repudiating in one season the provocative statements that had earlier gained him the notice—if often the irritated notice—of his

---

* *Skeptical Engagements*, page 124.

† *Is There a Text in This Class?*, seriatim, pages 180, 174.

peers. The detailed introduction to *Is There a Text in This Class?*, for example, traces the development of the notion of "interpretive communities" and is a veritable inventory of his own discarded positions, each abandoned for one slightly more extreme or, to use a word he favors in this book and elsewhere, "subversive."

Professor Fish's habit of denying the positions he had once forcefully insisted upon might simply be evidence of an unusual openness to criticism and willingness to change his mind when confronted with superior arguments. But a suspicious observer might wonder whether the driving force of his intellectual life was not a desire for truth so much as a desire for notoriety.* The question is whether blustering pronouncements like the one quoted above are products of momentary exaggeration—incautiously penned in the heat of debate—or whether they are the result of deliberate calculation and a striving for effect.

---

* Thus Professor Fish's latest book, *Save the World on Your Own Time* (New York: Oxford University Press, 2008), impishly suggests—or rather seems to suggest—that institutions of higher educations should eschew political engagement and concentrate on 1) introducing students to "bodies of knowledge and traditions of inquiry" and 2) equipping them with the requisite "analytical skills . . . that will enable them to move confidently within those traditions." I say "impishly" because what at first blush looks like a conservative plea for rescuing the humanities from politics turns out in the end to be a blueprint for the usual Left Eclecticism. No one who has followed the tergiversations of Professor Fish—who has spent his entire career undermining the traditions he now pretends to speak up for—will be surprised that in his peroration he tells us that Jacques Derrida, no less, provides the justification ("a deeply philosophical justification") for the "austerity" he urges.

III The new common sense

The essays that Professor Fish collected in *Doing What Comes Naturally: Change, Rhetoric, and the Practice of Theory in Literary and Legal Studies* effectively answer that and a good many other questions about the nature and lasting value of the work of this influential critic and academic entrepreneur. Part of a series from Duke anomalously called "Post-Contemporary Interventions," the volume contains twenty-two essays, all but three of which have appeared previously in one form or another.* After a long introduction setting forth the author's relativist credo, the book is divided into four sections: Meaning and Constraint, Professionalism, Consequences, and Rhetoric. The essays thus range freely over Professor Fish's standard repertoire. And as with everything Professor Fish writes, the pieces collected here are clearly written and display considerable wit and learning. Unlike

---

* This series, incidentally, is edited by the indefatigable Professor Fish and his colleague Fredric Jameson. One may safely hazard that the nonsensical phrase "post-contemporary" was the result of a search for something even more up-to-date, more fashionable, than "postmodern"—that ubiquitous but nonetheless catachrestic term that, as Professor Fish observes of those old workhorses "structuralist," "post-structuralist," and their cognates, has had something of a period flavor for some time now. The addition of the word "interventions" is obviously meant to impart an aura of decisive activism: as if the series comprised not mere books but political acts. An outsider cannot of course be certain about the genesis of the title, but in Professor Fish's defense it must be said that this aggressively barbarous phrase has all the earmarks of being Professor Jameson's brainchild.

many of his colleagues, at Duke and elsewhere, Professor Fish not only does his homework but also values clarity of expression. It is noteworthy, though, that none of the essays in this bulky volume concerns itself explicitly with a literary text considered as *literature*. About as close as we get to literature is an essay called "Transmuting the Lump," which deals with the changing critical fortunes of books XI and XII of *Paradise Lost*. But even here, the poem is adduced solely in order to illustrate the politics of literary taste in contemporary English studies.

True, literary texts are often *mentioned* in *Doing What Comes Naturally*. But Professor Fish, like so many of his colleagues, seems to have given up literary criticism in order to play at being a philosopher. Accordingly, several essays deal with what for lack of a better term one may call the philosophy of language. Some of these advance Professor Fish's views on rhetoric, about which more below. ("Rhetorical," he correctly notes, is "a master-word" in these essays.) Others explicate and criticize rival theories of language and meaning. Typical of the latter is a lengthy piece that compares the work of the doyen of French deconstruction, Jacques Derrida, and the British ordinary-language philosopher J. L. Austin. One would hardly have thought this a subject to inspire humor, but who can resist an incredulous smile when Professor Fish confides that "Derrida is very much a philosopher of common sense," that "one might even say, with the proper qualifications, that he is a philosopher of ordinary language"?*

In order to appreciate the extent to which Derrida is a philosopher of "common sense" and "ordinary lan-

---

* *Doing What Comes Naturally*, seriatim, pages 25, 57.

guage," consider this passage, of about average clarity, taken from the main article by Derrida upon which Professor Fish bases his claim:

> A written sign is proffered in the absence of the receiver. How to style this absence? One could say that at the moment when I am writing, the receiver may be absent from my field of present perception. But is not this absence merely a distant presence, one which is delayed or which, in one form or another, is idealized in its representation? This does not seem to be the case, or at least this distance, divergence, delay, this deferral must be capable of being carried to a certain absoluteness of absence if the structure of writing, assuming that writing exists, is to constitute itself. It is at that point that the *différance* as writing could no longer (be) an (ontological) modification of presence.*

Common sense? Ordinary language? I guess they really do talk different down there in Durham, North Carolina.

Doing What Comes Naturally also contains a half dozen pieces on the law, including three much-discussed attacks on the work of the legal theorist Ronald Dworkin ("Working on the Chain Gang," "Wrong Again," "Still Wrong After All These Years"), as well as, under the rubric "Professionalism," a well-known essay entitled "No Bias, No Merit." In this essay, Professor Fish argues against the policy many academic journals follow of accepting articles for publication only after they have been

---

* Jacques Derrida, "Signature Event Context," in *Limited Inc*, translated by Samuel Weber and Jeffrey Mehlman (Evanston: Northwestern University Press, 1988), page 7.

submitted to a blind peer review. Now there are plenty of reasons to be wary of this policy; often it seems blind in more than the desired sense of "impartial." But how many sought-after academics would admit that they are against it because it prevents them from cashing in on their reputations? "I am against blind submission," Professor Fish proclaims with characteristic bravura, "because the fact that my name is attached to an article greatly increases its chances of getting accepted. . . . I have paid my dues and earned the benefit of the doubt I now enjoy and don't see why others shouldn't labor in the vineyards as I did."*

It is important to note that Professor Fish's case against the policy of blind submission goes well beyond this expression of blatant self-interest. In fact, at the center of his animus toward blind submission is a contention that, in one way or another, surfaces in nearly every article in *Doing What Comes Naturally.* Professor Fish duly acknowledges that the intention behind the policy is to minimize bias and provide the proverbial "level playing field" for the hordes of academics hungry for publications to add to their resumés. But he rejects the idea that bias is a problem; more specifically, he rejects the idea that, given the limitations of human knowledge, the notion of bias is even *intelligible.* "Bias," he writes, "is just another word for seeing from a particular perspective as opposed to seeing from no perspective at all, and since seeing from no perspective at all is not a possibility, bias is a condition of consciousness and therefore of action."†

When he is not being deliberative provocative, Professor

---

* *Doing What Comes Naturally*, page 175.

† *Ibid.*, page 176.

Fish has a tendency to present the obvious as if it were a stunning discovery. In "Critical Self-Consciousness, Or Can We Know What We're Doing?"—one of the key essays in *Doing What Comes Naturally*—he explains how it is that even our best efforts to be impartial turn out to be biased. "We say to ourselves," he writes, " 'with respect to this matter I am going to put aside my interests, preferences, and biases; and consider the evidence and alternatives in an impartial manner'. " In his view, what this resolution overlooks is "the extent to which the specification of what is and is not an 'impartial manner' is itself an 'interested' act, that is, an act performed within a set of assumptions" about what will count as evidence. Hence, he concludes, it is an ineluctably *"partial"* view of the world.* Rightly understood, this would seem to be an unexceptionable point. For what does it portend except that our ideas have a history, that they arise in particular circumstances, and are the products of diverse situations? Does any of this dilute by one iota the ideal of impartiality?

The answer is no, but for Professor Fish, the insight that we are not gods, endowed with perfect knowledge, seems to have come as a shocking revelation. It leads him to one of his chief polemical points—a point made repeatedly in this volume: namely, that we are imprisoned by our interpretive schemes and hence any attempt to achieve critical distance on those schemes is doomed to failure.† Although Professor Fish presents this idea as a

---

* *Ibid.*, page 439.

† Indeed, this is a leitmotif in all of Professor Fish's later work. See *There's No Such Thing as Free Speech . . . and It's a Good Thing Too* (Oxford: Oxford University Press, 1994), page 18: "Whenever Reason is successfully invoked, . . . the result will be a victory not

hard-won discovery, in one version or another it has been gospel in the literary academy for several years. Whether one turns to Jacques Derrida with his insistence that "There is nothing outside the text" or to Professor Fish's colleague Fredric Jameson, who speaks of "the prison house of language," the notion that (to adapt yet another popular formulation) the limits of language exhaustively define the limits of the world is an unquestioned assumption in the all-questioning precincts of literary academia.

There was a time, however, when the academy was not so besotted with language. Traditionally, reflection was seen as a means of achieving critical distance on what Professor Fish calls our "interpretive schemes." Reflecting on our point of view, it was held, we in some sense transcend that point of view, appreciate its limitations, and entertain alternatives. But for Professor Fish, this sense of transcendence is an illusion. It could be achieved, he tells us, only "if the moment of self-reflection is in no way dependent on that from which it is to set us free" (i.e., our "deeply assumed norms and standards"). "Reflection," he concludes, "is just a fancy name for persuasion."* But why should we insist that reflection, in order to be effective, in order to be liberating, must be utterly free from the "norms and standards" out of which it arises? Does not the simple fact of our being able to entertain points of view very different from our own

---

for Reason but for the party that has managed . . . to get the reasons that flow from its agenda identified with Reason as a general category." The idea that truth might guide reason is something that Professor Fish just cannot abide.

* *Doing What Comes Naturally*, page 448.

show that we can meaningfully transcend our taken-for-granted interpretive schemes?

Like many of his colleagues who are impatient with "authoritarian" concepts like objectivity and disinterestedness, Professor Fish tends to prosecute his anti-traditional brief by caricaturing the opposition. As we have seen in the case of Professor Hartman's reconstruction of Paul de Man, one basic tactic is to postulate a kind of super-Cartesian whose view of what counts as knowledge is so stringent that it is inevitably defeated and whose defeat is then chalked up as a victory for the notion of deconstruction, interpretive communities, critical theory, etc. Faithful to this tradition, at least, Professor Fish assures us that for anyone who believes in objectivity,

> the trick then is to to think of sentences that would be heard the same way by all competent speakers no matter what their educational experience, or class membership, or partisan affiliation, or special knowledge, sentences which, invariant across contexts, could form the basis of an acontextual and formal description of the language and its rules.*

But who believes such sentences exist, outside the precincts of pure mathematics? And who believes that we need such a rigorous view of language in order to make sense of, say, impartial judgment? Just as Professor Fish's reader of *Paradise Lost* was rather a dim chap whose primary virtue was to bring glory to the reader-response view of literary criticism, so those who dispute his skeptical notion of interpretive authority are held to be

* *Ibid.*, page 320.

benighted souls who have never suspected that human knowledge is a fallible thing.

IV Don't worry, be happy

One of Professor Fish's neatest rhetorical gambits is to assure us that his radical view of meaning and interpretation is benign. Are you worried about making decisions on the basis of merit, not prejudice? Don't worry: because all judgments are prejudiced, decisions that claim to be based on merit are just as prejudiced as any others, only they are less self-consciousness, since they fail to recognize their own prejudices. Are you concerned about preserving the ideal of disinterested scholarship? Forget about it: "disinterestedness" is a chimera; and what is impossible or illusory can't very well be preserved. Professor Fish's favorite method of introducing such charming sophisms is by bluntly denying the obvious. "There is no such thing as . . ."—you name it: truth, merit, justice, facts. For example:

> there is no such thing as literal meaning, . . .
> there can be no such thing as theory, . . .
> there is no such thing as intrinsic merit, . . .
> Indeed, there is no such thing as a 'mere' preference in the sense that makes it a threat to communal norms, for anything that could be experienced as a preference will derive from the norms inherent in some community.*

---

* *Ibid.*, *seriatim*, pages 4, 14, 164, 11. And of course there is the title of his book *There's No Such Thing as Free Speech.*

Let us allow the first three of these pronouncements to stand as what they primarily are: verbal provocations, without (since we have just been assured that there is no such thing) literal meaning or intrinsic merit. But do let us pause to consider some of the implications of Professor Fish's dismissal of anything so scandalous as "mere" preference and his assurance that nothing "that could be experienced as a preference" can be "a threat to communal norms." First, note that he is not just making the unarguable point that our desires and preferences have a social component, that what we want is to some extent the product of the community we happen to find ourselves in. On the contrary, he believes that socialization (to borrow a phrase from the philosopher Richard Rorty) "goes all the way down." Like Rorty, Professor Fish maintains that there are no independent criteria to which we might appeal to justify, or to condemn, our beliefs or actions. Indeed, he is fond of declaring that phrases like "independent criteria," "disinterested judgment," and "intrinsic merit" are self-contradictory.

Yet, as is often the case in these essays, part of Professor Fish's purpose in denying the obvious is to sweeten his message, to reassure us that his view of language and meaning entails no important loss. If there are no such things as intrinsic merit or disinterested judgment to begin with then we need hardly worry about their corruption or loss. Of course, most of us have been taught the opposite. We believe, for example, that there *is* a difference between action based on "mere preference" and action based on principle, between acting in a way that is self-interested and acting for the sake of something greater than self-interest. We believe that there is such a thing as unprincipled behavior, based on "mere preference," and that such behavior can be dangerous. Professor Fish is in effect telling us that we are being too fastidious. Since, in his view, every decision and every action is inexpungably colored by undeclared interests, the effort to distinguish between preference and principle is otiose. Moreover, because all values, preferences, facts, desires, and principles are themselves products of some "interpretive community," " 'mere' preference" cannot be a "threat to communal norms." Professor Fish's slogan for this happy state of affairs is that "all preferences are principled."*

But think about it. Around the time that Professor Fish was telling us that "all preferences are principled," a gang of adolescent boys raped and brutally beat a woman in Central Park, leaving her for dead. The extreme youth of the attackers and the ghastly savageness of their crime assured that the case made national headlines. When asked why he had repeatedly beat the helpless woman about the head with a metal pipe, one of the boys is reported to have replied, "Because it was fun." In other words, there was no particular reason. It was a whim. He just felt like doing it. Not to worry, though: Professor Fish has informed us that since preferences always "derive from the norms inherent in some community," they cannot be a "threat to communal norms." On what grounds, then, do we condemn this act? Is our condemnation merely the expression of prejudice—the expression, that is to say, of unacknowledged values inculcated by our "interpretive community"? Would we want to allow that another point of view, one that sanctioned rape and brutality, might be equally legitimate and morally

---

* *Ibid.*, page 11.

234

compelling because it, too, derived from norms inherent in some interpretive community? Is Hitler to be exonerated because, after all, his preferences derived from the norms that won out in *his* interpretive community?

V Pulling the rug out from under yourself

Looming behind all of Professor Fish's startling denials and rhetorical antics is a single large claim about the nature of truth and meaning. In brief, there isn't any. That is to say, there isn't any if one insists that judgments of truth require independent criteria, that there must be external checks or constraints on meaning and interpretation. In Professor Fish's terms, this insistence is "formalist" or "foundationalist." He defines "foundationalism" as "any attempt to ground inquiry and communication in something more firm and stable than mere belief or unexamined practice." It follows that we are guilty of foundationalist thinking if we believe there are criteria or "constraints" on judgment independent of our particular situation.*

Although it is castigated under a variety of names— "objectivism," "formalism," "hierarchical thinking," even, for shorthand, "truth"—we have seen that what Professor Fish calls "foundationalism" has emerged as a prime whipping boy for many contemporary academic humanists. It has indeed emerged as one of the favored academic terms of contempt. We are thus treated to the darkly comic spectacle of (to employ Harold Rosenberg's memorable phrase) this herd of independent minds, safely

---

* *Ibid.*, page 342.

tenured within its ivy-covered walls, assuring each other in paper after paper, conference after conference, book after book that everything is a text, that reality is only a "social construction," that truth is merely a sociological convention.

Of course, the campaign against "foundationalism" comes in varying degrees of sophistication. Many literary academics simply parrot a set of impressive-sounding phrases culled from the writings of fashionable stars like Derrida, Foucault, Jameson, or from the primary precursor of these men, Friedrich Nietzsche, whose work is full of histrionic declarations like "there are no facts, only interpretations." (Is that, one is tempted to ask, a fact?) In these cases, one is dealing not so much with an argument as an *attitude*, a posture of skepticism that is often adopted more from intellectual laziness and fear of being unstylish than from conviction. As usual, Professor Fish presents a more complicated case. Like many of his academic colleagues, he repeatedly assures us that "there are no higher or more general constraints, only constraints that are *different*, constraints built into practices other than the one whose reform is now being contemplated."

But it turns out that Professor Fish is not your garden variety relativist; he is a relativist of a more sophisticated stripe. He recognizes that in order to make sense of judgment at all one has to appeal to something like criteria. It's just that he doesn't believe that criteria ever possess the independence traditionally imputed to them. Hence he insists there are "no constraints that are more than the content of a practice from which they are indistinguishable"; "whatever is invoked as a constraint on interpretation will turn out upon further examination to have been the product of interpretation." Hence, too, the frankly political aspect of his view of meaning: "It is first and last," he writes in his introductory chapter, "a question of *power* in relation to the putting of *constraints*."*

This set of ideas has been dawning on Professor Fish for years, and has now assumed the proportions of an *idée fixe*. It is indeed the lodestar around which all his critical work currently circles. As he notes in the preface to *Doing What Comes Naturally*, the essays therein collected, though ostensibly on diverse topics, are really "the same." All develop or defend or explain this one idea about the nature of truth and meaning. Not surprisingly, Professor Fish's preferred term for his outlook is "anti-foundationalism." He himself, he assures us, is a "card-carrying anti-foundationalist,"† and he thinks we should be, too. Not that he wants for company. While he is more rigorous in his exposition than most of his literary colleagues, Professor Fish is hardly alone in his anti-foundationalist sympathies. As we have seen again and again, though it travels under a variety of aliases, the anti-foundationalist creed has installed itself as the reigning ideology of American higher education in the humanities. Indeed, examples of well-known literary academics dissenting from the anti-foundationalist ethos are much harder to come by than those who champion it. Typical of the majority voice is the proclamation by Professor Fish's colleague Barbara Herrnstein Smith of a "radically contingent . . . conceptualization and discourse of 'reality,' 'validity,' 'justification,' 'reason,' 'truth,' 'facts,' and so forth," or Richard Rorty's endorsement of a "post-metaphysical" and "postreligious" culture in which "the sermon and treatise" are being replaced by "the novel, the movie, and the TV program" as the "principle vehicles of moral change and progress."*

In this context, it may be worth noting that one of the things Professor Fish is proudest of is the unusually wide range of his enemies. He is fond of reminding one that he is attacked as often by the Left as by the Right. The academic Left is unhappy with him because he is impatient with their claims for the practical consequences of "theory"—what he aptly calls "theory talk" or "theory hope." In accordance with the principle of knowing how far to go in going too far, Professor Fish outflanks most of his radical brethren, claiming that they aren't quite radical enough. They may have plowed through volumes of Derrida and Althusser and Habermas, to say nothing of Hegel, Marx, Nietzsche, and Heidegger; they may rail against the logocentric hegemony of an elitist patriarchal

---

* Barbara Herrnstein Smith, *Contingencies of Value: Alternative Perspectives for Critical Theory* (Cambridge: Harvard University Press, 1989), page 156, and Richard Rorty, *Contingency, Irony, and Solidarity* (Cambridge: Cambridge University Press, 1989), pages xiii–xvi. It is worth calling attention to Professor Smith's use of scare quotes. Obviously, she wishes to cast doubt on such conceptual dinosaurs as reality, validity, justification, reason, truth, facts, "and so forth." But it is useful to ask what reality, validity, truth, "and so forth" would be left in her own "discourse" once "*the realist/objectivist sense*" (as she contemptuously puts it) of these ideas is jettisoned. Readers interested in experiencing academic prose at its most self-important and intellectually pretentious may wish to wade through a few of the essays collected in *Contingencies of Value.*

faith in objectivity and science—but what good does it do them? In the midst of their orgies of disillusionment and skepticism, there is one belief they never abandon: the belief in theory itself, the belief that in some important sense theory *matters*. That is to say, they always assume that their current pet theory provides them with a critical purchase on language or the world that is somehow truer, better, more accurate than that enjoyed by their neighbors. Accordingly, Professor Fish charges that even "anti-foundationalist" theory (and is there any other kind in the academy?) is covertly . . . yes, *foundationalist*. And that, clearly, is not a charge calculated to win one friends in the humanities departments of our universities.

The academic Right, on the other hand, is unhappy with Professor Fish primarily because he is a relativist who believes that "political justifications are the only kind there are"* and because he consequently denies that traditional ideals like truth or justice—to say nothing of our old friends "intrinsic merit," "disinterestedness," and "objectivity"—have any meaning except as rhetorical gestures. Yet it would be a grave error to suppose that Professor Fish plies a middle road between the intellectual Left and the Right. Both the Right and the Left have misunderstood him, he complains, but it is clear that he regards some misunderstandings as more equal than others. He criticizes the naïveté of his Leftist colleagues and attracts their ire (a certain species of feminist seems to be especially exercised by his writings). But as a "card-carrying anti-foundationalist" his political sympathies—and remember, for Professor Fish there are no other kind—are all with them.

* *Doing What Comes Naturally*, page 340.

If this were not already clear enough from his anti-foundationalist ideas about meaning, truth, and interpretation, it becomes pellucidly clear whenever he steps out of his preferred role as radical epistemological proselytizer and discusses concrete issues of policy. Consider, for example, the very different ways he characterizes two articles by fellow academics in "Profession Despise Thyself: Fear and Self-Loathing in Literary Studies." The primary occasion for this lecture on the virtues of professionalism was a 1982 article by the eminent Harvard professor Walter Jackson Bate decrying the new faddishness and politicization that was erupting in English departments around the country. Naturally, Professor Fish has little patience with Bate's criticism. But it is instructive to compare his attack on Bate's piece with his treatment of another attack on the academy that appeared in 1982: this one by Columbia University's redoubtable PLO sympathizer and professor of comparative literature, the late Edward Said. No one acquainted with the work of Bate and Said will be surprised to learn that where Bate criticized the the profession for abandoning standards, Said criticized it for being overly narrow and insufficiently political. After spending several pages excoriating Bate for his small-mindedness, Professor Fish then turns, reluctantly, to criticize Said. Said must be criticized because he thinks something is wrong with the profession of English being professional. But Professor Fish is careful to describe Said's piece as "infinitely more attractive" than Bate's, claiming that it is "everything that Bate's is not: generous, learned, humane, compassionate, responsible."* Again, anyone familiar with

* *Ibid.*, page 212.

the work of these authors will recognize that this characterization is preposterous. Clearly, though, one tangible advantage of Professor Fish's policy of doing what comes naturally is that it relieves him of the chore of even attempting to be even-handed.

VI The new sophistry

The development of Professor Fish's anti-foundationalist campaign also explains a good deal about the direction his own work has taken. It explains, for example, why he has increasingly abandoned literary criticism for the study of rhetoric. Already in *Is There a Text in This Class?*, he concludes that

> the business of criticism was not (as I had previously thought) to determine the correct way of reading but to determine from which of a number of possible perspectives reading will proceed. . . . The business of criticism in other words is not to decide between interpretations by subjecting them to the test of disinterested evidence but to establish by political and persuasive means (they are the same thing) the set of interpretive assumptions from the vantage of which the evidence (and the facts and the intentions and everything else) will hereafter be specifiable.*

Given this interest in the art of persuasion—that is to say, in rhetoric—it is no wonder that Professor Fish should have increasingly turned away from literature toward legal texts to provide fodder for his theories. At least

---

* *Is There a Text in This Class?*, page 16.

since Plato, as the *Phaedrus* reminds us, rhetoric has been understood as having to do principally with "lawsuits . . . and of course public harangues."

In broad outline, Professor Fish's position is nothing new. Similar presuppositions about language can be found in certain strains of American pragmatism as well as in Ludwig Wittgenstein's late philosophy of language, especially in his theory of language games. And, as Professor Fish proudly acknowledges, the spirit and intellectual pedigree of his anti-foundationalist views hark back to the sophists of Plato's time. Like them, Professor Fish argues that "man is the measure of all things," that "justice" "means nothing but what is to the interest of the stronger party," etc. Here is Professor Fish's own version of Thrasymachus's claim: "Does might make right? In a sense the answer I must give is yes, since in the absence of a perspective independent of interpretation some interpretive perspective will always rule by virtue of having won out over its competitors."* In other words, whatever interpretive scheme happens to have "won out" is not only victorious but is therefore *right*.

It is hardly surprising that Professor Fish has attracted many disciples in the academy. Yet for all its professional cachet and shock value, his position is far from convincing. For one thing, as with the sophists before him, there is an insurmountable contradiction at the heart of the Fish course on meaning. It is this: he cannot claim truth for his own theory without at the same time denying the "anti-foundationalist" principles upon which it is based. He rightly points out that the various aspects of his anti-foundationalist creed are closely connected, noting that

---

* *Doing What Comes Naturally*, page 10.

the "first step down the anti-formalist road," the denial of literal meaning, "contains all the others." But then how are we to understand that denial? Is it . . . *true?* Or is it merely an interpretive gesture? As with every thoroughgoing relativist since Protagoras, Professor Fish faces the problem of not being able to assert his position without self-contradiction. He hastily assures us that this is an objection that is "easily gotten around." But is his response convincing? Does it help to say, as he does, that, yes, there is a foundation for his relativistic position, but it is only "rhetorical," based on evidence that is "cultural and contextual"?* Waffles, anyone?

Like the relativistic theories of his colleagues, Professor Fish's anti-foundationalist view of language and interpretation is most grievously deficient when it comes to science and the idea of objective truth. The insistence that all our notions of truth are products of particular interpretative communities does not go very far in accounting for the cogency of scientific discourse, nor, in fact, for the everyday notion of empirical truth. It is difficult, for example, to see how the truth of the assertion "The sun is shining" is culturally contingent or relative to the presuppositions of the interpretive community one happens to inhabit.

It must also be said that, *pace* Professor Fish, science offers us not just "another" perspective on the world but, in a way that can be precisely specified, a higher, more precise, more objective perspective than that provided by ordinary language. This is not to deny that the view of the world furnished by scientific rationalism is deeply reductive; indeed, it is reductive *in principle*, excluding as

---

* *Ibid., seriatim*, pages 25, 29.

far as possible any reference to the fluctuating, uncertain realm of values and sense perception. Nor is it to deny that the concept of objectivity itself is the product of a particular culture and assumptions about the nature of truth. Of course it is. But the fact that all our concepts and theories have a history does not by itself gainsay their truth or validity. Nor does the fact that the idea of objectivity happened to arise out of a particular interpretive community mean that its application is limited to that community. The truth of Euclidean geometry is hardly limited to the Greeks, nor the truth of algebra to the Arabs. Moreover, the very power that science has given us to predict, manipulate, and control reality shows that its truths, though reductive, are genuinely universal.

Like so many "transgressive" academics today, Stanley Fish suffers from a bad case of what the Australian philosopher David Stove identified as "cognitive Calvinism." Just as Calvinists, convinced of the total depravity of human nature, believe that "if an impulse is one of ours, it is bad *because* it is one of ours," so anti-foundationalist academics believe that "any knowledge *we* have could not be the real thing, *because* we have it." As Stove points out, there are many versions of this argument. All proceed illegitimately from tautology ("We can only know things as they are known to us . . .") to Protagorean skepticism (". . . therefore, we cannot know things as they really are").* Similarly with the idea of disinterestedness. It is a simple tautology that "All a man's interests are interests of his." But from this it by no

* David Stove, "Idealism: A Victorian Horror-story (Part Two)," in *Against the Idols of the Age*, edited by Roger Kimball, (New Brunswick: Transaction, 1999), page 187.

means follows—as Professor Fish and his like-minded colleagues would have us believe—that "All our actions are self-interested." Such an inference, to quote David Stove again, "belongs to exactly the same class as the atrocious (though ever popular) inference from 'Whatever will be, will be,' to 'All human effort is ineffectual.' "

> The possible objects of a man's interests, motives, or desires, are inexhaustibly various. Among them may be, to wreak revenge on a particular man, to gain the love of a particular woman, to serve his country, to experience the love of God, to understand contemporary physics, to witness the sufferings of others, to relieve the sufferings of others, to acquire money, to write a great book . . . the list is endless. But it can perfectly well happen, and often does happen, that a man pursues one or more of these 'particular passions' without regard to his own interests; indeed, to the manifest injury of those interests.*

It is important to stress that the implications of Professor Fish's anti-foundationalist fantasies are not confined to abstract matters of epistemology. As he acknowledges early on in *Doing What Comes Naturally*, the effects of the anti-formalist, anti-foundationalist creed he champions are "almost boundless." We have seen, however, that notwithstanding this admission he is also everywhere at pains to assure his readers that "when you get to the end of the anti-formalist road nothing will have changed except the answers you might give to some traditional

---

* David Stove, *Darwinian Fairytales: Selfish Genes, Errors of Heredity, and Other Fables of Evolution* (New York: Encounter Books, 2006), pages 134–135.

questions in philosophy and literary theory." "The dangers of excessive interpretive freedom, of 'masked power,' of random or irresponsible activity," he writes, "are *unrealizable*, because the conditions that would make them the basis of a reasonable fear—the condition of free subjectivity, of 'naturally' indeterminate texts, or unprincipled authority—could never obtain." Once again, we find there is nothing to worry about: "nihilism is impossible" and of course "it is unnecessary to combat something that is not possible."*

But in fact there is a great deal to worry about. For not only is the anti-foundationalist creed wrong, it is—as Professor Fish himself has been eager to declare—subversive. Not least, it is subversive of the intellectual foundation of liberal democratic society. Indeed, Professor Fish blithely notes that the entire tenor of anti-foundationalism is subversive of "a general assumption of liberal thought," namely, the ideal of disinterested knowledge.† For if one can no longer cogently distinguish between impartial judgment and *parti pris* lobbying, between dispassionate description and partisan propaganda, one can no longer make sense of the moral and intellectual ideals upon which our society is based.

And this brings us back to that "master-word" of Professor Fish's later work: rhetoric. What we see at work throughout is a deliberate attempt to supplant reason by rhetoric, truth by persuasion, by the simple device of denying that there is any essential distinction to be made between them. This would be troubling enough if it were confined to literary texts; extended to legal texts and

* *Doing What Comes Naturally, seriatim*, pages, 26, 138, 139.
† *Ibid.*, page 348.

basic political concepts like justice, it is nothing short of disastrous.

There was a time when one studied rhetoric in order to equip oneself to employ its resources effectively for the sake of truth and justice and to inoculate oneself against rhetoric's seductive charms. For Professor Fish, however, rhetoric is all there is. This has always been the contention of professional rhetoricians, from the time of sophists like Thrasymachus, Callicles, and Protagoras, down to contemporary sophists like Rorty, Fish, and their many disciples. Plato rightly condemned rhetoric as a "shadow play of words" that was concerned with semblance, not reality. Does it help to be told that Plato's qualms were groundless because "there is no such thing as" reality or facts or literal meaning or truth? (Given the impressive material triumphs of Professor Fish & Co. at Duke, one cannot help recalling that Plato also remarked the astounding amounts of money that sophists make.)

Considered as a representative instance of what contemporary academic culture holds up as exemplary work in the humanities, Professor Fish's writings are more reasoned but no less radical than most. By the time he published *Is There a Text in This Class?*, in 1980, he was already far down the anti-formalist, anti-foundationalist road. Like most errors, this one did not improve with time. Regarding *Doing What Comes Naturally* with its updated litanies, one can hardly do better than to quote one of Professor Fish's own condemnations: Still wrong after all these years.

More generally, however, his recent work illustrates the extent to which academic literary studies have abandoned the most elementary distinctions of taste, judgment, and value. It is one of the clearest symptoms of the decadence besetting the academy that the ideals that once informed the humanities have been corrupted, willfully misunderstood, or simply ignored by the new sophistries that have triumphed on our campuses. We know something is gravely amiss when teachers of the humanities confess— or, as is more often the case, when they boast—that they are no longer able to distinguish between truth and falsity. We know something is wrong when scholars assure us—and their pupils—that there is no essential difference between the disinterested pursuit of knowledge and partisan proselytizing, or when academic literary critics abandon the effort to identify and elucidate works of lasting achievement as a reactionary enterprise unworthy of their calling. And indeed, the most troubling development of all is that such contentions are no longer the exceptional pronouncements of a radical elite, but have increasingly become the conventional wisdom in humanities departments of our major colleges and universities.

CHAPTER SEVEN

The Real Crisis in the Humanities

Live with your century, but do not be its creature; render to your contemporaries what they need, not what they praise.
—Friedrich Schiller, *On the Aesthetic Education of Man*

I The new establishment

THE OVERHEATED rhetoric and pose of besieged defiance that one regularly encounters in the academy may suggest that those railing against, say, "European dominance" or "white, male, WASP hegemony" (to recall Cornel West's memorable phrase) are isolated figures on the margins of academic power. Unfortunately, the opposite is the case. Far from being the work of a minority, these voices represent the new academic establishment of tenured radicals. Often they are among they most highly paid professors—the professors for whose services leading universities engage in heated bidding wars. Nor is the influence of these professors confined to the present moment. At many prestigious institutions, they are precisely the people helping to shape the future by making faculty appointments, overseeing promotions and other preferments, and devising the educational program in the humanities—efforts at self-propagation that virtually assure their continued influence for another generation.

The truth is that when the children of the Sixties received their professorships and deanships they did not abandon the dream of radical cultural transformation; they set out to implement it. Now, instead of disrupting classes, they are teaching them; instead of attempting to destroy our educational institutions physically, they are subverting them from within. Thus it is that what were once the political and educational ambitions of academic renegades now appear as ideals on the agenda of the powers that be. Efforts to dismantle the traditional curriculum and institutionalize radical feminism, to ban politically "unacceptable" speech and propagate the tenets of deconstruction and similar exercises in cynical obscurantism: The directives fostering these and other radical developments now typically issue from the dean's office or faculty senate, not from students marching in the streets.

It would be difficult to imagine a more revealing illustration of the new academic establishment at work than the one Williams College offered at its two-day fall convocation ceremonies in September of 1989. The festivities were held not only to mark the beginning of term and confer various academic prizes and honors but also to inaugurate the new Center for the Humanities and Social Sciences at Williams. The highlight of the event was an evening panel discussion devoted to the question, "Crisis in the Humanities?" Members of the panel included Houston A. Baker, Jr., whom we met in Chapter One; the renowned Jacques Derrida (who died in 2004); Werner Gundersheimer, a specialist in Renaissance European history who had been recently appointed director of the Folger Shakespeare Library in Washington, D.C.; the historian Gertrude Himmelfarb, professor emeritus of history at the Graduate Center of the City University of New York; and E. D. Hirsch, Jr., of *Cultural Literacy* fame. These five—who were awarded honorary degrees at the convocation ceremonies the following day—were joined by two members of the Williams faculty: Mark C. Taylor, professor of religion and director of the Williams Center for the Humanities and Social Sciences, who acted as moderator for the panel, and Lynda Bundtzen, professor of English and chair of Williams's Women's Studies program.

What made this event noteworthy was not its novelty; similar panels have been convened at major universities for years now. Nor was the opening of Williams's Center for the Humanities and Social Sciences much news; there are already some three hundred such centers at colleges and universities across the country. And if Williams has only now acquired a humanities center, it is because only recently has the interdisciplinary humanities center securely enough entrenched itself in the academic mainstream to be an attractive ornament for a small, mainstream liberal arts college. No, the inauguration of a humanities center and a debate over the state of the humanities at Williams College are important not so much for their own sakes as for what they tell us about the progress that academic radicalism has made in transforming itself into the new academic establishment.

Nearly a thousand people—most of them students—crowded into Williams's elegant Chapin Hall to listen to the panel debate. Professor Taylor introduced the discussion by dwelling on the question mark that formed part of the title: Yes, we've all heard a great deal about the humanities lately, but is there really a crisis? And if so, what is it? Professor Taylor made it clear that he doubted that the popular perception that the humanities are in trouble was at all accurate. But he had no doubt about where to place the blame for that mistaken perception. In his view, the widespread sense that the humanities are in a state of crisis has largely "grown out of an extraordinary attack on recent tendencies in humanistic studies that had been carried out during the Reagan years and is continuing in the Bush administration." (He meant the administration of George H. W. Bush, of course, but I have doubt that he would say something similar about the administration of George W. Bush.)

Whether Professor Taylor actually believed that the Reagan and Bush administrations themselves had undertaken or otherwise abetted this alleged attack or whether he thought they merely provided a climate conducive to attacking the humanities was never made terribly clear. What was clear, however, was his deep antipathy to the voices that "are calling us back to what they regard as the traditional values of the Western humanistic tradition." Professor Taylor did not mention any names, but it was not long before the specters of William Bennett, Allan Bloom, and Lynne Cheney loomed large and threatening in the wings. For Professor Taylor, if there was a crisis in the humanities today, it lay not in the way the humanities are in fact pursued at our colleges and universities— where, we were given to understand, things were proceeding splendidly—but precisely in efforts by people like Bloom, Bennett, and Cheney to resuscitate those "traditional values of the Western humanistic tradition."

Professor Taylor's main supporting text was *Speaking*

for the Humanities—a document written, he assured his attentive audience, by a group of "the nation's leading humanists." Alluding to and quoting copiously from this report from the American Council of Learned Societies, Professor Taylor's remarks also conveyed a good deal of its spirit of arrogant and politically tinged condescension. Following the report, for example, he maintained that the people of the United States had always exhibited a marked anti-intellectual bias—hence, you see, it was not surprising that many people were uneasy with recent developments in the academy—and then proceeded to point out that the humanities are "inextricably bound up with philosophical and political traditions that many in today's world find problematic."

Professor Taylor passed on quickly to other matters; but let us pause for a moment to consider this last suggestion. What does it mean that a professor of religion and director of a center for the study of the humanities and social sciences should think that the humanities are inextricably linked to traditions that "many" find "problematic"? Which philosophical and political traditions, exactly, does he have in mind? Just who are the "many" taking issue with these traditions? And what does the euphemistic "problematic" imply? Again, Professor Taylor did not offer specifics. But his invocation of the legacy of Greece and Rome as the ultimate source of the humanistic tradition made it clear that he meant the philosophical and political traditions of the West—traditions that, in philosophy, developed the ideals of truth, objectivity, and disinterestedness, and that, in politics, are responsible for the rise of liberal democratic society. The "many" who dispute this legacy are of course Professor Taylor and his colleagues—that is, precisely those academics charged with teaching and preserving the humanities and the traditions upon which they are based.

What Professor Taylor was saying, then, is very close to the message of *Speaking for the Humanities*. It goes something like this: Recent attacks on the humanities have been misplaced; indeed, the humanities today are thriving; but there is the unfortunate detail that the philosophical and political ideas that gave rise to and have traditionally supported the humanities are essentially racist, sexist, and elitist—among other things—and so must be scrapped for something more enlightened. The institutional corollary to all this was unexpressed but also fairly obvious: More "research" is needed to discern and foster such enlightened alternatives; so please, you anti-intellectual, unenlightened populace who continue to labor under the prejudices of an outmoded tradition, please keep sending your children to college to be disabused of such prejudices and keep supporting us post-humanist humanists with grants from the National Endowment for the Humanities and other governmental institutions. Given his understanding of the humanities, it was little wonder that Professor Taylor should conclude his remarks with another echo of the ACLS report, reminding his audience that he considers the "stakes" in the controversy over the humanities to be primarily "social and political." Who could doubt it?

Instead of offering prepared remarks on the large issues that Professor Taylor had broached in his introduction, members of the panel were asked to respond individually to a series of questions that had been previously formulated by individuals from the Williams community and that Professor Taylor addressed to each of them in turn.

Some of the questions, and certainly some of the responses, tended to wander off the announced topic of the evening's discussion; but, taken together, some half dozen of the exchanges provided a veritable catalogue of the chief issues that define the controversy over the humanities today.

The first question, addressed to Professor Bundtzen, concerned the issue of the canon: how should it be defined and what is its importance for contemporary debate? Professor Bundtzen began conventionally enough by alluding to Matthew Arnold: he had been invoked by the authors of *Speaking for the Humanities,* she noted, and indeed the traditional idea of the canon could be summed up in Arnoldian terms as "masterpieces, the great works, those works deemed to be of lasting value and significance, important for critics to return to again and again." In this context she mentioned Samuel Johnson's notion that great works are those that continue to be read for a hundred years. But it soon became clear that Professor Bundtzen had little patience with this whole idea of the canon, at least as it has been traditionally defined. For who occupies its ranks? People like "Chaucer and Shakespeare and Milton"—those whom Professor Bundtzen repeatedly and contemptuously referred to as "the big guys" and "the big names": the likes of "Picasso, Matisse, Rembrandt" in painting, Nietzsche and Kant in philosophy. "It's like having a big list of names," Professor Bundtzen complained, working up to her main point: "The names, I hope you all noticed, are . . . *men.* They're white men; they're Western European. . . . [The canon is] the list of the white men who have created Western culture." One wasn't sure which she thought was worse, the sex of the creators or their creations. Professor Bundtzen went on to support the "feminist contention" that "surely there must be some women somewhere who did something that might be deemed of interpretive significance."

Having already encountered many variants of this position, we know that Professor Bundtzen's complaint is so predictable as to approach the status of a cliché. But she did not limit herself to lamenting the exclusion of women writers from the canon. Echoing academic feminists like Elaine Showalter, she also made a more radical point. "There is a way in which there is a canonization of unique genius," she told us, "and genius as it's attached to the male imagination: *Their* problems, *their* desires, what *they* love and *they* think is important, and *their* narratives and *their* stories, *their* events, *their* history, the way in which they paint their often female subjects." In other words, it's not only the predominance of men in the canon that Professor Bundtzen objected to, but also *the very criteria for inclusion* in the canon: the whole idea of "unique genius," for example, seemed specifically "male" to her, as did the problems, desires, stories, and so on that were expressed in works created by men. The possibility that there might be something *human* in these aspirations and achievements, something that transcended the contingency of gender, was rejected out of hand.

Professor Bundtzen's comments were nothing more than a commonplace expression of commonplace feminist sentiments; but of course they are so disturbing precisely *because* they have become commonplace. It is another measure of the triumph of radical feminism in the academy that ideas that were considered an extreme idiosyncrasy only a few years ago are these days taken for granted and repeated as gospel by professors everywhere. Thus even at an elite liberal arts institution like Williams, once an epitome of the small, rigorous traditional college, we have faculty propagating the notion that the "value" placed on "unique genius" in our culture is somehow distinctively "male" and therefore open to feminist dismantling.

Later in the evening, when the discussion returned to the question of the canon, Professor Bundtzen provided numerous additional examples of how far she has absorbed the conventional feminist ideology. Elaborating on her point about the essentially masculine nature of traditional aesthetic, intellectual, and spiritual criteria, she spoke of a "counter-canon" of women authors and questioned the high esteem that has been accorded to certain sorts of creative endeavor while being withheld from others. "When the Western male tradition was canonized," she informed us,

> certain values about individual genius were canonized, and mastery, and transcendence; and in other words the canonization of women authors [might be read] as a counter-canonization of different values. . . .[It would be] an enrichment of the canon overall to have a discordant woman's voice saying, "I'm not creating this poem for eternity," "I don't want to celebrate transcendent truth, I want to celebrate the little things in women's lives,. . . the small nurturing things that women do."

In the feminist reconstruction of the canon that Professor Bundtzen envisioned, then, allegedly "male" values like individual genius, transcendence, mastery, and truth must be put aside to make room for allegedly "female" values and the "discordant woman's voice" undertaking to champion "the small nurturing things women do." Concrete examples are always useful in these situations, but about as far as Professor Bundtzen went was to wonder "What did Dorothy *feel* like when she found herself at Tintern Abbey and what was her brother William doing with her?"

II Are you now or have you ever been conservative?

We shall return to Professor Bundtzen and her discordant woman's voice. But first, in order to get a fuller sense of the issues that were raised at Williams, let us consider the responses some of the other panelists gave to the questions that were addressed to them. The first question that was addressed to Professor Hirsch concerned the relationship between his book *Cultural Literacy* and Allan Bloom's *The Closing of the American Mind*. Professor Hirsch's work on cultural literacy had been widely associated with the spirit of *The Closing of the American Mind;* how, if at all, would he distinguish his position from Bloom's? And what does the enthusiastic public response to their books tell us about the educated public's attitude toward the educational mission of colleges today?

These questions were tailor-made for Professor Hirsch. Ever since the raging success of *Cultural Literacy* brought him not only fame but also the uncomfortable label "conservative," he has taken every opportunity to shake off the label and attempt to ingratiate himself with the academic Left. It was hardly surprising, then, that he should have responded that, "thank heavens," the question of his relation to Allan Bloom has finally become "obsolete." Though his name unfortunately had been linked with Bloom's when their books were first published, he said, people now understood that they were up to fundamentally different things. Bloom really was a conservative critic of new trends in the academy, whereas Professor Hirsch now declared that the new trends were, in his opinion, splendid; he just wanted more people to be able to participate in them, and so wanted young students to know enough to squeeze into college. The names that are now, and more appropriately, paired as being antagonistic to recent changes in the humanities, Professor Hirsch explained, are those of Allan Bloom and William Bennett—who, he told an amused audience, are known in some quarters as "the killer Bs." Moreover, he continued, "I presume that, on the simplest level, Bloom votes or least talks to Republicans and emotionally that has not been my own history." This, too, greatly entertained the audience—though Professor Himmelfarb had the bad taste to point out later that, in fact, Professor Bloom was a Democrat and talked to whatever groups invited him.

Professor Hirsch then went on to suggest that, while Allan Bloom's book was an embittered response to the student unrest of the late Sixties, his own work grew out of his study of reading and writing. *Cultural Literacy*, he said, was aimed primarily at disadvantaged children and sought to make the elementary point that some degree of shared knowledge was essential to academic success. What that shared knowledge should be, Professor Hirsch insisted, was another question entirely: he himself would certainly not wish to make invidious distinctions among various curricula. The important thing was not *what* was taught but, whatever it was, that it be shared. Continuing his effort at self-exoneration, he claimed to be "appalled" that his book had been read as a conservative tract. It was his "misfortune," he said, to enter the debate about education at a time when any effort at reform would be looked on with suspicion because it would seem conservative. What he really wanted, Professor Hirsch confided in his closing piety, was to give everybody an opportunity to go to college—an opportunity that did not now exist in American society.

Since questions are often more revealing than the answers they elicit, we may quote the next question, which was addressed to Professor Derrida, as much for what it tells us about the person who framed it as for the answer it received. "Does the very notion of crisis," Professor Taylor read aloud, "serve to reaffirm the institutional structures it apparently threatens, and, for those of us who feel that the humanities are hardly threatened enough, how optimistic should we be about the possibility of establishing a discourse which moves beyond the agonistic [i.e., contested], and apparently endlessly recuperable, language of crisis?" This is a classic so-to-speak "Derridean" question; whoever wrote it— and one cannot help suspecting Professor Taylor himself—is obviously well steeped in deconstructivist argot. Not only does it begin with a facile inversion of common sense (the prospect of a crisis actually "reaffirming" what it seems to threaten) and express a marked current of subversion ("those of us who feel the humanities are hardly threatened enough"), but also it uses an appropriately forbidding jargon ("discourse," "agonistic," "endlessly recuperable"); above all, Professor Taylor's question was everywhere at pains to place the emphasis on language, not on the reality language describes.

Not to be outdone at his own game, however, Professor Derrida's response was itself a consummate exhibition of deconstructivist legerdemain. Instead of addressing himself to the question, he began by posing questions of his own. He asked Professor Bundtzen whether she thought it was possible to stop the process of canonization once it had started. He himself, he said, did not believe that canonization could be stopped, for every attempt to stop it would simply lead to an alternative process of canonization, producing a "counter-canon" like the one Professor Bundtzen and so many others had proposed. One might wish to change what was "canonized," dropping, for example, the notion of the masterpiece. But this would not bring the process of canonization itself to a halt; it would merely channel it into a different route.

Before proceeding with Professor Derrida's response, it is worth pausing to note how far we have come from the notion of an academic canon with this talk of "canonization." Whatever the ecclesiastical roots of the term "canon," the process by which specific works are included in the literary canon is deeply different from the process whereby an individual is "canonized" as a saint by the Roman Catholic Church. Yet "canonization" has become a vogue word in the academy. No doubt this is partly because, poaching on the aura of religious canonization, it suggests something supernatural, *ex cathedra*, even—for many secular observers—inherently fraudulent. But it is always useful to track such misuses of language, and one cannot help pointing out that Professor Derrida's suggestion about "dropping" the notion of the masterpiece from discussions of the literary canon would be more or less like dropping the notion of "saint" from canonization in the religious sense—in other words, it would make a travesty of the whole idea of a literary canon, since a literary canon without masterpieces would be like a religious canon without saints. Jacques Derrida is hardly one to be detained by such details, however, and he went quickly on to ask Professor Hirsch what his earlier theories of interpretation revealed about his relation to Allan Bloom, and whether there was any essential connection between his current proposals for establishing cultural literacy and his theories of interpretation.

These were particularly naughty questions to put to E. D. Hirsch. Before Professor Hirsch burst upon the scene as the apostle of cultural literacy, he had acquired a certain reputation in the world of literary criticism as the author of *Validity in Interpretation*, not only a polemic against "radical historicism" and theories of linguistic indeterminacy—then still mostly of German, not French, extraction—but also a plea for the idea that texts possess a literal meaning that provides a criterion for valid interpretation. "There is clearly a sense in which we can neither evaluate a text nor determine what it means 'to us, today' until we have correctly apprehended what it means," he wrote in one characteristic passage.* Not that *Validity in Interpretation* won a particularly enthusiastic following: Proponents of "hermeneutics" and, later, deconstruction dismissed it as hopelessly reactionary while many of those who might have been sympathetically inclined toward the book's overall spirit regarded it as simple-minded. It became widely known, then, not so

---

* E. D. Hirsch, Jr., *Validity in Interpretation* (New Haven: Yale University Press, 1967), *seriatim*, pages viii, 209.

much because it was influential but because it was among the most clearly written and straightforward expositions of the minority view in the academy that there might be such a thing as literal meaning or, indeed, validity in interpretation. One tended to see it cited mostly as a straw man, a cardinal example of a thick-headed, overly literal approach to literary theory. Thus for someone as desperate as Professor Hirsch to disencumber himself from the "conservative" label, it must have been galling to be reminded of his former sins—especially by Derrida, who was at that moment the very incarnation of academic chic and whose entire *oeuvre* stands in the most glaring contrast to Professor Hirsch's own earlier ideas. Poor Professor Hirsch declared that people had once again been wrong to see him as "conservative," and then favored us with a little self-exposition according to which the argument of *Validity in Interpretation* was scarcely to be distinguished from the kind of relativism espoused by Stanley Fish. It was a pathetic performance.

For his own part, Professor Derrida then launched into a typical deconstructive gambit. We should not worry about the humanities being in a state of crisis, he said, because it is in the nature of the academy to be always in crisis. Noting that the etymology of "crisis" suggests choice or decision, he assured us that "the rhetoric of crisis" is "fundamentally optimistic" since it looks forward to a solution, a choice, a decision. In fact, the problem today is that the academy is no longer in crisis and hence "there is no choice, no decision to be made." But while Professor Derrida is obviously expert at the interpretive shenanigans that make things seem the opposite of the way they really are, his subsequent comments showed that—about certain subjects anyway—he is as interested as the next person in preserving the ordinary meanings of words. For he went on to say that even if there is, alas, no crisis in the humanities today, there are some serious problems. One important problem, he said, comes from outside the academy and concerns money. A great deal of money is being given to the sciences, while the humanities, having to make do with far more meager amounts, are in danger of being "marginalized." When it came down to talking about money, at least, Professor Derrida abandoned his customary intellectual high jinks and was perfectly straightforward. There was no attempt to make a lack of money seem like an abundance, or to show that the "margins" of this kind of "discourse" were really the center.

He was not quite so straightforward about what he identified as an "internal" problem that the humanities face today—namely, the problem of conservatives who want to preserve the traditional canon and fundamental values of the humanities. Recognizing the threat that this poses to the agenda of the new academic establishment, Professor Derrida resorted to paradox: The desire to preserve the traditional role of the humanities, he said, threatens to destroy the humanities "from within." Indeed, according to Professor Derrida, the only real way to rescue the humanities is to shoulder the "dangerous responsibility" of subjecting them to radical criticism, "to transform the canon, to enlarge the field." But lest it seem that he wanted simply to . . . well, to deconstruct the humanities, which after all would thus risk further "marginalizing" the humanities from sources of financial support, he hastened to assure us that "we all share the same respect for Shakespeare, for Milton, for others."

But do we? Does Professor Bundtzen, for example?

Wasn't Professor Derrida ignoring the fact that on many
American campuses, and indeed in many cases due to the
influence of his writings, "respect" is about the last word
one would choose to describe the prevailing attitude
toward Shakespeare, Milton, or other "Dead, White,
European Males" (DWEMs for short)? In fact, he wants to
have it both ways, to indulge in an all-out critical assault
on the traditional idea of the humanities and everything
they stand for, and yet, when the occasion calls for it, to
be able to mouth a few pious phrases about respect for
Shakespeare, Milton, and those unnamed "others."

III Who needs transcendent truths?

Such questions returned with renewed force when the
next panelist, the historian Gertrude Himmelfarb (the
panel's token conservative), responded to the first question that was addressed to her.

Asked to distinguish between political and intellectual
history as traditionally practiced and the new social history that has taken the academy by storm, Professor
Himmelfarb began by making a few observations about
the proceedings thus far. It was unfortunate, she said, that
the word "conservative" should have been introduced so
blithely into the discussion as a term of censure. For by
intimating at the outset that "conservative" means "bad,"
an overtly politicized framework for the entire discussion
had been established. Professor Himmelfarb acknowledged that most of the panelists would insist that
anyone wanting to preserve the traditional canon was already pursuing a political agenda of his own. But it
would be far more productive, she continued, if questions

about politics came in at the end of the discussion rather than at the beginning. Professor Himmelfarb also noted that she had many friends who, though they were very much on the Left politically, yet considered themselves "cultural conservatives" in educational matters. Given this, she suggested, a more neutral term like "traditional" or "conventional" would be preferable to "conservative" as a descriptive term.

Professor Himmelfarb went on to remind the audience that the moderator, Professor Taylor, had opened the discussion in a highly charged political manner by accusing the Reagan and Bush administrations of mounting "an extraordinary attack on recent tendencies in humanistic studies." What could this mean? After all, she pointed out, the very humanities center whose inauguration they were gathered together to celebrate was being supported by a generous grant from the National Endowment for the Humanities under the Bush administration. Is that the sort of "extraordinary attack" Professor Taylor had in mind?

And in response to Professor Derrida's call for greater questioning in the humanities, Professor Himmelfarb noted that questions were being asked on more than one side of the issue. Professor Derrida claimed to champion a rigorous questioning of authority, the legitimacy of tradition, and the nature and composition of the humanities. But were not others—including Allan Bloom, William Bennett, and Lynne Cheney—also asking hard questions about the humanities? Were they not questioning the authority of the dominant voices in the academy, the legitimacy of the attempt to delegitimate the tradition, the right of entrenched powers that would have us determine the nature and composition of the curriculum on purely political grounds? Of course they were. Why then, she asked, should such questions be dismissed at the outset as an "attack" on the humanities? Are not critics like Bloom, Bennett, Cheney, and others doing precisely what Professor Derrida and his like-minded colleagues would have their own students do: scrutinizing "contemporary modes of discourse"?

Professor Himmelfarb then turned to the question that had been addressed to her about the distinction between traditional intellectual and political history, on the one hand, and the new social history, on the other. She explained that the rise of social history, which concentrates on the texture of everyday life and the mundane activities of ordinary people, has tended to undermine the practice of traditional history, which was essentially "elite history," concerned with what she called high politics and great ideas. Indeed, she said, traditional intellectual and political history was precisely the history that had been enacted mostly by those Professor Bundtzen contemptuously referred to as "the big guys": great statesmen and military leaders in politics, great thinkers and artists in intellectual and cultural matters.

Speaking of "the big guys," Professor Himmelfarb then asked Professor Bundtzen whether she was not worried about fostering a new stereotype of women, one that might be "limiting, restrictive, even possibly demeaning"? For why shouldn't women as well as men be concerned with large questions? "What about the woman who does want to celebrate transcendence and uniqueness and genius and large things," Professor Himmelfarb asked, "and doesn't want to be confined to 'a nurturing role'? Is she to be illegitimized as a woman?"

This question elicited a great round of applause from

the audience but considerable confusion from the podium. An obviously stunned Professor Bundtzen replied that what she had said did not preclude the possibility of genius, though she did admit that she was "very reluctant" to use the phrase "transcendent truths"—after all, why should transcendent truths be "better or of greater value to us than the kind of truths we need to live our lives, which are not usually terribly transcendent from moment to moment or hour to hour"? One might wish to inquire a little more deeply into Professor Bundtzen's understanding of "transcendent truths." What "kind of truths," for example, did Professor Bundtzen think we needed "to live our lives"? This was not the occasion to ponder such details. Instead, in case there was any doubt about the matter, Professor Bundtzen declared that she would characterize herself as a feminist critic. As such, she did not want to leave us with the impression that she would confine women to "the small things," as she put it earlier. In fact, she particularly admired women authors who regularly challenged male authors on their own terms: "who discover that beneath the guise of this extraordinary genius and potency and all the terms that are traditionally associated with male genius, there are vulnerabilities and weaknesses and ways in which to create a dialogue with that male tradition."

Professor Bundtzen then went on to respond to Professor Himmelfarb's criticism of the way politics had intruded into the discussion. The problem is, she said, that if as an educator in the humanities you read that you should be "teaching transcendent truths" and you have difficulty with the very notion of transcendent truth then you feel under attack, especially if the definition of the humanities as having to do with transcendent truths is also tied to purse strings. What if, she asked, the Humanities Center at Williams decided that this year "we're not going to deal with transcendence, we're not going to deal with truths this year, we're going to deal with . . . I don't know, I can imagine another agenda which would not be outside the realm of humane studies." In that case the Humanities Center would no doubt find that their requests for money from the government would be denied—and that, she concluded, she would regard as a "truly political" act.

It must be said that Professor Himmelfarb responded to this bilge with great restraint. Did their application to the National Endowment, she wondered, say something to the effect that "this year we plan to deal with transcendent truths"? Did it not rather represent quite faithfully the program they have in fact been carrying out? One might ask, in addition, what the alternative to dealing "with truths" might be: dealing with untruths, perhaps? Is this an alternative within the realm of "humane studies" we would want humanities centers to pursue with public funds? Professor Bundtzen did not exactly reply to Professor Himmelfarb's question, although—no doubt searching for a safe way to reintroduce a note of political virtue into the discussion—she did offer the stunning *non sequitur* that "I do think a lot of people feel threatened by the Helms amendment recently." What a gift to the cultural Left the proposed Helms amendment was! Formulated in the wake of the controversy over federal funding for Robert Mapplethorpe's photographs of homosexual sado-masochistic acts, the proposed amendment would have imposed a ban on giving federal money to art deemed offensive to a wide range of groups. It had already been soundly defeated by the time Professor Bundtzen spoke out against it, but that didn't seem to matter. To declare oneself against the amendment was still to show that one was on the side of virtue. Indeed, Professor Bundtzen's comment showed that the Helms amendment, even though it never had a prayer of being passed in its original form, has continued to provide a wonderfully convenient icon for politically correct academics, artists, and other cultural figures to attack: where else these days can one bask in the aura of outraged virtue by risking so little?

IV A lesson in representative democracy

The discussion at Williams that evening proceeded with many other memorable insights. Professor Baker, for example, won a round of applause for noting that the phrase "shared values" reminded him of the black "sharecropper" who was always being exploited. Werner Gundersheimer assured us that the "contestations" in the humanities today over the canon, appropriate forms of language, and so on really derived from the "extreme vitality and diversity" the humanities now enjoy, not a crisis. And Derrida replied to the charge that deconstruction was fundamentally ahistorical by asserting that, on the contrary, deconstruction offered "the most historical approach" to history, and that, in fact, the techniques of deconstruction provided the best way to preserve the intellectual vitality of the university.

But the evening's single most dramatic moment came when Professor Baker decided to weigh in against Professor Himmelfarb. If he was short on coherence and consecutive reasoning, he nonetheless succeeded in making himself abundantly clear. He was troubled, he told the Williams audience, by the ease with which Professor Himmelfarb had seemed to score points against Professor Bundtzen using "what I call the Strom Thurmond strategy." He went on to explain what he meant with an anecdote. One day, after having heard Martin Luther King's famous "I Have a Dream" speech, Professor Baker turned on his television only to find Senator Thurmond exclaiming that "Negroes here have more refrigerators, more shoes, more appliances, than colored people anywhere in the world. Why are they out here marching? I just do not understand it." According to Professor Baker, Professor Himmelfarb's observation that the Williams Center for the Humanities and Social Sciences was supported by a grant from the National Endowment for the Humanities betrayed a similarly patronizing attitude, which he summed up as follows: "We've given you, even you . . . a grant, so how can we conservatives be politically motivated?"

Professor Baker then maundered on to consider Professor Himmelfarb's remark that she had many friends who were politically very liberal but who were conservative on cultural and educational issues. These were the sort of people, Professor Baker said contemptuously, "who speak Marxist and send their kids to elite prep schools." Such people might talk a good line, he explained, but when it came time "for Buffy or Cokie" to go to school, it was off to some elite institution like Choate for them. Of course, the idea that Professor Himmelfarb, the very embodiment of the modern Jewish intellectual, had such vacuous WASP caricatures in mind when she spoke of her liberal friends who happened to be cultural conservatives is almost as amusing as it is absurd.

By now Professor Baker was really warmed up. He more or less abandoned the attempt to frame an argument, letting himself be carried along by a gush of increasingly strident rhetoric. There were several notable elements in the oratorical collage he constructed. First, we were informed that "the fact is, the institutional site of authority is constituted by the National Endowment for the Humanities and the National Endowment for the Arts." "Authority" is always a term of reproach in the academy these days, of course, as is "institutional." So identifying the Endowments as the "site of institutional authority" is to suggest something particularly malevolent. Exactly what it portended was not clear, except that the phrase provided a kind of transition to Professor Baker's observation that "it is a fact that the people who run these institutions are not elected by voters in this room. President Reagan doesn't call you up and say, 'Hey, Houston, what do you think?' "

Professor Baker next told us that he saw no evidence that people like William Bennett, Allan Bloom, and Professor Himmelfarb had "immersed themselves in the very topics of inquiry that constitute our consensus" and charged that such people dismissed out of hand recent curricular innovations "precisely on the basis of gender, class, race, and sex." Professor Baker also opined (no doubt correctly) that Allan Bloom would not have much to tell us about the work of Frederick Douglass and other nineteenth-century American black writers or about the marvels of contemporary lesbian plays—though why Professor Bloom, a specialist in Plato and Rousseau, should have much to tell us about these subjects was not made clear.

We were now approaching Professor Baker's peroration. "Mr. Helms and that amendment have to do entirely with the institutional framework that I have discussed," he said, referring again (one conjectures) to the National Endowments as the "site of institutional authority." He then went on to issue a warning about those who criticize the dismantling of the traditional curriculum. "They are dangerous to all of us" and even, he said, to democracy. Why are those who criticize the politicization of the humanities dangerous? Professor Baker offered a few reasons, not all of which were immediately intelligible, but one that I did hear is that such people are dangerous "because they are conservative." Moreover, he charged, alluding to Professor Himmelfarb's description of traditional historiography, while this conservative view of education pretends to strive to be objective and to respect the facts, it really "assigns the values and makes the facts correspond to them"—in other words, though Professor Baker didn't put it so bluntly, it lies. He then squeezed in a few words about racial stereotypes and concluded in ringing tones by saying that while it may be too early to know whether all the new movements sweeping our campuses are right, we know "indisputably that what we have seen in the past is wrong." This remarkable performance was met by wild applause.

But what can we make of Professor Baker's denunciation? Consider only his observation that officials administering the National Endowments were not elected by the "voters in this room." It may be that Professor Baker is unacquainted with the mechanics of representative democracy. (After all, many, many officials are appointed with Professor Baker's consultation.) It's possible, too, that he has something to learn about the character of the American electorate. Does Professor Baker believe that the voters at large in this country favor spending their tax dollars to support university humanities programs that have frankly devoted themselves to a radical political agenda? Perhaps he really believes that most voters wake up thinking, "I wish the government would give more money to professors who spend their time criticizing the site of institutional authority in this country and teaching my children about lesbian plays"? Or maybe—since he, too, mentioned the Helms amendment—he is convinced that most voters want more federal money spent on exhibitions of photographs of sexual degradation and coercion? The fact is, it is impossible to know just *what* Professor Baker thinks about these or any number of other matters he touched upon; what is perfectly, clear, however is that he is blissfully unaware of how privileged and protected a position he and his colleagues occupy in our society, thanks precisely to their being insulated by the authority and largesse of the institutions they excoriate.

V   The collapse of the center

Perhaps sensing that he had let himself get carried away, Professor Baker later apologized to Professor Himmelfarb for comparing her to Strom Thurmond. He found nothing else in his declamation to retract, however, and as the assembled multitudes filed out of Chapin Hall a little later that evening his denunciations seemed to continue to echo. Professor Taylor had concluded by reassuring us yet again that even if there is a crisis in the humanities, it is "a sign of vitality rather than demise." Judging from snatches of conversation overheard after the discussion let out, the students were not so sure. Sentiment seemed to be running largely in favor of Professor Himmelfarb, not only with respect to the violence of Professor Baker's rhetoric but also with respect to the issues of feminism and the practice of history. Indeed, the proceedings at Williams that weekend reminded one that at many campuses today the political relation between undergraduates and the faculty has shifted in important ways since the late Sixties and Seventies. Increasingly, what one sees is not a radical student body importuning a recalcitrant faculty and administration for greater "diversity," relaxing of standards, and so forth, but a more traditionalist student body resisting the exhortations of a markedly more radical faculty. Often, the resistance expresses itself as simple indifference to the humanities: if studying the humanities has come to be an exercise in intellectual obscurantism and political sloganeering, well, there are other subjects worth pursuing. Is it any wonder that humanities enrollments have fallen off so precipitously in recent years?

The proceedings at Williams also reminded one of the extent to which the centrist position among our academic faculties has collapsed into a species of accommodating Leftism. There was, first, the continuing spectacle of Professor Hirsch busily dissociating himself from charges of conservatism and traditionalism. But an even more egregious example of this surrender to the Left was Werner Gundersheimer's convocation speech the following day. Though obviously meant to represent a "moderate" position mid-way between, say, Professors Himmelfarb and Baker, this historian and director of the Folger Shakespeare Library—a man whose very position would seem to require him to act as a guardian of one of the greatest writers in the literary canon—in effect showed how far the middle has capitulated to the radical extreme. His speech, entitled "'Our Battles join'd': The Struggle for the American Mind," had two chief messages: 1) New trends in the humanities, from deconstruction and feminism to radical curricular revision, are only so many signs of vibrancy and health; and 2) The real danger to the humanities comes from those who wish to preserve the traditional curriculum and the values it embodies.

Professor Gundersheimer was full of the requisite clichés and slogans: the humanities today were "enriched" by "diversity" and "innovation," they had "moved with the times" "by accepting new subjects and approaches into their curricula." He did speak with some nostalgia about the English professor of old whose task was to master the literature in his field and then teach and write about it "in plain, accessible English that any educated person could understand and appreciate." No doubt that was precisely the ideal once held up to and perhaps even espoused by Professor Gundersheimer himself. He admitted that it had long since been abandoned by fashionable academics, yet went on to assure us that, because "change is the only constant within existing academic disciplines," its loss was not a tragedy but an exciting new challenge.

At the center of Professor Gundersheimer's speech to the dutifully assembled Williams community was a solemn warning about attempts to reinstate a more traditional view of the humanities and what he called "the genteel ideal of plain talk in support of timeless verities." Predictably, Allan Bloom came in for particular censure because of his allegedly "simplistic attacks on colleges and universities." Yet Professor Gundersheimer was careful to assert that the problem went beyond Bloom and his followers. "Many distinguished scholars," he said, "see the flux of scholarship as a threat to the very substance of received doctrines, or what they are likely to call 'the truth.'" (One wondered what Professor Gundersheimer would be likely to call it.)

As a recent example of this "revolt against complexity," he quoted from a book review that had appeared recently in *The Wall Street Journal*.* The review was written by the late Edward Shils, the eminent sociologist who was then still teaching at the University of Chicago, and concerned *The Culture We Deserve*, a collection of essays on culture and the academy by Jacques Barzun, the venerable historian and emeritus professor at Columbia University. One of Professor Barzun's chief complaints in that book is that, in the name of specialization, much academic discourse in the humanities has mired itself in a jargon that is both trivial and unintelligible. Professor Shils seconded this criticism and took it a step further, castigating "the destructiveness of deconstruction," "that most chic of French academic exports, which preaches a nihilistic skepticism of language and that has now gained an almost unchallenged empire in American universities." Professor Shils went on to note that the collaboration of deconstruction and other instances of academic "theory" with "a smattering of Marxism and political antinomianism" had "ravaged" the study of the humanities.

Professor Gundersheimer was quick to ridicule Professor Shils's description of the state of the humanities. He

* Edward Shils, "The Sad State of the Humanities in America," *The Wall Street Journal*, 3 July 1989.

began by telling us that it was little more than an example of "the discourse of alienation" and "the old 'evil empire' gambit." (One can be sure that the damning allusion to President Reagan's epithet for the former Soviet Union was not lost on the audience.) He then proceeded with a few words about his own view of matters in the academy. Portraying himself as the embodiment of moderation, Professor Gundersheimer proposed the adoption of "common sense" as a fruitful antidote to extremes on both sides of the debate over the humanities. That might seem a worthy proposal—common sense being in notably short supply in the humanities these days—but lest anyone think he was suggesting something reactionary, Professor Gundersheimer explained that "I am of course prepared to believe that one person's common sense is another person's non-sense." In other words, he supports a wonderful version of "common sense"—what we might perhaps call a "deconstructed" version—that is common only to the individual who happens to hold it.

While this custodian of the legacy of Shakespeare never even mentioned Shakespeare's name, he did favor us with a few "axioms" that he claimed to find useful when thinking about the mission of the humanities. For example, we learned that the humanities do not thrive on sameness, but on "difference and conflict"; similarly, we discovered that "complexity in the world of ideas isn't scary. It's fun." "What *is* scary," Professor Gundersheimer pursued, "is reductionism. . . . Hitler knew exactly what art was. So does Jesse Helms." And it's the same way, apparently, with those who claim to know the "original intent of the framers of the Constitution"—that is to say, those who, like Judge Robert Bork, have fallen afoul of the Left. Professor Gundersheimer concluded by assuring us that although he was all in favor of conflict, he did think it would be "regrettable if the great issues that now divide us—the sanctity of the so-called canon; the referentiality of language; the legitimacy of new methods and subjects of inquiry—were to lessen the claims of humanists and social scientists to serious public attention."

The contrast between the message of Professor Gundersheimer's speech and the setting could hardly have been starker. Here we had the most traditional of academic ceremonies, replete with academic regalia and communal singing of "My Country, 'tis of Thee," providing the setting for a speech whose essential point was that the humanities can cut themselves off from both their foundation and their ideals and still be said to be thriving. What else are we to make of the evocation of a "common sense" that has a constituency of one? Or the contemptuous reference to "the sanctity of the so-called canon"? Or the suggestion that "the referentiality of language" is something the humanities today could just as well do without? Or the idea that "new methods"— meaning deconstruction and its progeny—and new "subjects of inquiry"—meaning everything from pulp novels to rock videos—are fit subjects for humanistic inquiry? Indeed, what else are we to make of the sum of Williams College's inquiry into the question, "Crisis in the Humanities"?

Professor Gundersheimer insisted that it would be "regrettable" were public interest in the humanities to falter. But why shouldn't it falter? Would it be surprising if the public spurned the claims of these new-style "humanists" and social scientists to "serious public attention"—to say nothing of serious public funding

—when those claims are often expressly at odds with the public interest in preserving and transmitting our intellectual and cultural heritage? Imagine: a New Historicist analysis of convocation ceremonies at small New England colleges "proving" that they were instruments of cultural repression, or a deconstructionist reading of "My Country, 'tis of Thee" showing that it was really a subversive or coercive text. Such exercises are legion in the academy; are they worth "serious public attention"? The point is not that Professor Gundersheimer is an especially important or radical figure on the academic scene; he is neither. Nor is his message at all out of the ordinary. Again, this is precisely the problem: that even an ordinary, self-proclaimed moderate should as a matter of course abandon moderation and adopt "moving with the times" as a criterion of critical judgment. The German poet-philosopher Friedrich Schiller exhorted us to render to our contemporaries what they need, not what they praise. It's good advice, but to be effective it requires not only insight but also the courage to think and act independently. The Williams panel was one of many recent events reminding us that, despite rhetoric to the contrary, such courage is in short supply in the academy.

The real crisis in the humanities today is caused by the collapse of a geninuely moderate center in the face of ideological pressure from a Leftist extreme. In the last few decades, what we have witnessed is the occupation of the center by a new academic establishment, the establishment of tenured radicals.

Postscript

I

W HEN *Tenured Radicals* was first published in April
1990, many critics—including some who were
generally sympathetic to the book's chief arguments—
wondered whether developments in the academy were
really quite as bad as I claimed. Surely, the argument
went, professors of literature who specialize in the rock
videos of Madonna are exceedingly rare; there can't be
many professors who devote their scholarly energies to
showing that *Paradise Lost* is a sexist document or that
The Tempest is an exposé of Western imperialism; are
there really more than a handful who maintain that there
are no compelling reasons for judging *Middlemarch* to be
a greater artistic achievement than the cartoons of Bugs
Bunny? And how many professors, really, would dismiss
the traditional notion of literary quality and the ideal of
disinterested scholarship as oppressive legacies of white
patriarchal culture? Surely such professors are a tiny

minority, freak or comical exceptions in an otherwise blandly moderate intellectual universe.

It would be consoling to think so. Unfortunately, subsequent developments in the academy have shown that if *Tenured Radicals* erred in its indictment, it erred on the side of understatement. It is not just that the peddlers of such politicized nonsense are in many cases among the most celebrated academics in the country: senior professors safely ensconced at Yale and Stanford, at Princeton and Harvard, Duke, the University of California, and other premier institutions, where they chair departments, sit on hiring, promotion, and tenure committees, and busy themselves developing and implementing radical curricular changes for their own and other institutions. That was already clear in the late 1980s. Nor is it simply that, unlike most of their moderate colleagues, such tenured radicals tend to be indefatigable proselytizers, bent on winning converts in their war of subversion against the traditional moral and intellectual values of a liberal arts education. This is troubling, to be sure, but it, too, has been obvious for some time. Nor, finally, is it news that even the most bizarre writings and proclamations coming out of the academy, instead of being regarded as exotic or repellent curiosities, are often instrumental in setting the terms of debate both in the classroom and within the profession as a whole. No one familiar with the kind of thing that passes for scholarship today will be surprised to discover—to take just one example—that the presentation of a paper called "Jane Austen and the Masturbating Girl" at the 1989 annual meeting of the Modern Language Association was matched by a paper at the 1990 meeting on "The Lesbian Phallus: Or, Does

Heterosexuality Exist?"* and, in 1994, "The Epistemology of the Queer Classroom."

All this is wearisomely familiar. What is new is the extent to which the constellation of radical trends that dominate the teaching of the humanities at many of our best institutions has found common cause in the rise of a new political ideology: the ideology of multiculturalism. Indeed, those interested in charting the course of this cultural fever will have noticed that the terms "multiculturalism" and "political correctness" have emerged as favored omnibus terms for these developments both in the academy and, increasingly, in the culture at large. Moreover, the multicultural agenda has provided common cause and something of a common vocabulary for an array of disciplines that are otherwise distinguished by quite different pursuits.

Still, partly because it has degenerated into something of a slogan, the term "multiculturalism" is apt to give rise to all manner of misunderstanding, and it is wise to begin by distinguishing between the adjective *multicultural* and the epithet *multiculturalism*. There is, first of all, the social fact that America, a country of immigrants, has always been a multicultural and multiethnic society. Indeed,

---

* This is the title of a paper in a session on "Lesbianism, Heterosexuality, and Feminist Theory" at the 1990 Modern Language Association meeting. The other papers listed for this session—which is by no means uncharacteristic of the offerings the MLA has seen fit to make available to its members—are "Mapping the Frontier of the Black Hole: Toward a Black Feminist Theory" and "Perverse Desire, the Lure of the Mannish Lesbian." *Publications of the Modern Language Association of America*, vol. 105, no. 6 (November 1990), page 1248.

it is our country's singular political achievement to have forged a society in which vast religious, ethnic, and racial differences are subordinated to the higher unity of national identity. Hence the once-defining image of America as a "melting pot."

The problem comes when this conciliatory vision of a multicultural society gives way to the ideology of multiculturalism. Here the politics of ethnic and racial redress is allowed to trump the sustaining unity. It happened in the 1910s, when a wave of ethnic militancy swept the country. Theodore Roosevelt was right to warn at that time that "The one absolutely certain way of bringing this nation to ruin . . . would be to permit it to become a tangle of squabbling nationalities." It is happening again now as the ideology of multiculturalism sweeps our schools and universities and infiltrates cultural life generally. As the historian Arthur Schlesinger noted in *The Disuniting of America*, his short but eloquent book on multiculturalism, "A cult of ethnicity has arisen both among non-Anglo whites and among nonwhite minorities to denounce the idea of a melting pot, to challenge the concept of 'one people,' and to protect, promote, and perpetuate separate ethnic and racial communities." It is in this sense, as Professor Schlesinger pointed out, that "the debate about the curriculum is a debate about what it means to be an American."*

We have all become familiar with the kinds of foolishness that the demand for multiculturalism and political correctness has brought to our schools and college cam-

---

* Arthur M. Schlesinger, Jr., *The Disuniting of America: Reflections on a Multicultural Society* (New York: Norton, 1991), *seriatim*, pages 15, 118, 17.

puses. The denunciation of Western civilization as inextricably racist, sexist, elitist, and patriarchal; the efforts by college administrations to enforce speech codes on college campuses; the blatant rewriting of history text books to soothe wounded ethnic feelings: all are transforming the nature of American society.

At the center of the multicultural ethos is the contention that all cultures are equally valuable and, therefore, that preferring one culture, intellectual heritage, or moral and social order to another is to be guilty of ethnocentrism and racism. Preferring Western culture and its heritage to others is held to be especially ethnocentric and racist. The thoughtless egalitarianism behind these ideas helps to explain the current academic obsession with the notion of "difference" and the widespread insistence that the differences that separate us—pre-eminently, differences of race, class, sexuality, and ethnic heritage— must be given priority over our common humanity.

This celebration of "difference" may sound like a prescription for tolerance and genuine pluralism. But in fact it has fostered a positively Orwellian situation in which "diversity" really means strict intellectual conformity, and "tolerance" is reserved exclusively for those who subscribe to one's own perspective. As has been widely reported in the press, attempts to enforce the ethic of "difference" have led to egregious violations of academic freedom and have poisoned the atmosphere for honest intellectual exchange at campuses across the country. Multiculturalism has provided a convenient umbrella for the smorgasbord of radical ideologies now regnant in the academy. Despite their differences, the one thing your literary deconstructionist, your Lacanian feminist, your post-structuralist Marxist, your New Historicist, and your devotee of what goes under the name of Cultural Studies can agree on is that the Western humanistic tradition is a repository of ideas that are naïve, repressive, or both.

The multicultural imperative proceeds on the assumption that all cultural life is to be explained in political terms, preeminently in terms of gender, race, class, and ethnic origin. In other words, categories of thought that have their home in the social sciences are imported into the arts and humanities and granted the status of golden explanatory keys. In good Marxist fashion, culture is denied autonomy and is reduced to being a coefficient of something else: class relations, sexual oppression, racial exploitation, etc. Questions of artistic quality are systematically replaced with tests for political relevance, even as the whole realm of aesthetic experience is "demythologized" as an insidious bourgeois fiction designed to consolidate the cultural hegemony of the ruling class. The thought that there might be something uniquely valuable about culture taken on its own terms, that literature, for example, might have its own criteria of achievement and offer its own distinctive satisfactions that are independent of contemporary political battles— none of this seems to matter or indeed to be seriously considered by our multiculturalist radicals.

Some partisans of multiculturalism will claim that in placing issues of gender, class, and race at the center of the humanities they are merely following a time-honored procedure for enriching their discipline by asking novel questions. Just as the New Critics of a previous generation enlivened literary criticism by focusing on verbal complexity, ambiguity, and irony at a time when philology and textual scholarship still ruled literary studies, so what we might call the New New Critics, marching under the banner of multiculturalism, are invigorating the humanities by concentrating on issues of gender, race, and class. The subjects addressed by their criticism may differ markedly from the subjects addressed by criticism of previous generations; the judgments made about what matters in literature and in life may differ radically as well; but that is only to be expected; in essentials, such critics are doing what humanists have always done: they are interpreting texts with the categories that seem most pertinent to contemporary experience.

So goes the argument when the new academic orthodoxy is challenged. But the crucial difference is that whereas the New Critics drew on the essentially literary resources of rhetorical analysis to give us a deeper appreciation of literature, multiculturalists employ the tools of ethnic and sexual redress in order to transform the study of literature into a species of political propaganda and virtue-mongering. Our appreciation of literature is not enhanced; it is canceled and replaced with something else. We are told that by concentrating on questions of gender, class, and ethnicity, multiculturalism provides new ways of looking at literature; in fact, literature per se never really comes into focus at all. The freedom that belongs to the exercise and experience of art is delivered over to a preordained set of political scenarios. The effect is to impoverish, not to enlarge, our experience. Furthermore, the notion that criticism is a free-floating activity, equally valuable whether applied to comic books or to the poems of Dante, underscores the deep cynicism that characterizes so much academic criticism today. It is as if what is actually said, believed, or advocated in our critical judgments is somehow incidental to the character of the humanistic enterprise—as if the value of a particular interpretation were independent of its truth!

Implicit in the politicizing mandate of multiculturalism is an attack on the idea of a common culture, the idea that, despite our many differences, we hold in common an intellectual, artistic, and moral legacy, descending largely from the Greeks and the Bible, supplemented and modified over the centuries by innumerable contributions from diverse hands and peoples. It is this legacy that has given us our science, our political institutions, and the rich and various monuments of artistic and cultural achievement that define us as a civilization. *Pace* the partisans of radical multiculturalism, Western civilization, far from being a narrow ideology, is a capacious register of human achievement, embracing everything from the lyrics of Sappho and the philosophy of Aristotle to the works of Dante, Bach, Newton, Jane Austen, and T. S. Eliot. Indeed, it is this legacy, insofar as we live up to it, that preserves us from chaos and barbarism. And it is precisely this legacy that the multiculturalist wishes to dispense with. Either he claims that the Western tradition is merely one heritage among many—and therefore that it deserves no special allegiance inside the classroom or out of it—or he denies the achievements of the West altogether. As a student at Williams College patiently explained to me when I lectured there about some of these issues, "You are telling us, Mr. Kimball, that we undergraduates ought to focus our attention on the monuments of Western civilization. But you don't seem to understand that Western civilization is responsible for most of the world's ills."

The sources of the multicultural animus against the West are varied. In its more radical versions, as the historian Diane Ravitch has pointed out in a perceptive essay on the subject, multiculturalism "has its roots in the ideology of ethnic separatism and in the black nationalist movement."* This form of multiculturalism denies the ideal of the United States as an integrated society in which peoples of different races, creeds, and ethnic backgrounds can live together in a state of social harmony. The multiculturalist replaces the traditional integrationist image of our society with the ethnically and racially divisive image of the United States as a kind of salad or mosaic: a potpourri of essentially unassimilable elements. Despite occasional rhetoric to the contrary, the multiculturalist scorns the motto *e pluribus unum*—out of many heritages, one society—in order to bolster ethnic, racial, or class-oriented fiefdoms. It follows that the multiculturalist will also have little patience with the idea of universal humanity. Corresponding to the attack on the idea of a common culture is a rejection of the idea of a common humanity. The multiculturalist rejects the idea that our identity as human beings transcends our membership in a particular class, race, or gender. On the contrary, for the multiculturalist what is important is not what binds us together but what separates us. And what separates us—be it gender, ethnicity, class, or race—is used as a totem to confer the coveted status of victimhood upon certain approved groups.

* Diane Ravitch, "Multiculturalism," *The American Scholar*, Summer 1990, page 342.

II

In order to appreciate what is at stake in the debate over multiculturalism, consider the phenomenon of Afrocentrism. The basic contention of the movement is that Western culture is largely a bastardization of African, and especially Egyptian, culture, which in a highly innovative piece of ethnography is said to have been predominantly black. Consequently, black Americans—sometimes referred to as "diasporan African people"—are enjoined to discard "the preponderant Eurocentric myths of universalism, objectivity, and classical traditions" and reclaim their proper intellectual, cultural, and spiritual legacy by returning to African sources. What might be left of culture after dispensing with "universalism, objectivity, and classical traditions"—in other words, with rationality, science, and history—is never really discussed because the truly radical nature of the enterprise is never brought to light. One hears the call for Afrocentrism on many campuses, but—what is even more disturbing—it has so far been most successful in influencing high school curricula.

The journalist Andrew Sullivan provided an introduction to the subject in his account of the Second Annual Conference on the Infusion of African and African-American Content in the High School Curriculum. As Sullivan pointed out, the impetus for the conference was the Afrocentric aim to rid black education of "white influences" and "to transform the high school curriculum by giving it an exclusively Afrocentric base."*

---

* Andrew Sullivan, "Racism 101," *The New Republic*, 26 November 1990. Subsequent quotations from this conference are taken from Mr. Sullivan's article.

A fantasy? In Portland, Oregon, a version of the Afrocentric curriculum, informed by a document called *African-American Baseline Essays*, has already been adopted. Similar documents are planned for other "geo-cultural" groups. The Portland curriculum, which has come to serve as a national model for curricular trans-formation, is being adopted at schools in Pittsburgh, In-dianapolis, Atlanta, and Washington, D.C. In New York, a task force presided over by Thomas Sobol when he was State Education Commissioner recommended sweeping changes in the teaching of history in New York schools in order to accommodate ethnic pressure groups and to root out what Commissioner Sobol called the "hidden as-sumptions of white supremacy" in the textbooks cur-rently used.*

And what is taught? Like much about Afrocentrism, it is beyond satire and would indeed be funny if it were not in earnest. In its simplest terms, the doctrine of "Afrocentrism" claims that many of the great achieve-ments of classical civilization were stolen from black Africa. It is the belief of Afrocentrists that Greek philoso-phy and science and political theory were largely pilfered from African sources. A subsidiary claim is that many famous historical figures—Socrates and Cleopatra, for example—were black. How could the world have labored for centuries in ignorance of such monumental cultural pillage? According to the Afrocentrists, it was no acci-dent. They claim that the black African contribution to world history has been systematically covered up by a white conspiracy to deny the black race its place in the

* See Heather Mac Donald, "Multiculturalism Triumphant: The Sobol Report," *The New Criterion*, January 1992, pages 9–18.

sun, as it were. In *African-American Baseline Essays*, students learn about the great "African-Jewish" scientist and philosopher Maimonides. Old Testament history is conveniently rewritten to portray the ancient Hebrews as guests, not slaves, of the Egyptian pharaohs. It is suggested that the "so-called Pythagorean theorem" was discovered—like just about everything else—by the ancient Egyptians. There is even a section on ancient "Egyptian Metallurgy and Electrical Engineering." Sullivan reports that ninth graders are to immerse themselves in the study of Egyptian hieroglyphics, cleansing rituals, and numerology. Students are taught that Greek philosophy was plagiarized from black African Egypt (Plato and Aristotle, it turns out, are figures of derision for Afrocentrists) and, more generally, that "all Western knowledge is a corruption of Egyptian, i.e., black African thought, and must therefore be junked." One charming participant in the conference explained this point as follows:

> When we adopt other people's theories, we are like Frankenstein doing other people's wills. It's like someone drinking some good stuff, vomiting it, and then we have to catch the vomit and drink it ourselves. . . . The Greeks gave back the vomit of the African way. . . . Don't become the vomit-drinkers!

Leave aside the objection that it was not Victor Frankenstein but his monstrous creation that the speaker has in mind here: who would expect someone who considers the Western European tradition of literature and philosophy to be a kind of vomit to bother to acquaint himself with any of it firsthand? The real problem is the

blinding ideological animus suffusing the movement. In its extreme forms, anyway, Afrocentrism reminds one of nothing more than Evelyn Waugh's portrait, in his novel *Scoop*, of the Consul-General from the fictional African country of Ishmaelia haranguing passersby in Hyde Park:

> "Who built the Pyramids?" cried the Ishmaelite orator. "A Negro. Who invented the circulation of the blood? A Negro. Ladies and gentlemen, . . . Who discovered America? . . . As that great Negro Karl Marx has so nobly written . . . Africa for the African worker, Europe for the African worker, Asia, Oceania, America, Arctic and Antarctica for the African worker."*

Instead of being a novelist's wicked parody of certain fringe elements, the movement for Afrocentricity is an influential ideology affecting the curricula in high schools and colleges across the country.

Afrocentrism is one of many forces in the academy today demanding that historical truth be sacrificed in the name of "diversity."† But while diversity may in some

---

* Evelyn Waugh, *Scoop* (Boston: Little, Brown, 1938), pages 65, 68.

† Examples of historical revisionism undertaken in the name of redressing real or imagined grievances are rife. Thus, for instance, on October 9, 1996 Governor George Pataki of New York signed a bill into law stipulating that henceforth high school students must be taught not only about the Irish potato famine of the 1840s (in itself a reasonable enough stipulation) but also that the famine was "the result of a deliberate campaign by the British to deny the Irish people the food they needed to survive" and hence that it bears comparison with Nazi genocide. In fact, as Mary E. Daly, professor of Modern Irish History at University College, Dublin, noted in her

cases be a social desideratum, its claims do not, as the classicist Mary Lefkowitz noted in *Not Out of Africa*, her definitive evisceration of Afrocentrism, "extend to truth." No commitment to social justice and black pride can transform Socrates into a black man or Cleopatra into a black woman. Professor Lefkowitz notes that our brutal century has been rich in illustrations of where "history-without-facts can lead us, which is right back to the fictive history of the kind developed to serve the Third Reich. It is not coincidental that ours is the era not just of Holocaust denial but of denial that the ancient Greeks were ancient Greeks and creators of their own intellectual heritage."* Afrocentrism is one particularly virulent species of "history-without-facts."

III

There is something grimly ironic about the spectacle of our new multiculturalists using ethnocentrism as a stick

---

essay "The Operations of Famine Relief, 1845–57," "every famine alert appears to have enlisted assistance from both government sources and private charities." *The Great Irish Famine*, edited by Cathal Póirtéir (Dublin: Mercier Press, 1995), page 124.

* Mary Lefkowitz, *Not Out of Africa: How Afrocentrism Became an Excuse to Teach Myth as History* (New York: Basic Books, 1996), page 49. It is hardly surprising that *Not Out of Africa* was excoriated by the politically correct academic establishment. Professor Lefkowitz provides an illuminating backward look at the book's reception in *History Lesson: A Race Odyssey* (New Haven, Yale University Press, 2008).

with which to beat the West. After all, both the idea and
the critique of ethnocentrism are quintessentially Western.
There has never in history been a society more open to
other cultures than our own; nor has any tradition been
more committed to self-criticism than the Western tradition: the figure of Socrates endlessly inviting self-scrutiny
and rational explanation is a definitive image of the
Western spirit. Moreover, "Western" science is not exclusively Western: it is science plain and simple—yes, it is
"universal" science—which, though nurtured and developed in the West, is as true for the inhabitants of the
Nile Valley as it is for the denizens of New York. That is
why, outside the precincts of the humanities departments
of Western universities, there is a mad dash to acquire
Western science and technology. The deepest foolishness
of multiculturalism shows itself in the puerile attacks it
mounts on the cogency of scientific rationality, epitomized
poignantly by the Afrocentrist who flips on his word
processor to write books decrying the parochial nature of
Western science and extolling the virtues of the "African
way."

Despite the racist character of Afrocentricity, it pleases
advocates of multiculturalism to present it and other
forms of politicized scholarship as prime examples of
freedom, diversity, and tolerance. In order to understand
what our tenured radicals mean when they use such
words, let us remind ourselves of the ingenuous student
from the University of Pennsylvania who made the mistake of expressing her "deep regard for the individual,"
only to be reprimanded by a university administrator who
told her that the word "individual" "is a 'RED FLAG'
phrase today, which is considered by many to be RACIST."
As Professor Alan Charles Kors of the University of Pen-

nsylvania has noted, the real lesson to be drawn from this episode—as from the many similar episodes that could be cited—is that the university "is a tolerant and diverse community, and if you do not agree with its particular notions of tolerance and diversity, it will gladly re-educate you."*

We were given a good sense of how the virtues of tolerance and pluralism have been faring in the academy when some professors at Duke University decided to establish a chapter of the National Association of Scholars in 1990. The NAS is a group of tradition-minded teachers and scholars whose motto is "For Reasoned Scholarship in a Free Society." Among the faculty who organized the Duke chapter of the NAS was James David Barber, the eminent political scientist whose impeccable liberal credentials include leading a successful fight against establishing the Nixon library at Duke and serving as president of Amnesty International. Nevertheless, as soon as word got out that a chapter of the NAS was being established at Duke, the redoubtable Stanley Fish, who was then chairman of the Duke English department, sent an anguished letter to a student newspaper, *The Chronicle*, in which he warned, among other things, that the NAS is "widely known to be racist, sexist, and homophobic."

Professor Fish was apparently so worried that reasoned scholarship in a free society might come to Duke that he also took it upon himself to write to the provost "advising him," as Dorothy Rabinowitz reported in her article in *The Wall Street Journal* on the affair, "that faculty

---

* Quoted in Alan Charles Kors, "It's Speech, Not Sex, the Dean Bans Now."

belonging to the NAS should not be appointed to key committees involving tenure or curriculum decisions."*
Professor Fish denied proposing this. But he had made the error of sending copies of this missive to a handful of trusted colleagues, one of whom was upset enough at the suggestion that basic civil rights of Duke faculty members should be summarily abridged to suit Professor Fish's politics that he made the contents of the letter public. Hearing of Professor Fish's denial, an editor at *The Chronicle* commented, "It was really strange to hear him say that. We had the letter with his own words asking just that, right in front of us." But then we must remember that Professor Fish proudly identifies himself as a sophist, one who, in the classical formula, "makes the stronger argument appear weaker, the weaker argument appear stronger." Perhaps he should remind himself that what works between the covers of a contemporary text of literary criticism is not always so convincing when exposed to the steady, if pedestrian, light of common sense.

Embarrassing and, indeed, disappointing as Professor Fish's exhibition is—one might have expected a modicum of principled behavior from so gifted a scholar—what is most revealing about this new controversy at Duke is that those organizing support for the NAS are not archconservatives but, by any conventional measurement, liberals. "What's happened to Duke," said one observer, is "the remaking of a mainstream university into a radical one—with terrible consequences—and I speak as a man who campaigned for George McGovern." The episode drama-

---

* Dorothy Rabinowitz, "Vive the Academic Resistance," *The Wall Street Journal*, 13 November 1990. Unless otherwise noted, quotations regarding this controversy are from Ms. Rabinowitz's article.

tizes the extent to which the traditional, moderate center of university life has been occupied by the new radicalism. As another scholar at Duke—one not, incidentally, affiliated with the NAS—put it: "Today they have something they should call the House *American* Activities Committee because people and ideas that are pro-American or pro-Western are now treated on the campuses as though they were some sort of subversive evil."

Notwithstanding the charges blithely hurled by Professor Fish and his allies against those supporting the NAS—"racist, sexist, and homophobic," for starters—the real battle that is now shaping up is not between radicals and conservatives but between radicals and old-style liberals. Or perhaps one should say that the classical liberal position—which fought for the ideals of quality, disinterested scholarship, and for advancement according to merit, not adherence to a given political line—is now castigated as conservative and reactionary. Professor Fish, for example, has gone to great pains to demonstrate that "there is no such thing as intrinsic merit," only conventional opinion.

The result is that at many institutions any middle ground has been abolished. On the one side we have the remnants of the much besieged liberal tradition attempting to maintain traditional standards of civility and scholarship. On the other side we have the ruling academic claque, the tenor of whose educational philosophy was vividly summed up by Stanley Hauerwas, a well-known professor of theological ethics at Duke. When the controversy over the NAS broke out, Professor Hauerwas disparaged the educational goals of the NAS, explaining in a local newspaper that "The canon of great literature was created by high Anglican ---holes to underwrite their so-

cial class.""* Edifying, is it not, to acquaint oneself with
the table talk of our contemporary academic theologians?

Professor Hauerwas's comment reminds us that a
major issue in the whole debate over multiculturalism—as
indeed in the controversy at Duke over the establishment
of the NAS—centers on the question of the proper content
of a liberal arts education. For both better and worse,
discussion of this question in recent years has crystallized
around the word "canon."

On the positive side, putting the traditional literary
canon at the center of the debate effectively called attention to some of the more egregious assaults on the
humanities in our colleges and universities. When professors of literature begin teaching Louis L'Amour—to say
nothing of the rock videos of Madonna—instead of
Henry James, when students begin reading Frantz Fanon
instead of John Locke in their political philosophy classes,
something has gone terribly wrong. And it is well to
remember that instances of such pedagogical frivolity are
now increasingly the rule, not the exception. A major
legacy of the 1960s in the academy has been the destruction of standards. The very idea that some works might
be more worth reading than others, together with the
ideal of excellence that informs it, is regarded with
suspicion as "hierarchical" and "elitist."

Nowhere has this been more apparent than in the attack
on the canon. Between the introduction of works of
popular culture into the humanities curriculum and the
unending search for works by authors of the requisite
gender, skin color, sexual orientation, or ethnic heri-

* Pam Kelley, "For Duke Profs, the Hot Debate Is What to Teach,"
The Charlotte Observer, 28 September 1990.

tage—between, that is, the trivialization and the politi-cization of the curriculum—the substance of a liberal arts education at many institutions has suffered catastrophic damage. Henry Louis Gates, Jr., chairman of Harvard's Afro-American Studies Department, was simply stating the truth when he noted in 1989 that "ours was the generation that took over buildings in the late 1960s and demanded the creation of Black and Women's Studies programs, and now . . . we have come back to challenge the traditional curriculum."* The consequence of the development that Professor Gates so candidly described is that many liberal arts majors are being graduated having read little more than a handful of popular novels, a bit of esoteric literary theory, and various works that confirm their chosen ideological prejudices. The great works of the tradition remain, literally, a closed book.

Nevertheless, there are reasons to be uncomfortable about the prominence that the word "canon" has as-sumed in the debate over the future of the humanities. For one thing, by concentrating on *what* is taught critics have sometimes tended to slight the question of *how* teachers are approaching the material they teach. Few would deny Jane Austen a place in the canon; but "Jane Austen and the Masturbating Girl" does not exactly raise one's hopes for responsible pedagogy. Plato and Aristotle belong in any liberal arts curriculum, but not as examples of how the white race has corrupted the wisdom of black Egypt. No author is immune to the depredations of ideologically motivated criticism, which is to say that our

* Henry Louis Gates, Jr., "Whose Canon Is It Anyway?" *The New York Times Book Review*, February 26, 1989, page 44.

concern for the integrity of the canon must be a concern for responsible teaching as well.

It must also be said that the scramble to draw up approved reading lists has had the unfortunate effect of suggesting to some that those supporting the canon wish to impose a changeless tablet of previously certified texts on unsuspecting students. In fact, no serious commentator believes—or has said—that the canon is a sacrosanct catalogue of books that may never be altered or added to. But this is not to deny that there is a body of works from the Western tradition that should form the core of a liberal arts education, works that embody what the late Roger Shattuck, one of our leading scholars of modern French literature, called "accepted versions of greatness," "scales of human eminence, qualities to admire and perhaps to emulate."* Of course, the number of books belonging to this core is far larger than the most voracious student could hope to master even if he or she were granted several lifetimes. In this sense, "being educated" is an ideal any one person can only aspire to. Yet when it comes to the content of a liberal arts education— when it comes, that is, to the works and authors one should study in the four years of one's undergraduate career—decisions have to be made. The criterion is first of all not whether a given work is included on some imaginary Received List of Great Books but whether it has proved to be of permanent interest. Some works have demonstrated their insight, beauty, or truth to so many educated people for so long that failing to read them is

* Roger Shattuck, *Perplexing Dreams: Is There a Core Tradition in the Humanities?*, American Council of Learned Societies Occasional Paper No. 2, 1987, page 6.

tantamount to consigning oneself to the ranks of the ill-educated. My own view is that a liberal arts education should concentrate as rigorously as possible on works that have proved to be of permanent value; in practice, that means that few if any contemporary works should be part of the undergraduate curriculum. This is not to say that students should not read contemporary fiction and criticism, or that they should not go to the movies, listen to contemporary music, and generally immerse themselves in the life of the moment. In fact, any young person who is intellectually alive and curious will do all these things as a matter of course. The bottom line is that contemporary culture should not form the basis of a college education. One should look to the past, not to the streets, for the substance of the liberal arts curriculum.

Some critics of *Tenured Radicals* have complained that the book fails to outline alternatives to the morass it describes—where by "alternatives" most seem to mean reading lists. But unless one subscribes to the ethos of multiculturalism, which looks to cultural politics instead of intellectual substance to dictate educational policy, the question of what one should read is not an esoteric matter. Nor is the rationale for a liberal arts education. One reads as much of what has stood the test of time as one can, beginning if possible with the oldest and most influential books of the Western tradition; and one does so because one desires the gifts of a liberal education: knowledge, intellectual freedom, and a cultivated appreciation of the traditions that have been instrumental in forming our culture. If that sounds like a list of clichés, well, it is—just as any true description of what matters in education will be. It is in the nature of generalizations about life's difficult choices to be perfectly obvious, which is perhaps why they are so often confounded by those making a profession of sophistry.

John Searle, a professor of philosophy at the University of California at Berkeley and one of the most thoughtful critics of *Tenured Radicals*, put the conventional rationale for liberal education with consummate simplicity when he observed that

> there is a certain Western intellectual tradition that goes from, say, Socrates to Wittgenstein in philosophy, and from Homer to James Joyce in literature, and it is essential to the liberal education of young men and women in the United States that they should receive some exposure to at least some of the great works in this intellectual tradition; they should, in Matthew Arnold's overquoted words, "know the best that is known and thought in the world." The arguments given for this view—on the rare occasions when it was felt that arguments were even needed—were that knowledge of the tradition was essential to the self-understanding of educated Americans since the country, in an important sense, is the product of that tradition; that many of these works are historically important because of their influences; and that most of them, for example several works by Plato and Shakespeare, are of very high intellectual and artistic quality, to the point of being of universal human interest.[*]

Until recently, as Professor Searle notes, this description of the substance of liberal education would have seemed so obvious as to have been a "platitude"—which we

[*] John Searle, "The Storm Over the University," *The New York Review of Books*, 6 December 1990.

might define as a statement sufficiently self-evident that
its utterance is superfluous.

IV

It is a measure of how drastically things have changed
that in the academy today Professor Searle's vignette
would, as he acknowledges, generally be regarded as
"wildly reactionary." Indeed, I can think of few major
universities that would dare to endorse it, even as an
educational platitude. (Seismic shifts in a culture's values
show up first in its choice of platitudes.) From Socrates to
Wittgenstein? From Homer to Joyce? Where are the
women, the blacks, the Hispanics, the Asians? Furthermore, why should a liberal arts education focus on "the
best" that has been thought and said? What about
populations and points of view that have been "marginalized"? What about popular culture? What about
Madonna? What about the tradition essential to *un*educated Americans? Moreover, who says that America is a
product of the white, male, Eurocentric tradition outlined
above? What about native American influences? What
about Africa?

And so on. A swamp yawns open before us, ready to
devour everything. The best response to all this—and
finally the only serious and effective response—is not to
enter these murky waters in the first place. As Nietzsche
observed, we do not refute a disease. We resist it. And yet
there are two issues that must be engaged. The first concerns the often-heard charge of "elitism." The traditional
notion of a liberal arts education is unquestionably elitist

in the sense that it focuses on the pinnacle of human cultural and intellectual achievement. It must also be admitted that not everyone is either interested in or capable of taking advantage of a liberal arts education conceived of in this way. In a deeper sense, however, the impulse behind a traditional liberal arts education is radically democratic. For its riches are in principle available to anyone with talent and energy, regardless of class, gender, skin color, ethnic origin, etc. The real tyranny is to deprive students of the best that has been thought and said in the name of one or another version of political rectitude. The second issue that must be engaged concerns the last item in Professor Searle's inventory, the fundamental question of "universal human interest." To speak of universal human interest is to acknowledge faith in a community of human endeavor that transcends the contingencies of race, gender, ethnic heritage, and the like. As the multiculturalists realize, some such faith is central to the tradition of liberal education; this is one reason they are so eager to repudiate that tradition. Many commentators have pointed out that the demography of the United States is changing so rapidly that by the year 2000 slightly less than half the population will be white. Already in certain areas more than half the population is non-white. Shouldn't the liberal arts curriculum acknowledge this change by questioning the priority still granted to Western culture and by including more literature by blacks, Hispanics, Asians, etc.? The multiculturalists think so.

Demographics notwithstanding, the truth is that the United States, by virtue of its history, its political institutions, its major cultural affiliations, and its dominant language, is essentially a Western society. And short of a major cataclysm, it will remain so. Donald Kagan, the eminent classicist who was dean of Yale College in the late 1980s and early 1990s, deftly summed up the case for the European basis of American culture in an address delivered to incoming freshmen in 1990. The United States does enjoy a common culture, Professor Kagan noted, one that is

> itself various, changing, rich with contributions of Americans who come or whose ancestors came from every continent in the world, yet recognizably and unmistakably American. At this moment in history an objective observer would have to say that it derives chiefly from the experience of Western Civilization, and especially from England, whose languages and institutions are the most copious springs from which American culture draws its life. I say this without embarrasssment, as an immigrant from a tiny country on the fringe of the West, without any connection to the Anglo-Saxon founders of the United States.*

Because the roots of our society are so deeply embedded in Western culture, being ignorant of that culture means being ignorant of oneself. Consequently, as Dean Kagan argues, "It is both right and necessary to place Western Civilization and the culture to which it has given rise at the center of our studies, and we fail to do so at the peril of our students, our country, and of the hopes for a

---

* Donald Kagan, "E Pluribus Unum," an address delivered to the freshman class at Yale College in September, 1990. The address is reprinted in the January 1991 issue of *Commentary*.

democratic, liberal society emerging throughout the world today."

The emergent democracy to which Dean Kagan refers with justified pride is essentially a Western phenomenon. But alongside the triumphs of hope and liberty we have seen in Eastern Europe, the Soviet Union, and elsewhere, we must place the many foreboding signs of resurgent nationalism, ethnic separatism, and ancient racial hatreds that have also been a prominent feature of recent history. It wasn't long ago that we were assured that the "end of history" was nigh: that a Western-style liberalism was on the verge of establishing itself the world over and that peace and amity were breaking out everywhere. But instead of that attractive version of the end of history, we are now witnessing what some have called the retribalization of the world: a violent turn against Western liberalism and its tradition of rationality, respect for individual rights, and recognition of a common good that transcends the accidents of ethnic and racial identity. Given this situation, it is all the more imperative that we educate our students in the Western tradition, that we teach them about the virtues of our society and its democratic institutions. Such education is the staunchest bulwark against the forces of disintegration we are facing.

The multiculturalists rant on about the repressive, inequitable nature of U.S. society. It is instructive to note, however, that people all over the world continue to flock here. They do so not because they believe the United States is perfect, but because they believe that the Western democratic institutions that govern this society will allow them greater freedom, economic opportunity, and personal dignity than they are likely to find anywhere else in the world. The multiculturalists notwithstanding, the choice facing us today is not between a "repressive" Western culture and a multicultural paradise, but between culture and barbarism. Civilization is not a gift; it is an achievement—a fragile achievement that needs constantly to be shored up and defended from besiegers inside and out. These are facts that do not easily penetrate the cozy and coddled purlieus of the academy. But they are part of the permanent challenge that any civilization must face. This was something that Evelyn Waugh understood with exceptional clarity. "Barbarism," he wrote in a somber moment in 1938,

> is never finally defeated; given propitious circumstances, men and women who seem quite orderly will commit every conceivable atrocity. The danger does not come merely from habitual hooligans; we are all potential recruits for anarchy. Unremitting effort is needed to keep men living together at peace; there is only a margin of energy left over for experiment however beneficent. Once the prisons of the mind have been opened, the orgy is on. There is no more agreeable position than that of dissident from a stable society. Theirs are all the solid advantages of other people's creation and preservation, and all the fun of detecting hypocrisies and inconsistencies. There are times when dissidents are not only enviable but valuable. The work of preserving society is sometimes onerous, sometimes almost effortless. The more elaborate the society, the more vulnerable it is to attack, and the more complete its collapse in case of defeat. At a time like the present it is notably precarious. If it falls we shall see not merely the dissolution of a few joint-stock corporations, but of the spiritual and material achievements of our history.[*]

Tenured Radicals is about the privileged beneficiaries of the spiritual and material achievements of our history who, out of ignorance, perversity, or malice, have chosen to turn their backs on the culture that nourished them and made them what they are. It is about intellectuals who have defiled reason with sophistries, and teachers who have defrauded their students of knowledge. Because of the times we live in and the hard choices we face as a society, it is, above all, a cautionary tale.

* Evelyn Waugh, "Conservative Manifesto," in *The Essays, Articles, and Reviews of Evelyn Waugh*, edited by Donat Gallagher (Boston: Little, Brown, 1984), pages 161–162.

Acknowledgments

A S A WRITER grows older, not only do his intellectual debts multiply but he also tends to become increasingly cognizant of those benefactions. At twenty-five, it is easy to take the intellectual furniture of your life for granted. At fifty, you realize just how much you had *taken* for granted—how much, I mean, that you call your own are really the unacknowledged dispensations of friends, teachers, colleagues, and critics. *Tenured Radicals* had its origin in some disconnected essays I wrote for *The New Criterion* at the urging of my colleague Hilton Kramer. It was Glen Hartley who discerned a figure in the carpet and suggested a book on the politicization of academia. The late, lamented John M. Olin Foundation helped to make it possible for me to do so. Along the way, Erich Eichman's keen editorial eye was invaluable. Alexandra Kimball has aided me in this and in earlier editions in ways too manifold to enumerate. Ivan R. Dee generously acceded to the idea of this expanded and updated edition. I am also grateful to Robert Paquette and James Piereson for their helpful criticisms. Hilton Kramer, to whom I rededicate the book, has been my staunchest intellectual ally, friend, and benefactor for more than two decades. I am profoundly grateful to them all.

Index

Acconci, Vito, 125
Adams, Hunter, liv
African-American Baseline Essays, 291–292
African-American Studies, xv, xxiii–xxiv, xxxii
Afrocentrism, l, liv, 290–295
Alexander Hamilton Institute for the Study of Western Civilization, xli–xlii
Allardyce, Gilbert, 104
Althusser, Louis, 53, 107–108, 123, 238; *Lenin and Philosophy and Other Essays*, 107
American Civil Liberties Union (ACLU), of Michigan, 110–111
American Conservative, The (journal), xxxi–xxxii
American Council of Learned Societies (ACLS), xli, 66, 215, 252–253, 302
American Council of Trustees and Alumni, xli
American Enterprise (journal), xliii
Amis, Kingsley, xv
Andersen, Kurt, xxxiii
Anderson, Brian C., *South Park Conservatives: The Revolt Against Liberal Media Bias*, xi

Anti-foundationalism, *See* Foundationalism
Architecture, Ch. 5 *passim*
Arendt, Hannah, 202; "The Crisis in Education," 119–120; *The Origins of Totalitarianism*, 117–118
Aristotle, 37, 288, 292, 300; *Metaphysics*, 3
Arnold, Matthew, 5, 72, 81, 97–99, 103, 255, 303; "The Function of Criticism at the Present Time," 118–119; "The Literary Influence of Academies," 119

Arrowsmith, William, 24
Artforum (journal), 133–134
Auden, W(ystan) H(ugh), 70
Augustine, St., 57; *Confessions*, 61
Austen, Jane, lviii, 7, 219, 282, 288, 300
Austin, J(ohn) L(angshaw), 226
AWARE (Actively Working Against Racism and Ethnocentrism), 111–112

Bach, Johann Sebastian, 288
Bahti, Timothy, 156
Baker, Houston, xxxiii–xxxv, 2,

Index

5, 39, 44–46, 54, 105, 250, 270–275
Balch, Stephen H., 52
Banks, William M., 24
Barber, James David, 296
Barr, Alfred H., Jr., 139
Barthes, Roland, 123
Barzun, Jacques, *Begin Here: The Forgotten Conditions of Teaching and Learning,* lix; *The Culture We Deserve,* 277; *The House of Intellect,* xv
Bataille, Georges, 123, 146
Bate, Walter Jackson, 240
Beckett, Samuel, 200
Benglis, Lynda, 125
Benjamin, Walter, 123, 138, 140, 144
Bennett, William J., 6, 52, 57, 66–68, 71, 117, 214, 252, 259, 266–267; *To Reclaim a Legacy: A Report on the Humanities in Higher Education,* 21–26, 67, 97–100
Berger, Brigitte, 38
Berger, Joseph, 5
Bernstein, Richard, *Dictatorship of Virtue: Multiculturalism and the Battle for America's Future,* 11
Bhabha, Homi, 144–145
Black studies, ix, xxiv, 5, 46
Blackmun, Harry A., 13
Bloom, Allan, 6, 64, 66, 214, 252, 262, 266–267, 272, 276–277; *The Closing of the American Mind: How Higher Education Has Failed Democracy and Impoverished the Souls of Today's Students,* xv, lxii, 20–21, 80, 258–259; *Giants and Dwarfs: Essays 1960–1990,* lii
Bloom, Harold, 184
Bohr, Niels, xxvi

Bolshevik revolution, 126, 130
Bork, Robert, 278
Boston Globe, The, xxviii–xxx
Bourdieu, Pierre, *Reproduction in Education and Society,* 50–51
Brandeis University, xiv
Bricmont, Jean, *Fashionable Nonsense: Postmodern Intellectuals' Abuse of Science,* lv
Brodhead, Richard, xxx
Brooke–Rose, Christine, 87
Brooks, David, xxix
Brooks, Peter, 31, 47, 52, 66, 97, 99, 114, 116–117, 119
Browne, Sir Thomas, 148
Buchloh, Benjamin H. D., 139
Buchsbaum, Ralph, *Animals Without Backbones,* xxiv
Buck, Pearl, 5
Bugs Bunny, 4
Bundtzen, Lynda, 251, 255–258, 261, 264, 267–271
Burroughs, William, 219
Bush administration, 252, 266

Camp, 203, 213
Canon, debate over the, 2, 4–5, 15, Ch. 1 *passim,* 65, 116, 264–265, 270, 276, 279, 299–301; and counter-canon, 9, 257; formation, 101–106, 255–256, 261, 298; relation to Roman Catholic canonization, 261–262
Carroll, Vincent, xxx
Carter, Jimmy, 131
Cassirer, Ernst, 167; *The Philosophy of Symbolic Forms,* 167–168
Cavell, Stanley, 4, 82
Cézanne, Paul, 125
Chaplin, Charlie, 200
Chaucer, Geoffrey, 255

Index

Cheney, Lynne V., 6, 68, 214,
252, 266–267; *Humanities in
America*, 66
Chodorow, Nancy Julia, 84–85
Churchill, Ward, xvi–xxiii,
xxxviii, xli; "Some People
Push Back," xvi
Churchill, Winston, 26
City Journal, xi
Cleopatra, 291, 294
Cliff's Notes, 27–28
Clinton, Bill, xli
Cocteau, Jean, 222
Colquhoun, Alan, 182
Commentary (journal), 52, 100,
110, 306
Constitution of the United States,
the, 45, 58, 112
Cooper, Roy, xxvii
Coop Himmelblau, 204
Copjec Joan, 124
Courbet, Gustave, *The Quarry*,
88, 92
Crews, Frederick, x, 5–6, 127,
178; *The Critics Bear It Away:
American Fiction and the
Academy*, 5–6; *Skeptical
Engagements*, 62–63, 223;
Postmodern Pooh, 6
Curie, Marie, xxvi
Currah, Paisley, xiv
Crimp, Douglas, 124
Critical Inquiry (journal), 123,
153
Critical Race Studies, 35
Culler, Jonathan, 37, 66,
114–116, 153; *On
Deconstruction: Theory and
Criticism after Structuralism*,
liv–lv
Cultural literacy, 16–23, 26–29,
251, 258–259, 262
Cultural Studies, lvi, 66, 73, 76,
216, 286
CUNY, Brooklyn College, xiv

Curriculum, changes to the
traditional, ix–x, xlix–l, liii,
lvi, lix, 5, 8, 14, Ch. 1 *passim*,
65, 72, 98–99, 104, 115, 250,
266, 273, 276, 284, 290–291,
297, 299–300, 302, 305;
setting a, 23, 114; *See also*
Canon, Stanford University

Daly, Mary E., 293–294
Dante, 57, 288
Darwin, Charles, xxvi
Davis, Douglas, 195
Davis, Natalie Zemon, 82
Deconstruction, Ch. 4 *passim*;
and architecture, Ch. 5 *passim*
de Graef, Ortwin, 149, 152
Delgado, Richard, liii
de Man, Paul, 33–34, 37, 123,
148, Ch. 4 *passim*, 231;
*Allegories of Reading: Figural
Language in Rousseau,
Nietzsche, Rilke, and Proust*,
149, 160, 167; *Blindness and
Insight: Essays in the Rhetoric
of Contemporary Criticism*,
158; *Wartime Journalism*,
150–151
Derrida, Jacques, xliii, lv, 10, 33,
79, 123, 152–154, 156–158,
179, 224, 226–227, 230, 236,
238, 250, 260–267, 270;
Limited Inc, 227
Detlefsen, Robert, 111
Dewey, John, 48
Diacritics (journal), 123
Dickinson, Emily, 219
Didi-Huberman, Georges,
143–144
Doane, Mary Ann, 142
Douglass, Frederick, 272
D'Souza, Dinesh, *Illiberal
Education: The Politics of
Race and Sex on Campus*, liv,
lxii, 11–12

313

Duchamp, Marcel, 116
Duke University, 2, 35, 218,
  296–299; Department of
  English, 7, 217–221,
  225–226, 247, 282, 296;
  lacrosse scandal at,
  xxvii–xxxv, xliv
Dworkin, Ronald, 227

Eichmann, Adolf, xvi
Einstein, Albert, xxvi
Eisenman, Peter, 182, 185–194,
  196–198, 200–201, 203–204,
  207, 212–213; *Houses of
  Cards*, 187–192
Eisenstein, Sergei, *October*, 126,
  129
Eliot, George, 42; *Middlemarch*,
  281
Eliot, T(homas) S(tearns), 288
Ellis, John, *Against
  Deconstruction*, 10; *Literature
  Lost: Social Agendas and the
  Corruption of the Humanities*,
  lvii, lx–lxii, 19, 37
Emory University, speech codes
  at, 110–111

Fanon, Frantz, 25, 58–62, 145,
  299; *The Wretched of the
  Earth*, 59–61
Faraday, Michael, xxvi
Farber, Daniel A., *Beyond All
  Reason: The Radical Assault
  on Truth in American Law*,
  liv
Feminism, liv–lvi, 14, 30–31, 38,
  41–44, 143, 275–276; radical,
  25, 37, 41, 250, 256
*Feminism and Geography: The
  Limits of Geographical
  Knowledge* (book), lv
Ferguson, Margaret, 47, 49–54,
  105, 133
Film, 61, 125–126, 129–130,

137–138, 142, 146, 200;
  feminist, 142
Financial Times, xii–xiv
Fineman, Joel, 144
Finn, Chester, 110
First Amendment issues, *See* Free
  speech
Fish, Stanley, 7, 103, 263,
  296–298, Ch. 6 *passim*; *Doing
  What Comes Naturally:
  Change, Rhetoric, and the
  Practice of Theory in Literary
  and Legal Studies*, 221,
  225–232, 234–235, 237,
  239–240, 242–243, 245–247;
  *Is There a Text in This Class?
  The Authority of Interpretive
  Communities*, 217, 223,
  241–242, 247; *Professional
  Correctness: Literary Studies
  and Political Change*, 221;
  *Save the World on Your On
  Time*, 224; *Surprised by Sin:
  The Reader in Paradise Lost*,
  216, 222–223, 231; *There's
  No Such Thing as Free Speech
  . . . and It's a Good Thing
  Too*, 229, 232
Flaubert, Gustave, *Madame
  Bovary*, 36
Foucault, Michel, xliii, liii, lvi,
  53, 123–124, 144, 184, 236
Foundationalism, 235–236; and
  anti-foundationalism, 237, 246
Fox, Nicholas, *Postmodernism,
  Sociology and Health*, 35
Fox-Genovese, Elizabeth, 23, 25,
  59
Frampton, Hollis, 125
Frecero, John, 82
Free speech, and academic
  freedom, xvii–xxii,
  xxxvi–xxxvii, 11, 109–112,
  229–235
Free Speech Movement, xxxvii

Index

Index

Index

Orwell, George, 70, 285; *1984*, xxxvii, 75

Paolozzi, Eduardo, 203
Paquette, Robert, xviii, xlii
Parini, Jay, ix
Parsons School of Design, 82; architectural debate at, 181, 195–203
Pasolini, Pier Paolo, 146
Passeron, Jean-Claude, 50–51
Pataki, George, 293
Patterson, Annabel, 219
Patterson, Lee, 219
Peirce, Charles Sanders, 184
Performance art, 138
Perloff, Marjorie, 23, 25
Photography, 128, 137–142
Picasso, Pablo, 255
Piereson, James, "The Left University," xlvi
Plath, Sylvia, 41
Plato, 18, 57, 74, 272, 292, 300, 303; Callicles (character), 247; *Phaedrus*, 242; *The Republic*, lvii, 103; Thrasymachus (character), lvii, 214
Podhoretz, Norman, 100–107, 117
Political correctness, xxvii, xxxv–xxxvi, xl, xlii, xlvii, li, liii, lvii, 10–11, 42, 88, 113, 283–284
Postcolonial Studies, 76
Post-structuralism, ix, lviii, 5, 30–31, 62, 121
Princeton University, xxiv, xli, xlvi, li, 39, 55, 100, 282; architectural education symposium at, 181–203; Madison Center, xli
Protagoras, 243
Pynchon, Thomas, *Gravity's Rainbow*, 125
Pythagorean theorem, 292

Queer Theory, xliv, 7, 76

Rabinowitz, Dorothy, 296–297
Race, issues of, xxiv, xxvii, xxxiii, liii–liv, lvii, lx, 9, 11, 18–19, 25, 35, 40, 44, 57, 72, 74, 94, 101, 105–114, 141–146; *See also* Afrocentrism, Multiculturalism
Ravaisson, Felix, 93
Ravitch, Diane, 289
Ray, Man, "Monument to de Sade," 137
Reader response, 216, 231–232
Reagan, Ronald, 22, 79, 131, 135, 252, 266, 272, 278
Reconstructing Individualism: Autonomy, Individuality, and the Self in Western Thought (book), 82–83, 85–88, 93–96
Rembrandt, 255
Representations (journal), 123
Responses: On Paul de Man's Wartime Journalism (book), 150, 156–157
Riffaterre, Michael, 32, 36, 38
Roberts, Selena, xxix
Robespierre, Maximilien, lii
Rocky Mountain News, xxxi
Rodchenko, Aleksandr, 130, 205
Romanticism, lix
Roosevelt, Theodore, 284
Rorty, Richard, 77, 233, 247; *Contingency, Irony, and Solidarity*, 3, 237–238
Rosenberg, Harold, 235
Rosenberg, Susan, xvi, xix, xli, xlvi
Rosovsky, Henry, 104–105
Rousseau, Jean-Jacques, lii, lix, 160, 272; *Confessions*, 166
Rowe, Colin, 184
Rupp, Christy, 135
Russian avant-garde, 126, 129, 206, 209–120

Index

Said, Edward, 144–145, 240
Salmagundi (journal), 22, 26–27,
  55, 62–63
Sartre, Jean-Paul, 59
Schama, Simon, *Dead Certainties
  (UnwarrantedSpeculations)*,lv
Schiller, Friedrich, *On the
  Aesthetic Education of Man*,
  249, 280
Schlesinger, Arthur M., Jr., *The
  Disuniting of America:
  Reflections on a Multicultural
  Society*, 284
Scholes, Robert, 22–27, 29
Schwarzenegger, Arnold, xii
Science, attacks on, li, liv–lv, lvii,
  lxi
Scott, Geoffrey, *The Architecture
  of Humanism: A Study in the
  History of Taste*, 211
Scruton, Roger, "On Humane
  Education," lvi, lxi
Scully, Vincent, 114–116
Searle, John, xlix–l, 303– 305
Sedgwick, Eve Kosofsky, 7, 219
Semiotics, 124; applied to
  architecture, 182
September 11, xi
Shakespeare, William, xxxiii, xlv,
  lviii, 4–5, 18, 28, 255,
  264–265, 278, 303; *Romeo
  and Juliet*, 27; *The Tempest*,
  75, 281
Shattuck, Roger, *Perplexing
  Dreams: Is There a Core
  Tradition in the Humanities?*,
  301
Sherry, Suzanna, *Beyond All
  Reason: The Radical Assault
  on Truth in American Law*,
  liv
Shils, Edward, xix–xx, 277
Short, Thomas, 43, 77
Showalter, Elaine, 1, 39–44, 46,
  57, 256

Shroud of Turin, 143
Silber, John, *Architecture of the
  Absurd: How "Genius"
  Disfigured a Practical Art*,
  205; "Poisoning the Wells of
  Academe," xviii–xix
Silverglate, Harvey A., *The
  Shadow University: The
  Betrayal of Liberty on
  America's Campuses*, xviii, li,
  11
Simon, John, *The Sheep from the
  Goats: Selected Literary
  Essays*, 81
Sischy, Ingrid, 133
Sisk, John P., 23
SITE, 196, 199–201
Smith, Barbara Herrnstein, 7,
  215–216, 219, 237;
  *Contingencies of Value:
  Alternative Perspectives for
  Critical Theory*, 238
Smith College, xii–xiv, xxxviii, 11
Smithson, Robert, *Spiral Jetty*,
  125
Sobol, Thomas, 291
Social Text (journal), 123
Socrates, lix, 291, 294–295,
  303–304
Soir, Le (newspaper), 150, 156,
  159–160, 163, 173, 176
Sokal, Alan, *Fashionable
  Nonsense: Postmodern
  Intellectuals' Abuse of Science*,
  lv
Sontag, Susan, lx, 81, 213
Sophistry, 214–248, 303
Speaking for the Humanities
  (American Council of Learned
  Societies report), 66–78, 87,
  114, 119, 215, 254–255
Speech codes, *See* Free speech
Spencer, Richard Bertrand,
  xxxi–xxxii
Springsteen, Bruce, 4

320

Index